Minds at War

MINDS AT WAR

Nuclear Reality and the

Inner Conflicts of

Defense Policymakers

STEVEN KULL

Basic Books, Inc., Publishers   New York

Library of Congress Cataloging-in-Publication Data ·

Kull, Steven.
  Minds at war.

  Bibliography: p. 319.
  Includes index.
  1. Nuclear warfare—Decisionmaking.   2. Military
policy—Decisionmaking.   3. Nuclear warfare—
Psychological aspects.   4. Military policy—Psycho-
logical aspects.   I. Title.
U263.K85   1988   355'.0217   88–47674
ISBN   0–465–04610–X (cloth)
ISBN   0–465–04611–8 (paper)

CONTENTS

PREFACE

BEFORE I BEGAN STUDYING Soviet-American security issues, I spent more than a decade practicing psychotherapy. This experience has, of course, conditioned my approach to the problems of international security. It may be valuable for me to describe, in advance, how my orientation as a psychologist makes the present study somewhat different from a traditional analysis of policymaking.

This study is not primarily a review of historical events, nor is it a critical evaluation of policies, leading up to an alternative proposal. Instead, it focuses on the *psychological processes* involved in making defense policy. More specifically, it focuses on what happens as policymakers attempt to cope with the profound changes in international relations engendered by nuclear weapons—that is, nuclear reality.

The distinction between this kind of analysis and a more traditional critical analysis is particularly apparent in the approach to inconsistencies in the statements of policymakers—something I will be paying particular attention to. A traditional perspective tends to regard inconsistent statements as arising from either disingenuity or a lack of intelligence. In the discourse of policy criticism, the way to undermine an opponent's position is to demonstrate how it is inconsistent. However, from a psychological perspective, inconsistent statements may tell us something important about the difficulties a policymaker is having in coping. If at one moment a policymaker recognizes fundamental features of reality and at another moment seems to ignore or deny them, this suggests a significant psychological conflict. Such conflicts and the fragmented behavior they produce can interfere with effective adaptation.

A criticism people often level at clinical psychologists is that they tend to focus on the negative. In this study I must plead guilty to this charge. I have actively sought indications of suboptimal forms of coping in defense policymaking. This doubtless puts a disproportionate emphasis on the problems in the thinking of defense policymakers. I worry that individual defense policymakers whom I quote will feel unfairly treated. However, given the paramount role that nuclear defense policy plays in the fate of the world, it does not seem inappropriate to be very exacting in the analysis of the thinking of defense policymakers. In taking on such responsibilities, such individuals should also be willing to accept this kind of scrutiny. It is in this spirit, I believe, that individual defense policymakers allowed me to study their perceptions. And for this willingness I express my profound respect. My intention in examining their inconsistencies is not to embarrass but to increase understanding of the inner conflicts that operate in defense policymakers and in the general public as well.

By focusing on such problems, I do not mean to imply that all thinking about defense policy is dominated by their effects. As I will illustrate, I believe there is also a vigorous stream in both American and Soviet defense thinking that is effectively adapting to nuclear reality. This was apparent in the interviews I conducted with defense policymakers and in published literature.

I also do not mean to imply that if all of these psychological conflicts were solved, then all other difficulties in coping with nuclear reality would evaporate. There are many objective difficulties in dealing with this condition quite independent of the psychological conflicts of defense policymakers. Nevertheless, the process of adaptation is not moving forward as easily as it might, and perhaps these psychological factors have a significant retarding effect. Based on my experience in psychotherapy, it would seem that a greater understanding of how these psychological conflicts operate and how they shape behavior may facilitate the process of adaptation.

ACKNOWLEDGMENTS

IT IS A PLEASURE to take this opportunity to discharge some of the pent-up feelings of appreciation I have for the many people who have helped me in the process of researching and writing this book. In the course of entering into what was for me a new field, I was the beneficiary of many favors.

Two individuals who were particularly generous and helpful were Richard Smoke and Alexander George. Richard Smoke guided me into the field of international security and nuclear strategy when I was still a practicing psychologist. He encouraged me to initiate this project and continued to give me advice and rigorous feedback right through to the very last draft. Early in the project Alexander George invited me to Stanford University and has been constantly available with his uniquely warm and humorous guidance—a quintessential mentor. He read every draft with care, precision, and remarkable insight.

Robert Jervis and Robert Lifton were also very helpful. Robert Jervis, whose work greatly influenced the conceptualization of this project, invited me to spend some months at the Institute of War and Peace Studies at Columbia University. His insights and comments on the manuscript were invaluable. My interaction with Robert Lifton was very rich. He sometimes understood what I was trying to say better than I did, and made sure I understood as well.

Other individuals who gave me valuable ideas and/or read parts of the manuscript include David Bernstein, Coit Blacker, George Breslauer, Arthur Macy Cox, Morton Deutsch, Gloria Duffy, Lynn Eden, Jerome Frank, David Holloway, Robert Holt, John Mack, Ted Postol, Condoleeza Rice, and Alan Tonelson.

I am indebted to numerous sources of financial support. The CS Fund and the Ploughshares Fund took the initial step of funding a project that in its original formulation may well have looked like something of a long shot. Other funding came from the Carnegie Corporation of New York, the Threshold Foundation, Rockefeller Family Associates, National Community Funds, and W. H. and Carol Ferry. During the later stages of writing the book I was also assisted by an award from the Social Science Research Council of an SSRC-MacArthur Foundation Fellowship in International Peace and Security.

Deserving special thanks is the Center for International Security and Arms Control at Stanford University. I was in residence at the Center as a research fellow for three years and received varying degrees of financial support from the Center as well as constant intellectual support.

I also wish to thank the Moscow Institute for the Study of the U.S.A. and Canada, of the Academy of Sciences of the USSR. The Institute was my gracious host during one of my trips to Moscow.

More than being simply an editor, Richard Liebmann-Smith at Basic Books was a real friend and cohort. Linda Carbone, also at Basic Books, was unflaggingly serene and helpful as she steered the book through production.

Over several years Kristen Coston faithfully and tirelessly transcribed thousands of pages from the interview tapes, typed the manuscript, and did library research. Edita Hanley did library research and made translations from Russian sources. Jeff Urdin, Felicia Wong, and Elinor Stutz also assisted in various ways.

During my many stays in Washington, D.C., Wayne Silby generously lodged me in his home.

Finally, like so many authors, I want to take this opportunity to make some slight amends for the demands that writing this book has placed on my wife, Wendy Grace. Perhaps most demanding was my habit of getting up in the middle of the night to write down a new idea. She has been marvelous and steadfast; the book flourished in the context of her sustaining qualities.

Minds at War

CHAPTER 1

The Problem of Adapting to Nuclear Reality

IN THE YEARS immediately following World War II, there was a widespread expectation that in the future the major nations of the world would show greater restraint in their military competition. It was hoped that the devastation of the war had had a sobering effect. But, more important, it was assumed that the extraordinary destructiveness of atomic and, later, hydrogen weapons would ultimately raise the probable costs of war so high that no sane leader would consider the probable benefits worth the risk. This was particularly salient in the Soviet-American relationship. It was foreseen that these countries, and thus the alliances they led, would soon be in a condition of mutual vulnerability. Both countries, even after absorbing an all-out surprise attack, would still be able to retaliate with such devastation that the original attack would be essentially fruitless. There was an assumption that once this condition was established, it would lead to mutual restraint in the levels of armament and in the use of military force, thereby lowering the risk of war.[1]

Since that time, some of these expectations have been fulfilled. The United States and the Soviet Union have restrained themselves from using force against each other in situations that might, in fact, have led them to do so in a pre-nuclear era. Substantial effort has been invested in arms control—some treaties have been signed and, for the most part, have been closely observed. Both sides have signed documents stating that given the condition of mutual vulnerability, it is no longer legitimate to use force for anything other than defensive purposes.

At the same time there is a widespread perception that considering the dangers involved, this progress has been very slow, and in a number of ways events have moved in an antithetical direction. Both powers continue to use their military force—or the threat of it—in a struggle for relative control or influence around the globe. Notwithstanding extensive negotiations for arms control, the numbers of weapons in their nuclear arsenals have proliferated at a staggering rate—at present each side has well over twenty thousand nuclear weapons. Rather than jointly structuring their arsenals into a stable configuration to discourage a first strike, both sides have developed weapons that give an advantage to the initiator. Despite the annihilating consequences of nuclear war, both sides still have military doctrines that aim to achieve an advantageous outcome in the event of a war.

In a somewhat bizarre way, leaders on both sides have denounced this state of affairs. They take every opportunity to point to the other side as the primary culprit, yet they also describe the situation as a whole in the language of psychopathology. Former Secretary Leonid Brezhnev called the arms race "dangerous madness";[2] former President Richard Nixon has called it "insane."[3] President Ronald Reagan has described the "vicious cycle of threat and response which drives arms races" as "tragic."[4]

And yet, despite a palpable desire to find a better adaptation to the condition of mutual vulnerability, both sides have felt compelled in various ways to continue acting in a traditionally competitive fashion. The aim of this book is to understand more fully why this is the case.

The focus of investigation will be primarily on the American side of the equation. This asymmetry is derived entirely from the availability of data and not from a belief that the problems being studied arise more from the American than from the Soviet side. Furthermore, there will be some investigation of the Soviet perspective (chapters 11 and 12), and the concluding chapter will draw together a more complete perspective of the problem as a whole.

The Adaptive Stream

Since the detonation of the first atomic bomb, there have been two major streams* in American defense thinking. One has recognized the profound change in the role of military relations between states and the necessity for a major adaptive response. The other has downplayed the significance of nuclear weapons and asserted the continuing viability of traditional military principles.

One of the original spokesmen for the adaptive stream was Bernard Brodie. In a 1946 book he edited, *The Absolute Weapon,* Brodie recognized that ultimately other countries besides the United States would have atomic weapons. He predicted that there would be no reliable means of defense against such weapons and that both sides would be vulnerable to strikes against their cities. In such a context the role of military force would fundamentally change. Brodie wrote, "Thus far the chief purpose of a military establishment has been to win wars. From now on its chief purpose must be to avert them. It can have no other useful purpose."[5]

It was not long before some government policymakers began to arrive at similar conclusions. In 1949, shortly after the Soviets exploded their first atomic bomb, George Kennan, then director of the Policy Planning Staff in the United States Department of State, formulated what would become some of the key concepts in the adaptive response to the condition of vulnerability. Recognizing the widespread devastation of an atomic war, he wrote that war should "not negate the principle of life itself." He counseled "that we not fall into the error of initiating, or planning to initiate, the employment of these [atomic] weapons . . . thus hypnotizing ourselves into the belief that they may ultimately serve some positive national purpose." Atomic weapons should only serve "purposes of deterrence and retaliation." He ar-

---

*Although this will be elaborated in subsequent chapters, I should clarify in advance that the "streams" identified here are not the same as "schools" of thought. While there may be some defense thinkers who almost exclusively espouse ideas from one or the other stream, most individuals engage in lines of thinking drawn in varying degrees from both streams. The tension between these streams is, at times, played out between different groups of people. However, as I will attempt to demonstrate, the tension also arises from ambivalence *within* individuals. This kind of ambivalence may be one of the reasons that leaders on both sides denounce the nuclear arms race and yet continue to participate in it.

ticulated what would later be called the doctrine of "minimum deterrence," saying that the American arsenal should have only "what it would take to make attack on this country or its allies by weapons of mass destruction a risky, probably unprofitable and therefore irrational undertaking for any adversary."[6]

Although many military writers have argued that the United States was not in a condition of mutual vulnerability with the Soviet Union until the 1960s, it appears that key American officials perceived this condition as obtaining already in the 1950s. President Dwight D. Eisenhower said in 1954, "Atomic war will destroy civilization. . . . If the Kremlin and Washington ever lock up in a war, the results are too horrible to contemplate." And later, "It would literally be a business of digging ourselves out of the ashes, starting again." Even in a counterforce war (that is, one limited to attacks on military targets) there would be "no significant differences in the losses we would take."[7]

In light of this condition, Eisenhower supported putting limits on the size of the American arsenal regardless of the size of the Soviet arsenal. He wrote in 1956:

> War implies a contest . . . when you get to the point that contest is no longer involved and the outlook comes close to destruction of the enemy and suicide for ourselves . . . then arguments as to the exact amount of available strength as compared to somebody else's are no longer the vital issues.[8]

And:

> If you get enough of a particular type of weapon, I doubt that it is particularly important to have a lot more of it . . . if in the judgment of responsible officials the United States had adequate power to deter the Soviets from making an attack . . . there [is] no justification for adding additional . . . weapons just for the purpose of trying to match in numbers those of the Soviets.[9]

In 1960, when Eisenhower was informed about the possible rate of increase in strategic nuclear weapons for the upcoming years, he is reported to have been astonished and asked sarcastically, "Why don't we go completely crazy and plan a force of ten thousand?"[10] (Ironically, this is approximately the size of the current American strategic arsenal.) How many times, he asked rhetorically, "could [you] kill the same man?"[11]

During the 1960s this kind of thinking was further elaborated by then Secretary of Defense Robert McNamara. To describe the military relationship between the superpowers, McNamara coined the term *Mutual Assured Destruction,* or *MAD.* This meant that even after absorbing a surprise attack designed to disarm the other's arsenal, either side would have the capability to inflict "unacceptable damage" on the other side. McNamara worked to define precisely what percentage of the Soviet population and industrial capacity the United States would need to be able to destroy to constitute unacceptable damage. The percentages ranged from 20 percent to 33 percent of the population and from 50 percent to 75 percent of the industrial capacity. Given that the United States was able to fulfill such criterion, McNamara promoted the idea of limiting the size of the American arsenal accordingly.

In the later 1960s there was a growing consensus, effected significantly by the recognition of the condition of MAD, that the United States should seek to put relations with the Soviet Union on a more stable basis. This led to the policy of "détente," defined by one of its key architects, Henry Kissinger, as "mutual restraint, coexistence and, ultimately, cooperation."[12] This policy reached its zenith with the signing of the first Strategic Arms Limitation Treaty (SALT I) and a joint statement on the Basic Principles of Relations between the Soviet Union and the United States. SALT I included an Interim Agreement limiting strategic offensive weapons and an open-ended agreement banning antiballistic missiles. This latter agreement was particularly significant because it, in effect, made explicit the condition of mutual vulnerability and committed both sides to refrain from trying to upset it through defensive systems.

The Basic Principles of Relations recognized the fundamental significance of the condition of mutual vulnerability. Because nuclear weapons had created fundamental changes in the utility of military force, both sides affirmed the need to conduct their relations in a manner that eschewed the use of military force for unilateral advantage. The agreement said that the two countries

7

will proceed from the common determination that in the nuclear age there is no alternative to conducting their mutual relations on the basis of peaceful coexistence. Differences in ideology and in the social systems of the USA and the USSR are not obstacles to the bilateral development of normal relations based on the principles of sovereignty, equality, non-interference in internal affairs and mutual advantage.

. . . The USA and the USSR attach major importance to preventing the development of situations capable of causing a dangerous exacerbation of their relations. Therefore, they will do their utmost to avoid military confrontations and to prevent the outbreak of nuclear war. They will always exercise restraint in their mutual relations, and will be prepared to negotiate and settle differences by peaceful means. Discussions and negotiations on outstanding issues will be conducted in a spirit of reciprocity, mutual accommodation and mutual benefit.

Both sides recognize that efforts to obtain unilateral advantage at the expense of the other, directly or indirectly, are inconsistent with these objectives. The prerequisites for maintaining and strengthening peaceful relations between the USA and the USSR are the recognition of the security interests of the Parties based on the principle of equality and the renunciation of the use of threat of force. . . .

The USA and the USSR regard as the ultimate objective of their efforts the achievement of general and complete disarmament and the establishment of an effective system of international security in accordance with the purposes and principles of the United Nations.

Several years later, in 1975, similar principles were reiterated in the Helsinki Accords, signed by the United States, the Soviet Union, and thirty-three other nations.

In addition, there were concrete efforts to structure the American arsenal in less provocative ways. This generally focused on stopping the development of nuclear weapons with high enough levels of accuracy to destroy missile silos and command and control centers. It was argued that if the United States had such a capability, the Soviet Union would be encouraged to launch their missiles (lest they lose them) as soon as they received warning (perhaps incorrect) that American missiles were on their way. In a more general way, it was argued that weapons with counterforce capability (that is, the ability to destroy missile silos and command and control centers) were destabilizing—they might give one side an incentive to launch first in a crisis situation, to get in the first salvo for fear the other side would try to do the same thing. Influenced by such considerations for several years in the mid-1970s,

Congress refused to legislate funds for the new, highly accurate Mark-12A warhead (though it did eventually do so).

Another key aspect in the adaptive approach to arsenal design has been to enhance stability by maintaining mutual restraints on strategic defenses. A strategic defense system would be so technologically difficult that it would probably never succeed in offsetting the condition of vulnerability. Furthermore, countermeasures would be highly effective and less expensive than the defensive effort. More important, though, the effort to achieve strategic defenses could create uncertainty about the condition of mutual vulnerability. One side may mistakenly believe that it has acquired the ability to inflict a disarming first strike. This may lead it to be inordinately bold in its general use of force or even to consider making such a first strike. Also, one side might believe that the other side thinks it is close to acquiring a disarming first-strike capability, leading the first side to consider a pre-emptive strike. To prevent such ambiguities and to avert an arms race in space, the United States and the Soviet Union signed the Anti-Ballistic Missile (ABM) Treaty in 1972. More recently, proponents of this kind of thinking have had to work especially hard to counter a reemerging interest in defenses connected with President Reagan's Strategic Defense Initiative (popularly known as "Star Wars").

The Traditional Stream

In contrast to the adaptive stream in American defense thinking, the traditional stream resists the notion that the condition of mutual vulnerability implies fundamental changes in the way the United States relates to military force. Instead, it insists, military force continues to be a viable instrument of policy between nuclear armed powers. Concepts about the significance of relative force levels and the possibility of achieving an advantageous outcome in a superpower conflict are still considered applicable in a nuclear context.

Perhaps the most visible root of this line of thinking was a 1950 joint State and Defense Department review of U.S. foreign and defense policy, National Security Memorandum No. 68, or NSC-68. Then Secretary of State Dean Acheson said that the purpose of NSC-68 was to "bludgeon the mass mind of 'top government' " so as to reverse a perceived softening trend.[13] The authors of NSC-68 (principally Paul Nitze) not only called attention to the threat of Soviet expansionism potentially emboldened by its newly acquired atomic capability but also suggested that the United States could use its military force to "induce a retraction of the Kremlin's control and influence."[14] It was asserted that "it is clear that a substantial and rapid building up of strength in the free world . . . [will be effective to] check and to roll back the Kremlin's drive for world domination."[15] Such a strategy could even "foster the seeds of destruction within the Soviet system."[16]

There were profound reservations about agreements to control atomic energy and conventional weaponry. "If, contrary to our expectations, the Soviet Union should accept agreements promising effective control of atomic energy and conventional armaments . . . we would have to consider very carefully whether we could accept such agreements."[17] Negotiation was rejected as a central instrument of policy, though it was important to appear to be open to it. "In conclusion, negotiation is not a possible separate course of action but rather a means of gaining support for a program of building strength."[18] In general there was a concern that those with a more conciliatory orientation might be offended by plans "to conduct offensive operations to destroy vital elements of the Soviet war-making capability and to keep the enemy off balance," and therefore "emphasis should be given to the essentially defensive character" of the measures proposed so as to "minimize, so far as possible, unfavorable domestic and foreign reactions."[19]

At the time NSC-68 was written, the United States was not yet in a position of nuclear vulnerability. Nevertheless, since the Soviets acquired an assured destruction capability, the kind of thinking characterized by NSC-68 has persisted. Such thinking rejects the notion that mutual vulnerability calls for fundamental changes in defense thinking. The fact of mutual vulnerability has rarely been questioned. Traditional defense concepts have been simply asserted, implying that they continue to be fully applicable in a nuclear context.

An example of such thinking is the concern for relative force levels, or the balance of strategic forces. In contrast to the concept that the United States needs only the capability to retaliate effectively, a strong voice in American defense thinking has insisted that the United States must maintain levels of forces at least equal to the Soviet Union's. This argument is consistent with the traditional concern for relative military strength—an implicit assumption being that the distribution of military power is a key indicator of the probable outcome of a military conflict. Despite high levels of overkill on both sides, this concern for relative capabilities has persisted.

When the Soviet Union was clearly inferior to the United States, this concern was not so widely vocalized. However, as the Soviets began to approach overall equality with the United States and even to exceed it in some categories, relative capability became a growing issue. By the time of the SALT I ratification debate, it had become particularly prominent. Influenced by the more adaptive stream of thinking, American arms control negotiators allowed the Soviet Union to have a larger number of weapons in certain categories. Besides the overall security of the American retaliatory capability, Soviet numerical advantages in some categories were more than compensated for by other American advantages. Nevertheless, a powerful group of senators complained loudly about these numerical inferiorities. Ratification of SALT I was accomplished only with the passage of the Jackson Amendment, which called for all future treaties with the Soviet Union to be designed on a more strictly equal basis. Since then, the secretary of defense and the Joint Chiefs of Staff have consistently embraced the policy of "essential equivalence" in the size of the United States's nuclear forces relative to the Soviet Union's. Such thinking has pervaded arms control negotiations so deeply that the major part of negotiations has centered on the problem of defining exactly what equality is in each situation— not an easy task given the asymmetries in the structure of the Soviet and American arsenals.

The emphasis on maintaining equality has not necessarily signaled a lack of interest in the traditional goal of achieving superiority relative to the Soviet Union. However, in a political context heavily oriented to the notion of equality, it has become necessary to present proposals in terms of the maintenance of equality. This has not been difficult to do; by focusing on arsenal categories in which the United States was behind and ignoring those in which the United States was ahead, it is possible to pursue de facto superiority in the name of equality.

Furthermore, in numerous instances the interest in superiority has been stated explicitly. In the mid-1970s several members of the Committee on the Present Danger* embraced the goal of superiority. Lieutenant General Daniel Graham said, "Do I advocate superiority for the United States? I say yes."[20] Jeane Kirkpatrick, later appointed ambassador to the United Nations, said, "I am willing to be just as generous as we possibly can be so long as that's consistent with maintaining clear supremacy."[21] The 1980 platform of the Republican party called for military superiority relative to the Soviet Union. And in 1981 Defense Secretary Caspar Weinberger said, "Now we've got to regain" the position that the United States held in the 1950s when it had "a degree of superiority" which made it "safe."[22]

Traditional thinking has also persevered in the key area of war termination. According to the adaptive stream in American defense thinking, it is not possible to achieve an advantageous outcome in a military conflict between nuclear-armed powers. When both powers have such high levels of secure destructive capability, an all-out war would lead to general annihilation. When both sides always have the capability to escalate to the next higher level, a limited war would most likely not stay limited if either side seeks an advantageous outcome. Nevertheless the traditional stream has argued that in the event deterrence fails, the United States should aim for the traditional goal of an advantageous outcome defined in terms of relative levels of damage or actually prevailing over and subduing the opponent—indeed the United States might have to consider initiating nuclear use in a preemptive fashion.

In the 1950s, before the condition of vulnerability obtained, such thinking was entertained in a relatively unambiguous fashion. A declassified Statement of Policy by the National Security Council from 1953 stated, "if war comes," the goal would be to "go on to victory" over the Soviet Union. It also specified the goal "to win general war."[23] In the same year, then President Eisenhower wrote:

> we would have to be constantly ready, on an instantaneous basis, to inflict greater loss upon the enemy than he could reasonably hope to inflict upon us . . . but if the contest to maintain this relative position should have to continue indefinitely . . . we would be forced to consider whether or not

*The Committee on the Present Danger is a private organization guided by a philosophy similar to the one expressed in NSC-68 and cofounded by Paul Nitze, a principal author of NSC-68. Ronald Reagan was a member of the committee and when elected president, appointed other members to many key posts in his administration.

our duty to future generations did not require us to *initiate* war at the most propitious moment that we could designate [emphasis in original].[24]

After the United States became vulnerable to large-scale nuclear strikes, the language used to describe such goals became ambiguous, but the goals persisted nonetheless. Unclassified statements, such as the United States Military Posture and reports of the secretary of defense to Congress, have consistently spoken of aiming for "favorable" termination (defined by the Department of Defense as "the United States and its allies emerg[ing] with relative advantage irrespective of the circumstances of initiation, response, and termination").[25] The goal of "favorable" termination was even enunciated by the relatively pacific President Jimmy Carter.[26] The Reagan administration, particularly in its first term, was considerably more explicit, speaking of the goal to "defeat aggression"[27] and to "prevail" even under the condition of a prolonged nuclear war.[28] In response to criticism, Defense Secretary Caspar Weinberger retorted categorically, "You show me a secretary of defense who is not planning to prevail and I'll show you a secretary of defense who ought to be impeached."[29] In short, as Robert W. Tucker notes, "no administration has been able to disavow the prospect of emerging from a nuclear conflict with some kind of meaningful victory."[30]

United States military writings have also expressed this traditional line of thinking and have explicitly rejected the notion that the emergence of nuclear weapons should alter American war objectives. The United States Army's 1971 field manual (FM 100-30) asserts, "The introduction of tactical nuclear weapons onto the battlefield neither negates the principles of war described in FM 100-5 [the basic Army field manual] nor causes the development of new ones."[31] The United States Army field manual FM3-87, published in 1980, states even more unequivocally, "The U. S. Army must be prepared to fight and win when nuclear weapons are used."[32] General John Ryan, the Air Force chief of staff, writes, "If deterrence were to fail, we must have forces adequate to prevail in a nuclear conflict."[33] Army General Donn A. Starry has written:

the purpose of military operations cannot be simply to avert defeat, but rather, it must be to win. . . . Enemy leaders must be made to understand clearly that if they choose to move militarily, no longer will there be a status quo ante bellum—something to be restored. Rather, the situation they themselves have created is one which will be resolved on new terms.[34]

He makes it clear that such objectives are not to be limited to conflicts with non-nuclear foes but are to include Warsaw Pact forces as well and that nuclear weapons should be used against advancing troops well before they even approach the front line of North Atlantic Treaty Organization (NATO) troops.

In addition to these more overt instances of advantage-seeking concepts, there is a large body of strategic literature that is a bit more ambiguous on this point. This literature, concerned with the idea of fighting a limited war with the Soviet Union, rarely specifies explicitly the character of the termination. However, a careful reading of the most influential treatise, Henry Kissinger's *Nuclear Weapons and Foreign Policy*, reveals that the goal of limited nuclear war—in at least some cases—is to achieve an advantageous outcome. Written in 1957, Kissinger's thesis is predicated on the assumption that the Soviets would soon acquire an assured destruction capability, and unconditional surrender would be no longer possible as a U.S. war objective. Nevertheless he rejects the notion that it is necessary to abandon the concept of using military force, even nuclear force, to wrest some assets from the Soviet Union.

> The West has accepted several contractions of its sphere without resorting to all-out war . . . [the Soviets] too might accept local withdrawals without resorting to all-out war . . . we may be in a position to reduce the Soviet sphere. A strategy of limited war is more likely to achieve this objective than the threat of a total nuclear war. . . . Thus if we could develop forces capable of conducting limited war and of getting into position rapidly, we should be able to defeat the Soviet Union or China in local engagements. . . . The prerequisite for victory in a limited war is, therefore, to determine under what circumstances one side may be willing to run greater risks for winning than its opponent will accept to avoid losing.

Despite the elegance of his logic, however, Kissinger appears unable to explain how the United States can reliably determine whether the Soviet Union will back down. In the end he simply calls for a willingness to take high-risk gambles despite extraordinary stakes: "the strategy outlined . . . will not be easy to implement . . . it requires strong nerves. We can make a strategy of limiting war stick only if we leave no doubt about our readiness and our ability to face a final show-down."[35] At a later date Kissinger pulled back from this line of argument. However, it has continued to play a significant role in American defense thinking.

Another element in the traditional stream in American defense thinking is the interest in targeting nuclear military assets, especially missile silos and command and control centers. The orientation to destroying military assets is, of course, a classic principle in military strategy. In the early 1960s, before the Soviets were firmly perceived as having achieved a secure assured destruction capability, there was substantial interest in the notion of "limiting damage" to the United States in the event of a nuclear war. This would be done primarily by destroying Soviet missiles before they could get off the ground and by destroying the command and control centers that direct the launching of weapons. As the Soviets clearly acquired an assured destruction capability, the idea of damage limitation declined. It was recognized that the Soviets would always have enough surviving capability to inflict high levels of damage making the goal of limiting damage pointless. There was also concern that such a policy might encourage the Soviets to go to a launch-on-warning policy.

Nevertheless, the interest in destroying missile silos and command and control centers has persisted. As the Soviets have hardened the protective shells around these targets, weapons with higher levels of accuracy have been required to destroy them. And indeed, the major American investments in nuclear weapons over the last ten to fifteen years have been in weapons with the requisite accuracy to supply what is called "hard-target kill capability" (the Mark-12A warhead, the MX, the Pershing II, cruise missiles, the D-5).

Attacking such hardened targets has also become more complicated in recent years. Soviet tracking capabilities now can identify the target of incoming warheads with enough time to launch a targeted missile before it is struck. Soviet command and control centers can also launch the weapons under their control before being destroyed. The net effect of striking at hard targets may well be to put the Soviets in a use-them-or-lose-them position, thus increasing the probability that the weapons in question will be fired. Despite such problems, the traditional interest in destroying Soviet military assets continues.

The most recent proposal to emerge from the traditional stream is the Strategic Defense Initiative (SDI), or "Star Wars." In a speech on March 23, 1983, President Reagan called for a system of strategic defense so effective that it would undo the condition of nuclear vulnerability. Despite a strong consensus in the scientific community that such an objective is unfeasible,* the concept has persevered and has been reiterated by President Reagan and members of his administration (see chapter 9). This proposal differs from other elements in the traditional stream. While consistent with a traditional orientation in seeking to restore the role of defense in military planning, it does not ignore the condition of vulnerability. Rather, it recognizes the condition and seeks to undo it through technological means. This effort should be distinguished from attempts to find a new adaptation to the condition of vulnerability. This may be the goal of some SDI advocates, but some key architects of the program have made it clear that their objective is to restore the situation that the United States was in around the time NSC-68 was written. Caspar Weinberger, giving testimony in support of SDI to the Senate Armed Services Committee, said, "If we can get a system which is effective and which we know can render their weapons impotent, we would be back in a situation we were in, for example, when we were the only nation with the nuclear weapon."[36]

Alternative Explanations

As these two streams in American defense thinking became apparent to me, a particularly perplexing question emerged: Why is the traditional stream so persistent when it seems to be in such conflict with so many features of the reality engendered by nuclear weapons? I entertained numerous explanations, all of which seemed inadequate for

---

*In a survey taken in 1986 of the members of the National Academy of Sciences in fields relevant to SDI, 94 percent estimated that SDI could not provide "effective defense of the U.S. civilian population," even if the Soviets do not employ countermeasures against the defense system. Assuming the Soviets do employ countermeasures, this figure goes up to 98 percent. Only 4 percent said that the odds of success are better than even that SDI would be "survivable and cost-effective at the margin." It is doubtful that the United States government has ever pursued a large-scale project deemed unfeasible by such a large proportion of its scientific community. ("Strong Opposition to SDI Found in National Academy of Sciences," *Cornell University News* [October 30, 1986], 29)

a number of reasons. Fully addressing each of these explanations would require an entire book. Nevertheless, I will share a few of the salient reasons why they left me dissatisfied.

ECONOMIC INTERESTS

One of the most common explanations for the persistence of the traditional U.S.-Soviet military competitiveness focuses on the large sectors of the American economy benefiting from it. These economic interests, it is argued, actively seek to influence both the public, by promoting attitudes that lead to competitive policies, and the policy-makers, by exerting financial leverage. It is in the interest of this economic sector to obfuscate nuclear reality so as to promote traditional behavior. This explanation is not easy to dismiss. Economic self-interest is a powerful force shaping human behavior, and indeed a good deal of money is made from defense spending. If one retraces historically a specific weapons deployment decision, one would very likely find the defense industry actively lubricating the decision-making process at numerous key junctures.

But while this explanation does supply some insight, it is inadequate in a number of ways. At the systemic level it is not clear why the defense industries should be so influential. Defense spending represents only about 7 percent of the Gross National Product. This means that 93 percent of the economy is in competition with the defense industry. Even given that some industries produce in both the defense and the nondefense sectors, it is clear that the majority of the economy, from a strictly economic point of view, would be interested in minimizing the level of defense spending. Therefore, logically, any economic interest seeking to promote defense spending should be at least equally countered by economic interests resisting it.

Putting aside the systemic argument, one can argue that the defense industries are simply better organized and buy influence through political action committees and lobbying efforts. Here again, though, the defense industries are not the only well-organized interest group trying to influence legislation. Certainly teachers are equally well organized and equally motivated and yet are considerably less successful.

It has also been argued that the defense industries have been particularly influential through control of the mass media, biasing the presentation of information to encourage the public to support a more competitive foreign policy. I have not encountered any direct evidence that the defense industries have had an inordinate influence on the media as compared with other economic interests. And I have not been convinced that the presentation of information is so consistently biased in directions that would point to high levels of defense spending. I have been more convinced by the simpler assumption that the media follows its own economic interests, which lead them to present information that will attract the public's attention and thereby increase the market share of the specific media outlet.

Looking more specifically at the individuals who generate the key ideas that shape American defense policy, I see little reason to believe that their behavior is primarily determined by economic self-interest. Most of these individuals, highly intelligent and capable, likely forgo the substantially higher salaries available outside the relatively modestly remunerated field of defense policymaking. Doubtless there are individuals who move back and forth between government and defense industry positions and make handsome incomes. However, this is not always the case and it is not at all clear that this is the pathway to the highest possible economic rewards, nor do individuals who follow such a path gain the maximum influence over policy. From what I know about the individuals who have been the most influential in shaping American defense policy, on the whole they have not made remarkable sums of money.

One more important point is that the policymaking community, even its more hawkish branch, does not always promote policies that would most enrich the defense industries. For example, in the 1950s there was a re-evaluation of American defense policy that led to what was called the "New Look." According to this policy, the United States would refrain from trying to match the Soviets with expensive conventional capabilities and instead would emphasize relatively less expensive nuclear weapons. Even though this policy inevitably resulted in relatively lower levels of defense spending (and was advertised as such), it was generally embraced by the policymaking community.

IDIOSYNCRASIES OF POLICYMAKERS

Another popular concept is that individuals involved in the defense field persist in formulating competitive policies because they have idiosyncratic personalities. They are plagued by inordinate urges to be aggressive and to acquire power, they have a paranoid view of the Soviets, or they have a hyper-rationalism that robs them of common sense about the realities of nuclear war. While it is possible that defense policymakers, in these dimensions, may deviate from the norm to a marginal extent, I am not convinced that margin is very great.

More significantly, the proposals offered by these policymakers seem to be for the most part in step with the attitudes of the general public. While the majority of the public has often favored decreasing the size of the defense budget, at times it has favored expanding it. Overall the public seems to be marginally less ambitious about foreign goals than the policymaking community, but, again, this relatively minor discrepancy does not explain the general character of the policies adopted.

CYCLES OF FEAR AND MISPERCEPTION

A number of social scientists have applied to the Soviet-American relationship an interactive model that generally describes how certain volatile political situations can escalate into a crisis. Nation A, feeling fearful of the military potential of Nation B, takes defensive actions that are misperceived by Nation B to be offensive in character. This generates fear in Nation B, leading it to take actions that are likewise misperceived by Nation A as offensive. In this way a cyclic interaction can start possibly leading to a crisis situation or even war.

While this model may be effective in explaining some specific historical events, it does not seem adequate to describe the general Soviet-American competition. Soviets and Americans, like people in general, are not only motivated by fear. They also have ambitions and, at times, aggressive intentions. When one side sees the other side build up its military capability, it is probably not entirely a misperception for the one side to discern something more than purely defensive intentions, whatever the other side claims. There is probably also an element of self-deception when the one side insists that its corresponding responses are entirely devoid of opportunistic considerations.

Another difficulty with the fear-driven model is its inability to account for the demonstrated willingness of the Soviet Union and the United States to risk war for certain political and economic goals even when the consequences would be devastating. This points to the fact that humans are not entirely dominated by a fearful desire for biological survival. In fact, they are surprisingly willing to jeopardize and even actively sacrifice their lives in the service of abstract goals. (That is why there is some credibility to the American and Soviet threats to use nuclear weapons.)

A more complete model of the Soviet-American competition must take into account the complex interaction of fearful defensive motives, ambitious offensive motives, and the idealistic willingness for self-sacrifice.

THE STRUCTURAL MODEL

Perhaps the most impressive theoretical model for the persistence of military competition in the Soviet-American relationship is based on an analysis of the game-theoretic structure of the relationship. In the game model most commonly used, two players have two options: to cooperate or to defect. Mutual cooperation produces mutual gain, while mutual defection produces mutual loss. When one player chooses defection and the other cooperation, the defector gains and the competitor loses. By adjusting the magnitude of the losses and gains in such a situation (the payoff matrix), game theorists assume they can model the interaction of the players. Likewise, by analyzing the behavior of nation-states in structurally similar situations, they assume they can deduce the payoff matrix that decisionmakers hold.

The payoff matrix most extensively studied is called "prisoner's dilemma." Here losses from joint defection are not as great as losses from unilateral cooperation, and gains from unilateral defection are greater than gains from mutual cooperation. Therefore, to minimize possible losses and to maximize possible gains (the "minimax" strategy), a player, game theorists predict, will choose to defect.

Lawrence Freedman writes: "The use of this game to illuminate an arms race is quite straightforward. If A devotes considerable resources to new weapons, at best he can gain a decisive lead over B and at worst he will deny B any advantage." As both sides reason in this fashion, the competition continually moves forward. In a way, this vision of the process has a tragic element to it because, as Freedman continues, "if A and B agreed on measures to dampen arms spending, then both could enjoy equivalent security at a lower cost."[37]

Such a model has been used to explain not only the Soviet-American arms race and the difficulty in achieving arms control agreements but also the general difficulty in moving toward any form of Soviet-American cooperation and mutual restraint. The assumption is that because the two nations are having such trouble negotiating, decisionmakers perceive a payoff matrix that rationally dictates competitive behavior. In such a situation it is almost impossible for either side to transcend its rational self-interest. Because it can only assume that the other side will pursue its rational self-interest, such an act would most likely lead to being taken advantage of—an unacceptable risk for a decisionmaker. This logic can be summarized in colloquial parlance: "If I don't try to get an edge on him, he's sure to get an edge on me."

This analysis is interesting because it may illustrate what, in fact, is occurring in the thinking of some policymakers. To that extent, it points to a possible program of empirical research.

There are problems, however, when this model is used to suggest that such cooperation is nearly impossible and that mutual defection is all but inevitable. Human behavior does not always conform to the elegant logic of game theory. In a laboratory setting, subjects frequently do not behave in a manner consistent with the predictions of game theory. People show individual differences and, perhaps more important, contrary to what the assigned payoff matrix might predict, sometimes people do cooperate.[38] They are particularly able to do so if they can talk to each other during the game.[39] Outside the laboratory examples abound in which individuals succeed in cooperating even when it requires their trusting the other party to not take advantage of them.

Let us take a partly hypothetical example. Imagine a remote town in the western United States during the middle of the last century when it was common for men to carry guns as part of their regular dress.[40] Despite the general recognition that life is more dangerous for everyone because of the constant presence of firearms, each individual could use a game-theoretic analysis that would lead him to be unwilling to relinquish his gun. Following a minimax strategy, he may reason that carrying his gun would minimize his probable losses should he encounter someone carrying a gun. He also may conclude that carrying the gun would maximize his possibility of gain should he be in need of money and encounter someone without a gun on a moonless night. Nevertheless, somehow westerners did eventually relinquish their guns, so that now it is relatively far less common for men in the western United States to carry guns.

A structuralist may object to this illustration on the grounds that the critical factor here is not the willingness to act cooperatively but the presence of a third party, law enforcement officials, that imposes a cooperative order. But while law enforcement officials do police compliance with the cooperative order, they do not create it. The cooperative order, or law, requires a general willingness to abide by it and to support the officers of the law in their efforts to deal with the minority of deviants. Should the number of deviants reach a critical mass, the law enforcement mechanisms would once again be powerless. In short, civilized society is held together by the willingness of most of its members to enter into cooperative relations.

It is sometimes suggested that while it may be possible to achieve cooperation between individuals, cooperation between states on matters of vital significance is close to impossible. Here again, the fact that there is no transnational entity capable of imposing order is cited as critical. But this problem is structurally the same as the problem at the individual level which somehow has been solved. Even more important, there are many cases in which nations have acted and do act in a cooperative fashion despite the problems inherent in interstate cooperation. Evidently there are factors other than the international structure itself that determine whether nations will cooperate or compete.

Perhaps most significantly, though, the structural approach does not account for some of the features of the Soviet-American military competition that are complex and even strange. In a game, theoretic model values are deduced from the players' behavior. In the Soviet-American competition, it is easy to deduce that the players believe they are pursuing a valuable advantage through their competitive behavior. However, this is not necessarily the case. For example, Robert McNamara presided over the largest buildup of the American nuclear arsenal, reaching, by most measures, the highest levels ever attained even though the Soviet arsenal was much smaller at that time. Nevertheless, McNamara argued repeatedly and convincingly that nuclear weapons beyond a certain minimal level (far below what was reached) were of no real utility and were even of negative value because they wasted so much money. Furthermore, contrary to the values of a competitive orientation, he applauded Soviet efforts to develop a secure retaliatory capability. Unless one assumes that McNamara's statements were simply cases of prevarication (which I do not), it is hard to see how such complexities can lend themselves to game theoretic analyses based on a unidimensional value system.

PERSEVERANCE

Another perspective on the persistence of the traditional stream in American defense thinking—one I initially found very promising—is the more psychological explanation that outmoded models of military relations between states have persevered due to cognitive rigidity and inertia. Hans Morgenthau, the realist political theorist, wrote in an article titled "The Fallacy of Thinking Conventionally About Nuclear Weapons":

> from the beginning of history to 1945, when mankind thought naturally in pre-nuclear terms, it developed certain conceptions about weapons and war, which have not yielded in the minds of certain theoreticians, or even in the minds of practitioners, when they have time to think in theoretical terms, to the impact of an entirely novel phenomenon, the availability of nuclear weapons and of what we call euphemistically a nuclear war. So we have a disjunction between the conventional ways we think and act about nuclear weapons and the objective conditions, under which the availability of nuclear weapons forces us to live. . . . We have tried, then, instead of adapting our modes of thought and action to the objective conditions of the nuclear age, to conventionalize nuclear war. . . . The idea that a nuclear war should necessarily end in a stalemate or in the mutual destruction of the belligerents is simply unacceptable to people who have made it their business to prepare for victorious wars. They are in the position of a banker or a business in general, whose purpose in life is to make a profit for his company, and all of a sudden he is faced with the contingency that the best he can hope for is to break even. He will never make a profit and pay a dividend on the stock of his company, which goes against his grain, against his nature.[41]

Robert Jervis elaborates this line of thinking in his book *The Illogic of American Nuclear Strategy*. He first explains that there has been what he calls "the nuclear revolution," derived from:

> the overwhelming power of the weapons and the existence of mutual second-strike capability, meaning that neither side can eliminate the other's retaliatory capacity by launching a disarming first strike.

Describing this as a profound change in the utility of military force, he writes:

In the past, states that were stronger than their adversaries could credibly threaten major war because if the other side did not comply, the threat could rationally be carried out. . . . Since states can no longer protect themselves, this is no longer the case.

However, Jervis notes that policymakers have trouble emotionally accepting this new condition and, in various ways, try to pursue security in a traditional fashion.

The changes brought about by nuclear weapons are so painful and difficult that it is not surprising that people react not by making the best of new realities, but by seeking alluring, if ultimately misleading, paths which they think will lead back to traditional security.[42]

He then describes a number of "attempted escapes" from the reality of the nuclear revolution. Borrowing from Morgenthau, he describes "the most significant and pervasive escape attempt" to be "conventionalization," which he defines as:

the attempt to treat nuclear bombs as though they were conventional weapons, to apply the same ways of thinking to them that applied to armaments in the prenuclear era. This view implies that there has not been a real nuclear revolution and . . . is intellectually attractive because it allows the analyst to use familiar concepts and apply ideas and arguments which have proven their utility over centuries of experience.

He then concludes:

But the denial of radical change cannot bring back the older world, and a policy that seeks escape in this way will make less and less sense as it becomes increasingly elaborate and precise.[43]

In many ways this perspective made a great deal of sense to me as a clinical psychologist. A major component of psychotherapy is helping clients see how they are applying to their life situation strategies that were appropriate at an earlier time but are no longer effective.

This phenomenon of "perseverance" has also been studied in experimental psychology. Summarizing the findings of a variety of studies, psychologists Lee Ross and Craig Anderson write:

it is clear that beliefs can survive potent logical or empirical challenges. They can survive and even be bolstered by evidence that most uncommitted observers would agree logically demands some weakening of such beliefs. *They can even survive the total destruction of their original evidential bases* [emphasis added].[44]

A similar pattern can also occur at a collective level. Thomas Kuhn has described the process of revolutionary change in the field of science.[45] According to Kuhn, science is carried out within the context of a prevailing paradigm that includes a general model of the nature of reality and specifies a mode of behavior for carrying out the business of science. At certain points, discoveries emerge that are anomalous— they do not fit inside the prevailing paradigm and even call the entire paradigm into question. Initially there are efforts to ignore or even suppress such anomalous evidence. Quantum physicist David Bohm has compared this phenomenon to the cartoon characters who walk off the edge of the cliff and continue to walk out into the air for a few steps buoyed by their refusal to recognize that they are no longer on solid ground. Eventually, though, reality catches up with the cartoon characters and they fall.[46] Likewise, in the field of science, as the body of anomalous evidence grows and as a younger generation of less-orthodox scientists gains more influence, the pressures for a new paradigm reach a critical mass and a revolution occurs.

This model of persevering cognitive structures did seem to explain much about the persistence of traditional military thinking in the nuclear age. (As we shall see it plays a prominent role in my analysis of the thinking of defense policymakers.) At the same time, though, I began to wonder whether it was really a complete picture. Even the most hard-line defense policymakers have fully available to them the information about the realities of nuclear weapons. On a closer reading of their writings, I found that they did not directly contest the reality of the condition of mutual vulnerability, though their references to it were in the context of complaints about its effect on American defense thinking. They formulated ideas and strategies that seemed to ignore the condition of mutual vulnerability, but they did not present a counterargument to explain how the condition did not obtain. (Because they seemed frustrated by the effects of the perceived condition on

American thinking, I presumed, if they had a good counterargument, they would have presented it.)

I also noted that individuals who clearly articulated ideas about the nature of nuclear reality also supported policies that were more consistent with the "conventionalized" thinking of the traditional stream. President Eisenhower, in the 1950s, vividly depicted the annihilatory consequences of an atomic war, calling into question the military utility of atomic weapons. Nevertheless he also made statements that are remarkably bold examples of conventionalization, such as "atomic weapons have virtually achieved conventional status within our armed forces . . . [and] I see no reason why [nuclear weapons] shouldn't be used just exactly as you would use a bullet or anything else."[47] He also called for seeking an advantageous outcome in an atomic war and considered a pre-emptive attack as an option. More recently, President Jimmy Carter, in his 1979 State of the Union message, clearly recognized the condition of mutual vulnerability and high levels of overkill, pointing out that just two nuclear-armed submarines were adequate to destroy every major and mid-sized city in the Soviet Union. Nevertheless, Carter initiated one of the largest nuclear buildups in American history. The Reagan administration has been noted for its inconsistency on the question of whether the United States should have a policy of seeking to prevail in a nuclear war. This was humorously depicted by Dan Wasserman in a cartoon in the *Los Angeles Times*. A reporter is interviewing Caspar Weinberger:

REPORTER: Mr. Secretary—does U.S. policy accept the idea that nuclear war is winnable?

WEINBERGER: Of course not—nobody in his right mind could believe that.

REPORTER: Because an all-out war with the Soviets would also wipe out the U.S.

WEINBERGER: Wanna bet?

Such apparent inconsistencies have also appeared in polls of the American public. In a 1984 poll, 90 percent of respondents agreed that "we and the Soviets now have enough nuclear weapons to blow each other up many times over"; 89 percent agreed that "there can be no winner in an all-out nuclear war"; and 83 percent agreed that even "a limited nuclear war is nonsense."[48] More recently, 69 percent agreed that "further increases and improvements in nuclear weapons would not give either the U.S. or the Soviet Union a real advantage over the other."[49] Nevertheless, 71 percent agreed that the United States "should continue to develop new and better nuclear weapons," and 57 percent agreed that it is necessary to maintain "a nuclear arsenal *equal to* [that of the Soviet Union] to guarantee America's national security [emphasis in original]."[50] And in general the public has supported defense budgets that are relatively large for peacetime.

Inner Conflict

The fact that individuals seem to recognize fundamental features of nuclear reality at the same time that they persist in supporting policies that seem inconsistent with it suggests that the difficulties in adapting to nuclear reality may not be entirely of a cognitive nature. People have the capability to fully grasp the new condition, but there is some resistance to doing so consistently and to adapting traditional policies fully to this new condition. This suggests there may be conflicting motives involved; one set of motives desires to adapt to the new reality and another to persevere in the pre-nuclear mode.

Of course, the motive generally given by defense policymakers for all their efforts is the pursuit of security. The efforts to recognize the changes engendered by nuclear weapons and to modify behavior accordingly, found in the adaptive stream, can certainly be interpreted as being motivated by security interests. However, it is harder to understand how some persisting traditional policies serve security. If we assume that these policies are, in fact, motivated by security concerns, then the policies may seem to be derived from a failure of intellect or the crusty perseverance of pre-nuclear thinking. However, if we assume that traditional policies serve interests other than security, then they may make a certain sense. Such motives may resist adapting defense policies to nuclear reality even if doing so might incrementally improve security.

The idea that there are motives that can enter into conflict with and even override security interests runs contrary to a popular model of human motivation. According to this model, the dominant human motivation is for survival with all other motivations being secondary. Nations, accordingly, seek security (that is, national survival) as their first priority. When investigators encounter behavior that seems to run contrary to security interests, the model prompts them to explain how the behavior, in fact, is consistent with security interests. For example, such behavior might be explained as a tactical move designed to produce a hidden end or as being derived from misperceptions that distort a clear assessment of costs and benefits. Such explanations often produce interesting insights.

However, such a model of human motivation should not be considered as adequate to explain all behavior. There are too many examples in which individual or collective security motives are overridden by other motives. Individuals sometimes commit suicide. Such behavior is not all that rare; in the United States approximately one out of sixty lives ends in suicide.[51] In some countries the numbers are considerably higher. Throughout history many individuals and groups have willingly sacrificed their lives in the service of abstract causes or as an alternative to modifying their religious customs. Nations frequently jeopardize their security in the pursuit of goals quite unrelated to their security, for example, goals related to religion or national pride. Polls of the American public's attitude about building nuclear weapons also suggest that security interests are not necessarily the most fundamental concern for all Americans. In a recent poll 68 percent agreed that "If we and the Soviets keep building missiles . . . it's only a matter of time before they are used." Nevertheless, 57 percent agreed that "The U.S. must not lose the arms race," and, as mentioned, 71 percent said "The United States should continue to develop new and better nuclear weapons."[52]

Analyzing defense policy in terms of such conflicting motives encounters certain problems. The discourse of defense policy is dominated by the assumption that survival is the preeminent human value. Even if traditional defense policies are consciously or unconsciously sustained by motives that conflict with security motives, we can well expect to hear defense policymakers rationalize their policies in terms of security interests, even if it is necessary to employ highly convoluted arguments to do so.

The phenomenon of perseverance may well dovetail with this rationalizing tendency. As discussed above, humans have an intellectual inertia that leads them to persevere with previously established conceptual models even in the face of substantial disconfirming evidence. By simply persevering in conventionalized modes of thinking, it becomes easier to sustain the argument that traditional policies serve security interests.

However, the fact that real security motives are also operating makes the phenomenon more complex. Security motives keep directing one's attention to elements in the environment that are relevant to security concerns even when such awarenesses undermine the rationale for traditional policies. The net effect may be to produce two disparate, though internally coherent, mindsets. One mindset attends to significant changes engendered by nuclear weapons and supports the search for adaptive policies. The other mindset ignores or discounts the evidence of such change and supports traditional policies. Because both underlying motives exist within a single person, it is possible for an individual to shift between these mindsets and ultimately to say and do things that seem quite inconsistent.

This model of an underlying conflict is, of course, only a hypothesis. Naturally, I recognized that there was a null hypothesis: that, in fact, policymakers are able to justify the policies in question in terms of security interests while still accounting for fundamental features of nuclear reality. If so, the inner conflict model would have to be severely reevaluated. For this reason, it was essential that I examine every possible rationale for traditional policies, even those that seemed far-fetched or convoluted. I was not satisfied with the rationales given in the defense literature; there were too many seeming logical flaws and unanswered questions. But perhaps they could be accounted for in ways that I was not able to grasp. Faced with this uncertainty, I came to feel it was necessary to carry out an interview study of defense policymakers.

To the extent that this model of inner conflict would be sustained by such a study, the interviews would also create the opportunity to address an equally important question: "What are the motives that conflict with security interests?" Perhaps policymakers would at some point abandon the effort to rationalize policies in terms of security interests and instead openly speak of other motives. If so, their comments might lend valuable insight into the underlying motives that sustain traditional policies.

CHAPTER 2

Design of the Study

THE FOCUS of this study was to learn how American defense policymakers rationalize certain defense policies that seem inconsistent with nuclear reality. These included the policies of:

1. Maintaining an American arsenal at least equal in size to the Soviet arsenal—that is, to maintain the balance
2. Seeking a relatively advantageous termination in a military conflict with the Soviet Union
3. Developing nuclear weapons with the ability to destroy hardened targets (that is, protected missile silos and command and control centers)
4. Developing strategic defenses as a means for eliminating population vulnerability.

These policies seemed inconsistent with numerous aspects of nuclear reality, including, but not limited to:

1. The existence of large and redundant nuclear arsenals capable of inflicting unacceptable damage even after absorbing an all-out first strike
2. The secure option, in a military conflict, for both the United States and the Soviet Union to escalate to unacceptable levels
3. The option to launch missiles that are (either directly or via the command and control center that controls them) threatened by incoming warheads
4. The extraordinary difficulty in meaningfully defending populations when such a small percentage of deliverable warheads would destroy such a large percentage of the population.

Design of the Study

Before proceeding into the details of the study, there are several points I want to underscore. First, this study is not *premised* on the assumption that these policies are necessarily inconsistent with nuclear reality. The study was prompted by my perception of this inconsistency but the purpose of the study was to discover how policymakers rationalize these policies. Naturally I wanted to know if their perception of nuclear reality was quite different from mine or if they had some crucial information that would alter my view. Would they deny that fundamental changes had occurred? Would they shift between recognizing nuclear reality pretty much as I perceived it and then promoting apparently inconsistent policies, without any real resolution? Did they recognize such inconsistencies? (My hunch was that some people did.) If so, how would they explain their continued support for the policies?

Second, I do not mean to imply that these policies are, themselves, the essential problem in the Soviet-American relationship. If all the policies in question were abandoned, if the U.S. arsenal was reduced to a minimal deterrent, if war-fighting objectives were scaled back with goals that were minimal and sought a symmetrical outcome, if hard-target capable weapons were eliminated, if the goal of protecting populations was abandoned, if all these things were done, they might well be very positive steps. But we would still be faced with the more fundamental question of how two great powers deal with the condition of mutual vulnerability. How do these powers resolve their conflicts if it is no longer viable to resort to force? Even more basic is the question of exactly what national security (and even national sovereignty) means in a condition of interdependence.

But though I am not suggesting that abandoning these policies would resolve the most essential problems, I am suggesting that these policies are symptomatic of the difficulties in dealing with nuclear reality. In each case, I am hypothesizing, these policies reflect some resistance to fully addressing nuclear reality and its fundamental implications. The psychological processes that sustain such policies may reflect some of the most basic obstacles to the more profound changes required for a more complete adaptation to nuclear reality.

Third, by focusing specifically on American defense policymakers I am not suggesting that these individuals are the primary source of the difficulties the United States is having in adapting to nuclear reality, that the idiosyncratic, psychological features of defense policymakers generate the essence of the problem. The problem itself is very much a systemic problem involving not only the American policymaking community but also the American public. I have focused on defense policymakers only partly because they play a disproportionately larger role than other individuals in shaping policy. More significant was my assumption that defense policymakers would most vividly and articulately display the collective psychological processes reflected in the policies being studied. While there may be some specific points on which the policymaking community differs from the general public, it is very possible that members of the public would ultimately arrive at similar positions if they gave each question more thought and still held to their basic orientation. Even though the public might be characterized as dissatisfied with the general condition of defense policy, it may be more correct to say that it is not happy with the objective condition or with any of the policy options presently available. It has not settled on an alternative policy direction in a consistent way. In short, my assumption is that defense policymakers reflect fairly well what might be called the collective psyche, complete with its tensions and contradictions.

To study the thinking of American policymakers, I began with a review of the defense literature written since the 1960s. This included the annual reports of the secretary of defense to Congress, the annual Military Posture Statements of the Joint Chiefs of Staff, numerous books written on nuclear strategy, selected articles from numerous journals that explore security issues, publications of prodefense organizations and think tanks, testimony from congressional hearings on defense issues, and public statements by defense policymakers in the press and the media.

This material alone was not adequate to answer the key questions of the study. I wanted to know not only the ostensible rationales offered but also how they stood in the mind of the defense policymakers and strategists. I was not entirely convinced they fully believed everything they said. Nor was I confident they were simply dissembling. I wanted to know how they would respond when the apparent inconsistencies in their positions were presented to them in a focused way. When writing, people have firm control over the development of an argument; they can nimbly avoid difficult areas. In the back-and-forth of an interview, it is harder to evade problematic issues. My goal was not, however, simply to uncover inconsistencies but to see if policymakers would generate more complex arguments to account for them.

Respondents*

As used here, the term *defense policymaker* refers broadly to individuals who are part of the community involved in formulating, evaluating, and carrying out defense policies. It includes individuals ranging from those who develop highly specific targeting plans, to academics who develop general theories, to the highest-level Pentagon officials who formally set policies, to legislators who decide what to fund. From the point of view of this study they are all part of the intellectual milieu of the defense policymaking community.

The individuals selected for interviewing reflected this broad definition. Easily identifiable were prominent individuals who have played a highly visible role in developing and executing American defense policy. I also drew from lists of officials at various levels in the Departments of Defense and State. From lists of congressmen and senators on defense-related committees, I selected those with "prodefense" voting records so as to find ones who would support the policies being examined. I selected a number of individuals in academia and various defense think tanks based on their publications in the defense literature. I asked for recommendations from a number of individuals who have been involved in the defense community. And finally, at the end of interviews I asked respondents to suggest other people to interview. A list of the institutional affiliations of the eighty-four individuals interviewed can be found in table 2.1.

Of the eighty-four respondents, only three were women. Because the defense policymaking community is extremely male-dominated, it took conscious effort to reach even this small number of women.

I used a variety of methods for approaching respondents. Most frequently it was a telephone call. The second most frequent was a letter. In a small number of cases, I asked an acquaintance of the

---

*The term *respondents* is used rather than *subjects* to avoid giving the false impression that this was a highly controlled, laboratorylike study.

TABLE 2.1

Interview Respondents Listed by Institutional Affiliation
(A = Active, F = Former)

Defense Department
    Secretaries (2F)
    Other High Level (3A, 2F)
    Middle level (15A, 5F)
Joint Chiefs of Staff
    Members (2F)
National Security Council
    Members (1A, 6F)
    Staff (1A, 1F)
State Department
    Arms Control and Disarmament Agency
        High level (3A, 2F)
        Middle level (1A)
    Other middle level (3A)
Presidential advisors (formal and informal) (5A)
Military
    Flag rank (2A, 2F)
    Other (1A, 2F)
Congress
    Senators (on defense-related committees) (2A)
    Representatives (on defense-related committees) (2A)
    Foreign policy aides (3A)
    Senate Armed Services Committee staff (1A)
    Senate Foreign Relations Committee staff (1A)
    House Armed Services Committee staff (1A)
Original key nuclear strategists from the 1950s and 1960s (6)
Rand Corporation (8A, 6F)
Scowcroft Commission members[a] (5)
Center for Strategic and International Studies at Georgetown University (4A)
Committee on the Present Danger (5A)
American Security Council (3A)
National Institute for Public Policy (2A)
Other think tanks (5A)
Livermore Laboratories (6A)
Members of private sector of defense industry (5A)
    Total respondents interviewed: 84[b]

---

[a]The "Scowcroft Commission" was a group of high-level defense thinkers (headed by Lieutenant General Brent Scowcroft) convened by President Reagan in 1982 to address broad issues related to strategic defense policy and the question of whether to deploy the MX missile.
[b]The totals from the above categories are greater because some individuals fell into more than one category.

potential respondent to write an introductory letter which I then followed up with a telephone call.

I presented myself as a research fellow at the Center for International Security and Arms Control at Stanford University, carrying out a study on the role of perceptions in American defense policy. Depending on the specialization of the potential respondent, I also included a specific reference to nuclear strategy or arms control. I then explained that I was interviewing people throughout different sectors of the defense establishment and mentioned some names of people already interviewed. In many cases I clarified at this point that the interview was on a nonattribution basis.

Procedure

At the beginning of the interview, I again described the study and answered any questions respondents had. Most had no questions; a small number wanted to know more about my purpose and my background. I gave a minimal amount of information so as not to bias the responses. Most respondents probably assumed I was a political scientist rather than a psychologist.

I asked permission to tape record, reiterating that the interview was on a nonattribution basis and that they would not be quoted by name without getting their approval. The great majority of people readily agreed. Some respondents refused to be taped; others agreed with some reluctance. Occasionally, respondents asked me to turn off the tape recorder when they wanted to say something controversial or highly critical of a particular individual.

I did not follow a list of questions; rather, I started with a very general question and then allowed the interview to move in a free-form fashion. There were a number of key policy areas that I wanted to explore (these are described below). In many cases the discussion spontaneously moved into these areas; in some cases I gently steered the discussion; on occasion I abruptly set a new direction with a strong question. Clearly, some respondents preferred talking about some issues more than others. Though I often pushed them a bit, for the most part I accommodated their preferences.

My participation in the discussion was generally considerably more than that of a passive listener. I pressed for more careful definitions and challenged assumptions. I brought in new information that was being overlooked and pointed to inconsistencies in their arguments. Whenever an answer was given I indicated interest and satisfaction and genuinely tried to understand their arguments.

The majority of respondents seemed to enjoy the interview process, often continuing the meeting longer than they had originally planned. In many cases they expressed their satisfaction with the interview, describing it as a "stimulating discussion" and sometimes even requesting that I return to continue it. Most wished me well in my research. In one touching moment a respondent invited me to bow my head with him as he gave a short prayer for my project. Only a few individuals seemed genuinely irritated by the challenging nature of the questions, so that the interview ended on an awkward, uncomfortable note.

Naturally, a key question is how the respondents perceived me and how this may have affected their responses. Obviously I was an academic associated with an institution oriented to arms control. The fact that I was an academic may have encouraged their presenting themselves as "defense intellectuals" by giving relatively more sophisticated rationales than they might have given in a public forum. This may have also led them, as we shall see, to disclose to a surprising extent their reservations about the military logic used to support certain policies. This level of discourse may also have been encouraged by my introducing the study as being on "the role of perceptions" in defense policy.

It is difficult to determine whether there was a biasing effect leading respondents to take positions they thought were consistent with my views. Respondents did try to determine my views on the subjects being discussed and occasionally made attributions to me. (I was surprised at how frequently they were mistaken.) Presumably because of my association with an arms control-oriented institution, they assumed that I was generally less than enthusiastic about a high level of defensive armament. Therefore they may have presented their views with a relatively moderate cast. When I sensed this might be occurring, I sometimes rephrased questions in a way that might make it easier for them to reveal a line of thinking they may have been restraining. I was also careful to nod to reinforce statements that I did not agree with, and only after they were completed did I begin to challenge them. Of course, for the most part respondents said many, many things that were quite inconsistent with my point of view. Nevertheless, biasing effects have been shown to operate in some very subtle ways, and the data need to be viewed in that light.

Furthermore, at times I did implicitly reveal my point of view on such issues as the viability of a certain scenario or specific factual matters related to the capability of a certain weapon system. This was particularly true when I sensed that respondents seemed to be making statements that they did not entirely believe. In such cases I refrained from nodding and with a certain facial expression and tone of voice indicated some dubiousness about their line of argument. Sometimes it made respondents press their arguments more vigorously—something I took as an indication of their earnestness. Other times they responded with a smile, became embarrassed, began to modify their argument, or even abruptly discounted what they had previously said.

Obviously, this methodology reflects my general theoretical orientation. I do not see defense planners as necessarily having completely coherent conceptual and attitudinal frameworks in their approach to defense issues. In general, people are not entirely consistent. Another key assumption is that the apparent inconsistencies in military thinking are at least partially derived from the complexities of adapting to the new conditions engendered by nuclear weapons. The character of the interview process reflects these assumptions. I did not simply accept a stated position at face value. I asked different questions that sometimes led to contrary positions. I probed to see how genuine the expressed attitude was. I pointed to inconsistencies and contrary evidence to see how respondents would resolve apparent contradictions. I nodded, looked surprised, smiled, frowned, made jokes, confirmed points, argued points, looked confused, and frequently did not respond at all. In other words, I used whatever interventions were available to draw out the rich complexity of their thinking and attitudes.

From a scientific point of view, such an approach has trade-offs. On one hand, the highly variable nature of the interview process makes such a study hard to replicate. On the other hand, it may be the one way to elicit the multifaceted nature of the phenomenon being studied.

Policy Areas Explored

Each of the policy areas explored in the interviews involved components of American defense policy that seemed inconsistent with nuclear reality. These included the policies of:

1. Maintaining a balance of nuclear forces relative to the Soviet Union
2. Seeking advantageous termination in the event of a nuclear war
3. Developing hard-target kill capability
4. Pursuing the elimination of population vulnerability through strategic defenses.

It is important to note that there have been some minor changes in American policy since these interviews were conducted between early 1984 and early 1987. A major topic of discussion in relation to the policy of developing hard-target kill capability was the rationale for the Pershing IIs and ground-launched cruise missiles. As of this writing, it appears quite certain that these missiles will be eliminated through arms control negotiations. Nevertheless, the general policy of developing hard-target capable weapons still stands, and the rationales given for the Pershing IIs and ground-launched cruise missiles are still a good reflection of the thinking that supports this general policy. Another, more subtle, change is in relation to the SDI program. Recently, spokesmen for the program have been downplaying the potential for protecting populations through strategic defense and putting more emphasis on the value of strategic defenses for enhancing deterrence. This is not a real change in policy. The official purpose of the SDI program continues to be the pursuit of population defense. Presumably, because the difficulty of attaining this objective has become increasingly apparent, there has been an incremental shift in the degree of emphasis.

MAINTAINING THE BALANCE

A major concept in American defense policy, and perhaps the most pervasive rationale for arms building, is the idea that the United States must maintain a balance of military forces in relation to the Soviet

Union. The concept of balance is not carefully defined. Sometimes it seems to mean a minimum of numerical equality in every weapons category. More often, though, there is an acceptance of some asymmetries in specific categories but a desire for general equality, described as "essential equivalence," "rough equivalence," or "essential parity." In some cases, "dynamic factors," such as the potential rate of growth or the extent of research and development, in addition to the already existing "static measures," play a central role in assessing the balance. Relative levels of types of capabilities (such as time-urgent survivable hard-target kill capability) also figure prominently in some assessments. Despite this complexity there is widespread adherence to the general principle that the United States must maintain a balance of nuclear forces relative to the Soviet Union. Such a principle pervades arms control negotiations, with both the United States and the Soviet Union rationalizing their own proposals in terms of equality and rejecting the other's proposals on the basis of unfavorable asymmetries. The requirement of balance has been explicitly stated in every administration since the Soviets have built their arsenal high enough for it to be a question.

It is not readily apparent why the United States should have such a concern for maintaining the balance. American nuclear strategy is based on the concept of deterrence—that an adversary should be dissuaded from aggression as long as the United States has the ability to impose costs greater than any potential benefits. Because nuclear weapons are able to impose such enormous costs, it is quite possible for these requirements to be met with a level of weaponry substantially lower than that held by the other side.

Naturally, in the design of an arsenal, there are considerations other than the simple destructive yield of weapons. It is essential to think about how many weapons would survive an all-out counterforce strike. It is also important to build some degree of flexibility into an arsenal to maintain variable options for specific scenarios that might arise. But here again, the requirements of survivability and flexibility do not necessarily point to the need for an arsenal the size of an adversary's.

When this concern for the balance emerged, respondents were asked if they believed that the United States has an assured destruction capability. Because if they did not, this concern for a balance was considerably more reasonable than if they did. I asked directly, "Are there important targets that are not adequately covered by our present survivable capabilities?" Assuming worst-case counterforce scenarios and accepting the most pessimistic assumptions, respondents were asked to assess the residual American capabilities and to evaluate whether such capabilities would effectively counter the cost-benefit analysis of even an ambitious, risk-prone Soviet. I also asked how Soviet capabilities, presently emerging or on a more distant horizon, might affect this general calculation.

Other scenarios in which new American deployments might be useful were also explored. One approach was to ask what mission these new deployments would serve in the event of a war, which allowed them to specify the scenario. This was followed by queries whether the United States already has capabilities suitable for the mission described and whether emerging Soviet capabilities would affect this condition.

When the response was that the United States does have an assured destruction capability and can already dispatch targets essential to any particular scenario, I returned to the question of why it is important to match Soviet deployments.

SEEKING ADVANTAGEOUS TERMINATION

Ever since the first atomic bombs were detonated, a strong voice in American defense thinking has been saying that the use of military force to seek political advantages from a superpower war has become obsolete. This belief has arisen primarily from the recognition of the potentially devastating effects of nuclear war. However, this attitude also extends to the use of conventional forces between nuclear powers. Given that both sides would always have the potential to escalate, if both pursued an advantageous outcome, a conventional military conflict would inevitably lead to a nuclear conflict. As a result, there has been a marked trend toward seeing military forces serving almost exclusively as a deterrent to military conflict.

Nonetheless, when faced with the question of what the United States should do in the event that deterrence fails, American policy tends to revert to a more traditional concept of the purpose of military force. Once deterrence fails, it is proposed, the United States should seek termination on terms that are advantageous to the United States. Such advantages have been described as being in the position to dictate the terms of termination, to release territory from Soviet control, to impose relatively greater destruction, or even to seek the overthrow of the Soviet government. In some cases, U.S. policymakers even consider initiating the use of military force in a pre-emptive fashion in anticipation of the breakdown of deterrence.

As discussed above, it is not entirely clear how the United States can reasonably pursue this goal as long as it remains vulnerable to devastating nuclear strikes leading up to and including strikes against population centers. While a war may in fact lead to an asymmetrical outcome, it is not clear how the risks inherent in the active effort of pursuing such an advantage would be proportional to the potential benefits.

In the interviews, I raised the issue of war-termination by posing the following question: "In the event that deterrence fails and the Soviet Union takes some aggressive action either in Central Europe or through a counterforce strike against the continental United States, in principle what should the goal of American actions be?" Some respondents answered in moderate terms, such as advocating a tit-for-tat strategy with the objective of restoring the status quo ante. Many respondents, though, did describe more ambitious, advantage-seeking objectives, sometimes saying flatly that the United States goal should be "to win." In these cases, they were asked for details of how such an objective could be pursued, how the United States in its war-planning could deal with the possibility that the Soviet Union, when faced with a disadvantageous outcome, would simply move the conflict to a higher level, even to striking at population centers.

DEVELOPING HARD-TARGET KILL CAPABILITY

Over the last decade, the primary new development in the American nuclear arsenal has been the emergence of weapons with the ability to destroy hardened targets, such as protected missile silos and centers of command and control. The ability to destroy these targets has emerged with improvements in the accuracy of American missiles. All of the weapons recently deployed or currently proposed—the MX, the Pershing IIs, the cruise missiles, and the D-5 missile on Trident submarines—are able to destroy hardened targets, and most arguments in favor of their deployment center on this capability.

It is not entirely clear that such a capability would be useful to the

United States. The ability to destroy even a substantial portion of Soviet missiles would not necessarily reduce the potential damage to the United States. A large number of Soviet nuclear weapons are in survivable basing modes (that is, they could not be destroyed by hard-target-capable weapons), and these weapons would be more than adequate for inflicting unacceptable damage.

More important, it is highly questionable whether even with these hard-target-capable weapons the United States would be able to destroy a significant number of Soviet missiles. The Soviets can determine which missile silo is being targeted by an incoming warhead with enough time to launch their missiles out from under the incoming missile.* While it is certainly a possibility that the Soviets might refrain from launching out from under, it hardly seems that an American decisionmaker could count on this.

Such a problem also emerges relevant to striking at command and control centers. If striking such centers would destroy their ability to launch a number of missiles, the Soviets, again, would be encouraged to launch those missiles. (If redundancy exists in their command and control system that would preclude such an incentive, then the value of striking these targets becomes questionable.)

In the interviews, the subject of hard-target kill capability arose very spontaneously. In reply to a question whether there are important Soviet targets not adequately covered by existing survivable American forces, a common answer was that hardened targets are not adequately covered. When asked for the military rationale for current deployments, respondents frequently placed emphasis on the improved ability to destroy hardened targets. I then asked why it is important to be able to destroy such targets and after they fully elaborated their rationale, I usually raised the problems described above—the impossibility of drawing down Soviet forces below the level at which they could inflict unacceptable damage and, more significantly, the probability that the Soviets would launch out from under incoming warheads. This was an attempt to ascertain if policymakers and strategists had rationales that assimilated these critical features of nuclear reality or if they were almost reflexively applying

---

*A small amount of the defense literature questions whether the Soviets have such a capability. However, the dominant view is that the Soviets do, and this was virtually unanimous among the respondents interviewed.

the traditional principle that it would be militarily logical to try to destroy an enemy's military assets.

ELIMINATING POPULATION VULNERABILITY
THROUGH STRATEGIC DEFENSES

Since President Reagan's now famous speech in March 1983 proposing the SDI program, the pursuit of strategic defenses has become a prominent element in American defense policy. The stated purpose of the Strategic Defense Initiative (SDI) has been to eliminate the condition of Mutual Assured Destruction (MAD). Naturally, such an objective would require the protection of a major portion of the civilian population. In the intervening years, however, there has been some ambiguity about whether this ambitious goal is, in fact, the goal of SDI or whether the real aim is to protect land-based intercontinental ballistic missiles (ICBMs). Nevertheless, when questioned directly, administration figures have reaffirmed the goal of protecting populations and eliminating MAD.

There are several problems with such an objective. Nuclear weapons are so powerful that only a small number would need to reach population centers for the damage to be unacceptable. Furthermore, the United States would never be able to stage a full-scale simulation of its strategic defense system using thousands of missiles. Therefore, an American leader would have trouble making choices based on the optimistic assumption that such a system would be highly effective even if the system performed well in limited simulations. Moreover, assuming that the United States could develop such a reliable system, it is doubtful that the Soviet Union would not develop countermeasures (the United States has already begun developing them for itself).

In the interviews, when respondents expressed support for SDI, these various problems were raised. The purpose was not to argue with respondents but rather to learn whether they had answers to these problems, whether they were reflexively following a traditional assumption that it is simply a good idea to protect against enemy forces, or if they had some other motive for SDI despite these problems.

Types of Rationales Offered

The rationales offered for the four policies described above fall roughly into three categories: rationales based on military force, rationales based on the strategic manipulation of perceptions, and rationales based on psychological needs.

RATIONALES BASED ON MILITARY FORCE

Most respondents spent at least some time trying to rationalize policies in terms of traditional military force, focusing on the objective capabilities that the United States would have in the event of a war and how they would interact with Soviet capabilities. The most common rationales focused on maintaining the military capabilities necessary for deterrence. This involved making certain that, given the disposition of forces on both sides, the Soviets could not arrive at a cost-benefit analysis that would make aggression appear attractive. Other rationales were not tied to deterrence but to the actual event of a war. Policies related to war objectives were presented as providing meaningful guidance in the midst of a war. The deployment of certain capabilities was rationalized as providing otherwise unavailable and useful options in the pursuit of such objectives.

Rationales based on military force will be explored in chapters 3 through 5 and part of chapter 9, each chapter devoted to one of the four policies described above.

RATIONALES BASED ON THE STRATEGIC MANIPULATION OF PERCEPTIONS

In the majority of cases, respondents at some point set aside—or, more commonly, flatly dismissed—the military basis for defense policies. Instead, they rationalized policies in terms of efforts to manipulate the perceptions held in peacetime by a variety of key audiences. Frequently such rationales were based on the assumption that widespread misperceptions exist about the nature of nuclear weapons and the role of military force in the nuclear age. Policies were recognized as being invalid from a military perspective but nonetheless politically necessary as a means of accommodating these general misperceptions. It was argued also that certain policies help to generate incorrect, or at least ambiguous, perceptions of the way American leaders think, and that such perceptions may be valuable for American interests.

Rationales based on the strategic manipulation of perceptions will be explored in chapters 6 through 8 and part of chapter 9, each chapter devoted to a specific policy.

RATIONALES BASED ON SATISFYING PSYCHOLOGICAL NEEDS

All of the rationales described above, while different in many ways, share a common theme—they all describe means of enhancing American security. There were, however, rationales based on the value of gratifying certain collective psychological needs. In some cases policies were seen as valuable because they fulfill competitive desires for status and prestige, maintain domestic morale, distract the public from the unnerving reality of the condition of vulnerability, or fulfill the inherent urge to be competitive.

These rationales will be explored in chapter 10.

Presentation of Findings

In the presentation of the interview findings contained in the following chapters, there are some unusual features. When describing specific rationales for policies, I make some comments that roughly describe the frequency with which these rationales appeared. The design of the study does not lend itself to making more precise, quantitative descriptions. I did not follow a fixed list of questions that could produce statistical findings. Due to time limitations and respondents' inclinations, all of the major policy areas could not be explored with every respondent. Furthermore, it would be difficult to enumerate the rate at which arguments were used because some subjects expressed the arguments vaguely or by implication. What this study primarily offers is a map of the pathways through the territory of defense thinking. My assessments of the rate of passage along these pathways is approximate and impressionistic. Nevertheless it seems worthwhile to include them accompanied by this caveat.

Another unusual feature of the presentation is that I do not limit myself to reporting on verbal expressions. At times I also describe subtleties expressed through affective tone and body language. It seems completely natural for me, as a psychologist, to include such observations. My friends who are political scientists tell me that though they find this unusual, they also grant me the privilege to include such observations because of my training and my fifteen years of experience as a clinician. I take the liberty of doing so because I think it is intrinsic to the problem being studied. The purpose of the study is not simply to report on the rationales given for policies but to explore how people account for policies that seem inconsistent with nuclear reality. In this context it becomes critical to note not only inconsistencies between different verbal statements but also ways in which affect and gestures communicate signals that are inconsistent. The problem of adapting to the fundamental changes engendered by nuclear weapons is more than an intellectual process and can have complex emotional repercussions. This study attempts to explore this adaptive process in just such a multifaceted manner.

CHAPTER 3

Maintaining the Balance

THE IMPORTANCE of maintaining a balance of nuclear forces relative to the Soviet Union is a recurring theme in American defense policy. This principle was at times explicitly stated in the interviews and at other times implicitly presented when respondents explained the need for a weapon system by pointing out that the Soviets had a corresponding system. When I probed into why it was necessary to maintain such a balance, a variety of answers were given. Some stressed the political significance of perceptions of the military balance (to be discussed in chapter 6). Others clarified that they were concerned not with the balance per se but with the ability to match the Soviets on each rung of the ladder of escalation (see chapter 4). Others, however, argued in support of maintaining the balance in terms of traditional concepts of military force. These arguments followed three different patterns. At times respondents simply asserted traditional, conventional principles in rationalizing the importance of the balance, ignoring the condition of mutual vulnerability and the redundancies in both arsenals. In some cases respondents directly questioned whether the United States even has an assured destruction capability, thus giving a logical military basis to the concern for a balance. Finally many respondents shifted between mindsets, at some points applying conventionalized concepts of military relations, at other times clearly recognizing that the existence of robust assured destruction capabilities made such concepts invalid.

Conventionalization

A recurrent indication of this tendency to conventionalize was the use of analogies from non-nuclear contexts. Several respondents compared superpower nuclear confrontations to fistfights between children. Principles that made sense in a rough neighborhood were used analogically to analyze superpower military relations. Relative physical size was seen as critical. Others used analogies from various conventional wars, stressing especially the role of relative capabilities in determining outcomes. In none of these cases was there any discussion of how these analogies might have limited applicability given the different potential consequences of a nuclear war, a conventional war, or a childhood fistfight. Although in some cases the analogies may have been a convenient mental habit, in at least one case, that of a congressman, it was explicitly asserted that they were completely applicable.

INTERVIEWER: But you're using analogies from conventional warfare there.
RESPONDENT: Strategic ain't a damn bit different.
I: That's a strong statement.
R: That's where we lose our concept sometimes. Basically, there's no difference.

In a variety of ways, such conventionalized thinking was used to support the idea that it was essential to maintain the balance. One of the more common patterns was to assert that a balance of forces, not a secure retaliatory capability, is intrinsic to deterrence. At times the concepts of deterrence almost become fused into a single concept, as in the statement of one respondent, "Balance . . . means to be strong enough to know you can deter the other guy."

This equation has also appeared in public discussion. In a 1984 address, President Reagan said, "As long as we maintain the strategic balance . . . *then* we can count on the basic prudence of the Soviet leaders to avoid [nuclear war] [emphasis added]."[1] Secretary of Defense Weinberger has written that "the critical point in deterring war and preventing aggression is maintaining a balance of forces." Weinberger went on to use pre-nuclear history as a basis for this assertion, "History has shown us all too often that conflicts occur when one state believes it has a sufficiently greater military capability than another."[2] Defending the Intermediate Nuclear Force (INF) deployments, British Prime Minister Margaret Thatcher told the House of Commons, "The principle is a balance in order to deter . . . we must achieve balanced numbers."[3] Sometimes the potential consequences of an imbalance have been put in dire terms. Ronald Reagan, during his 1976 campaign, said, "It is dangerous, if not fatal, to be second best."[4]

In some cases the concept of a strategic balance also fused with the traditional concept of the "balance of power." A congressman I interviewed explained:

> We used to use history, when I was in school, to talk about the balance of power. You don't hear as much about the balance of power as such any more. Today we talk about it more in terms of the power of the balance of forces. But it's all the same thing.

Also drawing on balance-of-power concepts, Eugene Rostow wrote, "Wars come about not when power is balanced but when power is unbalanced,"[5] and then went on to use this concept to support increased American arms building to secure this balance. It may well be that certain traditional balance-of-power concepts are quite applicable in a nuclear context. There are, however, new elements in the nuclear context that must be accounted for. In neither of the above cases was there evidence of such an effort. Balance-of-power concepts were simply imposed in a traditional and wholesale fashion.

At some point in the interview, I usually tried to find out if the respondent had a concept of a ceiling on the level of nuclear capabilities that would have real military utility—a point past which it would be useless to build as long as Soviet deployments did not significantly interfere with those capabilities. This idea appeared in some of the original formulations of deterrence theory and during the Nixon administration was termed the principle of "sufficiency." A surprising number of the people interviewed resisted the notion. Some of them even directly contradicted it. One presidential advisor flatly asserted that the United States should always build more nuclear weapons.

R: Because if you have a deterrent, the more you have the better deterrent you have . . .

I: Is it unlimited? Is more always better, or do you get to some critical point where—

R: No, more in relation to them is always better.

Sometimes the value of increased weaponry was seen as having a direct proportional relation to the number of weapons. In a discussion about the number of surviving warheads following an all-out Soviet strike, a congressman said, "If we had, instead of about three thousand, we had six thousand, we'd have twice the capacity to make certain that the Soviets understand they'd have losses which they might not have the tolerance to accept."

Frequently respondents were further queried why increased capabilities would be useful as long as the United States was able to wreak enough damage to deter a rational adversary. In some cases they avoided this question by making the Soviets an entirely unknown factor. For example, the above interview continued as follows:

I: And do you think three thousand warheads wouldn't be enough to be unacceptable to them?

R: I don't know. I can't think with a Soviet mind.

In many cases, though, it simply seemed to be taken as a given that superpowers adjust their behavior according to marginal shifts in the military balance—a reasonable argument in a conventional context but a more difficult one to make when states have secure and flexible second-strike capabilities. Nevertheless, some flatly asserted that states do adjust their behavior in this way and used pre-nuclear historical examples to support their point. They were quite uninterested in questions dealing with mutual vulnerability and even seemed to find them irksome. With one former high-level State Department official, who presented this view at length, I questioned why he seemed to regard the balance as so much more important than population vulnerability. To my surprise, he asserted that under no circumstances would an American president launch a nuclear attack knowing that as a result sixty million Americans would be killed. Nevertheless, he reiterated that relative capabilities would play a decisive role in a crisis, pointing to the Cuban missile crisis as evidence. (Based on his other comments, he did not seem to be making the argument that this imbalance was relevant because the Soviet Union did not have an assured destruction capability.)

Building on this point, he emphatically dismissed the British and French arsenals as "completely irrelevant" because they were relatively so small. Referring to his comment about an American president being deterred by the prospect of sixty million fatalities, I asked him if the British and French arsenals could kill sixty million Soviets. He agreed that they could, but, shaking his head, he nonetheless asserted that in the event of a Soviet invasion of Europe, "Pétain would be in power in France in no time." When I asked him if, as a Soviet leader, he would feel free to invade France in the face of the French nuclear threat, he looked at me impatiently and said, "You've been reading too much nuclear strategy—you and Tom Schelling."*

An underlying theme seemed to be that a balance was necessary for a retaliatory threat to be credible. For some reason there was a feeling that an imbalance made the vulnerability of American cities seem more vivid even though they would be equally vulnerable in a balanced condition. A 1983 publication from The Heritage Foundation, a conservative think tank, denounced the concept of a nuclear weapons freeze on the basis of American inferiority, warning:

> The problem is that under the current (im)balance, it has become increasingly less believable that the U. S. would . . . respond to a Soviet attack at all, because of the certain knowledge that the Soviets would still retain enough weapons to destroy the U. S. civilian population.[6]

A number of respondents also argued that marginal shifts in the balance affect not only potential Soviet behavior in a major confrontation but also the Soviet general level of adventurism. When I asked why it is important to maintain a balance of forces, a common answer was that it is necessary for deterrence. When asked what was being deterred, two high-level Pentagon officials said, using almost the same phrase, "Things like Afghanistan." Again, such a concept would make sense in a pre-nuclear context—the ability to do well in a potential war

---

*Thomas Schelling is a prominent and influential nuclear strategist. His work will be discussed in later chapters.

might make a state feel freer to take chances. This idea also seemed to be a given and not subject to refutation. When I pointed out some moves Khrushchev made when the Soviet Union was strategically inferior—moves that were bolder than those the Soviets have made since they achieved parity—these were dismissed as simply the result of Khrushchev's personality.

The idea that Soviet adventurism is influenced by the state of the balance has been particularly strong in the Reagan administration. In 1980, Reagan said, "Today we are not equal to the Soviet Union, and that is why they are able to cross into Afghanistan."[7] and that "if we instantly reverse our own course and set out to rebuild . . . I think it's possible to keep the Soviets from getting the kind of edge that would lead them to go adventuring against us."[8] In 1984, Secretary Weinberger claimed success on this front, attributing Soviet restraint in Poland and Afghanistan to improvements in the American arsenal. He said, "We have to think that that change in pattern of activity is related to the correct perception that the United States is regaining military strength."[9]*

Interviewing Vice President George Bush in 1980, Robert Scheer tried to challenge this general argument:

SCHEER: What is the connection between the possession of an MX missile system and being able to do something about problems like Afghanistan and Iran?

BUSH: The direct linkage is rather remote, but in the overall link-

---

*This kind of logic was also reported on in a *New York Times* "News Analysis" of March 27, 1986:

President Reagan believes he has succeeded in bringing about a more favorable Soviet-American balance of power, thus enabling him to act with greater freedom and decisiveness around the world, according to Administration officials. . . . To these officials, Mr. Reagan can afford to be more assertive because the United States is relatively stronger overall and the Soviet Union relatively weaker overall than five or eight years ago. . . . From the outset of his Administration . . . the Reagan language was strong, [but] his actions were generally cautious. They had to be because the prevailing view in the Administration was that the Soviet Union was militarily superior to the United States. In time, however, senior officials came to feel that their arms buildup was redressing the balance. . . . Now, the sense is that Moscow is on the defensive and that the United States can be somewhat more venturesome in challenging Soviet interests with less risk of a serious Soviet response.

(Leslie H. Gelb, "Reagan's Maneuvers," *New York Times*, March 27, 1986, A8).

age, as long as the United States is perceived to not be slipping behind the Soviets in forces, the Soviets will be constrained from adventure.

SCHEER: They were weaker in '68 than they are now.

BUSH: Much weaker.

SCHEER: In '68 they invaded Czechoslovakia. That was adventurism.

BUSH: But it doesn't follow that therefore, if we're weaker, that will constrain adventure. They're stronger today and they invaded Afghanistan.[10]

This argument is somewhat self-contradictory. If the Soviets will be adventuristic should the United States be relatively stronger *or* grow relatively weaker, then there is no basis for saying that perceptions of American strength will influence Soviet behavior.

Some individuals also said that it is proper for American behavior to be influenced by the state of the balance. The most critical change in relative capabilities cited was, of course, loss of the American capability to inflict a disarming pre-emptive first strike as the Soviets built up their nuclear arsenal. The United States could no longer confidently assert an ability to dominate the escalation process because the Soviets had gained the capability for unlimited escalation. Therefore, the United States had to become considerably more ginger in its use of force. What was particularly striking in the interviews, though, was that this critical change was not associated with the Soviets acquiring an assured destruction capability in the late 1950s or early 1960s but rather with the Soviets achieving parity in the 1970s. A former middle-level Pentagon official from the Carter administration explained:

R: I think the theory [of escalation dominance] has less validity today because if we were to use nuclear weapons in a limited way within the theater, the Soviets have the option of escalating. And—to use a cliché'd expression—we don't dominate the escalation process any more, as we did in the 1960s and in the late 1950s. . . . In fact, I used to say [we could] at one time, but I think it really doesn't hold up because if the other fellow has another chip he can put on the pile, you aren't any longer confident. . . .

I: At what point did you change that perspective?

R: I began to change in the late '70s because of a change in the military balance.

Along similar lines, it was also argued that by improving the relative standing of American defense capabilities, the United States could counteract some of these constraining effects of vulnerability. During the 1980 election Ronald Reagan expressed doubt that backyard bomb shelters could be effective but argued that "maybe there is a defense through having superior offensive ability."[11] He did not specify how he saw such offensive capabilities ameliorating the condition of vulnerability. Then in 1985, arguing against curtailing annual defense budget increases, he said, "The last thing we want to do is return our country to the weakened, vulnerable state in which we found it in 1980." He went on to say that "stronger and reinvigorated defense" had allowed the United States to be freer in its use of force, mentioning the invasion of Grenada and the response to the hijacking of the *Achille Lauro* as examples.[12] It was not entirely clear, however, how he saw these improvements in American defense translating into this greater freedom since these interventions did not require specific capabilities previously unavailable, nor had the improvements significantly altered any fundamental features of strategic reality.

At times in the interviews, the acquisition of a specific capability was seen as creating advantages that are difficult to understand in a nuclear context. For example, a high-level Pentagon official said, "We must be able to hold those [Soviet ICBMs] at risk so as to be able to deter them in the first instance." Here again, in a conventional context, in which weapons engage each other, improvements on one side might deter the other from taking action. However, American nuclear weapons cannot be used against already fired Soviet ICBMs. They can be used in a pre-emptive fashion against Soviet silos, but doing so does not fall into the category of promoting deterrence. It is also not clear how the ability to threaten pre-emption has a deterrent effect vis-à-vis the weapons being threatened. In fact, many specialists would argue the opposite— that threatening a missile creates an incentive to launch it so as to avoid its being caught in the silo.

In addition to these relatively explicit examples of conventionalized thinking, there was a more subtle way in which the strategic discourse was pervaded by pre-nuclear constructs. Respondents used terms and concepts that were much more appropriate to describe conventional rather than nuclear military relationships. Their statements seemed to imply that the condition of the balance was a significant reflection of the outcome of a possible war. Respondents frequently spoke of one weapon system "neutralizing" or "countering" another. A Rand Corporation analyst said, "The MX is a kind of equalizer for the SS-18. It is something to do the same thing to them." Such statements have appeared in public discourse as well. In 1977, then West German Chancellor Helmut Schmidt said in a major and influential speech that the strategic balance codified in SALT I "neutralizes [the superpowers'] strategic nuclear capabilities."[13] President Reagan asserted that "the only answer to these [SS-4, SS-5, SS-20]* systems is a comparable threat to Soviet threats."[14] Others spoke of nuclear weapons placed on specific territory to "protect" that territory.

In a conventional context these concepts are quite appropriate. Relative capabilities are a major indicator of the outcome of a potential conventional war. Conventional weapons do engage each other so that in a comparative analysis one set of weapons can be seen as "neutralizing" or "countering" another. Conventional weapons, in many cases, do "protect" territory from an advancing army. In a nuclear context, however, these concepts are far less applicable. The balance of capabilities is not the critical factor as much as is the capability to retaliate against important targets—a capability that has only a limited relationship to the relative number of weapons on each side. Nuclear weapons do not generally engage each other and therefore do not "neutralize" or "counter" each other† the way troop divisions and tanks do. Furthermore, nuclear weapons do not specifically protect the territory they are located on. Nuclear weapons do "protect" in the sense that they threaten retaliation for aggression, but in a military sense, where the retaliatory salvo originates is quite irrelevant.

When challenged on their use of such conventional terms, many

---

*SS-4, SS-5, and SS-20 refer to specific types of Soviet intermediate-range nuclear ballistic missiles.

†Nuclear weapons are, in some cases, used in a counterforce fashion to destroy other nuclear weapons. However, when the terms *neutralize* and *counter* were used, they were not generally used in this sense. The terms were, for example, most commonly used to describe the deployment of NATO INF weapons in response to the SS-20s. Because both of these weapon systems are mobile, none of them is intended for counterforce purposes against the other.

respondents quickly recognized that the terms were inappropriate and seemed to regard them as a kind of shorthand to describe more sophisticated concepts. They explained that specific weapons can be said to "counter" or "neutralize" their counterparts within the context of a refined ladder of escalation (a concept we will explore in chapter 4). And the location of the source of the retaliatory salvo, though militarily insignificant, might be significant politically and in terms of the credibility of the threat to exercise the retaliatory option (also to be explored in chapter 4).

In many cases, though, respondents did not appear to really mean these more sophisticated concepts. For example, when pressed to explain why the United States had to match a Soviet capability, they simply reiterated the fact that the Soviets had such a capability, as if this made the need for the weapon self-evident.

In some cases, they became more specific about weapon characteristics that need to be matched. For example, when a senator explained that the Pershing IIs and ground-launched cruise missiles (GLCMs) were necessary to balance the Soviet SS-20s in Europe, he was further asked why it was necessary to specifically have the politically troublesome Pershing IIs rather than just the GLCMs. He answered, as if it were self-evident, "Well, obviously the Pershings have a much shorter response period." But when asked to give a military rationale for this capability, he simply reiterated the need to match the Soviet capability.

I: What's the value for us in that?
R: Again, their SS-20s have short response as well.

In a similar exchange a congressman explained that the speed of the Pershing II specifically "checked" the use of the equally swift SS-20. In the ensuing discussion he did not give any explanation of how the relative speeds of the missiles would have a differential deterrent effect.

Questioning Assured Destruction

The vast majority of respondents readily recognized that the United States and the Soviet Union are in a relationship of mutual assured destruction, that is, both sides have the capability, even after absorbing an all-out first strike, to retaliate in such a devastating fashion that neither side could meaningfully benefit from such a first strike.* A very small number of respondents, however, challenged this idea. These arguments will be thoroughly examined because, unlike the less-considered conventional patterns of thought described above, they are a potential foundation for a strong argument that the strategic balance continues to be a critical military concern.

An examination of these arguments in this way does not mean to imply that countervalue targeting (that is, aiming at cities and targets with economic value such as factories) is the only or the best approach to deterrence. This is a question to be discussed in later chapters. The issue here is simply whether the United States has an assured destruction capability—a capability that, by definition, can be minimally derived from the ability to execute an annihilating countervalue strike.

Challenges to the notion that the United States has an assured

---

*Without going into too much technical detail, it may be useful to outline roughly the American "assured destruction" capability. The U. S. has more than 26,000 nuclear weapons. Approximately 11,000 of these are strategic—that is, they can be delivered against the Soviet Union in a short period of time. Virtually all of these strategic weapons have a greater destructive yield than the bomb that destroyed Hiroshima in 1945, and most have yields many times larger. Clearly such an arsenal is capable of inflicting "unacceptable damage" on the Soviet Union.

However, in assessing an "assured destruction capability" the measure is not the extant number of weapons but rather the number that would remain in the U. S. arsenal after the Soviet Union inflicted a surprise all-out strike designed to disarm the U. S. By the most dire scenario, the Soviet Union might destroy all U. S. land-based ICBM forces, the half of the bombers that are not on alert, and the half of the submarines in port at anytime. A huge number of technical complexities make it highly questionable that such a scenario is feasible. Nevertheless, even by this scenario the U. S. would retain more than 4,000 strategic warheads. However, some of these would be bombs—and given that bombers would face Soviet air defenses, there would be some attrition. A highly pessimistic assumption is that two-thirds of the bomber force would be destroyed, but even then, the U. S. would still have (or the Soviet Union must assume the U. S. would have) more than 3,000 deliverable warheads—a number that is generally regarded as destructive enough to inflict "unacceptable damage."

I should underscore that the outcomes described here, in the general strategic discourse, are on the extremely pessimistic end of the spectrum. Most strategic analysts feel that the U. S. would have (and that the Soviet Union must assume the U. S. would have) many more than 3,000 surviving weapons.

destruction capability have appeared very occasionally in the defense literature. For example, a publication of The Heritage Foundation rejected the notion of "overkill." Freeze advocates who use such concepts, it was argued, fail to consider the consequences of a Soviet first strike:

> ... the U. S. must be able to field enough weapons to demonstrate to Soviet military planners that it could cause unacceptable levels of damage to the Soviet Union even after sustaining the destruction of many of its strategic weapons in a nuclear surprise attack. That is why the overkill argument has so little validity when applied to U. S. strategic forces.[15]

By rejecting the overkill argument, the authors were implicitly arguing that the the U. S. does not have a robust survivable capability to inflict unacceptable damage.

In the interviews some respondents appeared genuinely confused about whether the United States has an assured destruction capability as, for example, was a congressman on a major defense-related committee.

R: I think that our [forces] have got to be up high so that the Soviets must recognize the fact that if they start something they can't win.

I: You don't think we have that now?

R: No, sir. Absolutely not. They've got three times the submarines, they've got seven times the airplanes, and they're ahead of us in lasers.

Although these figures on submarines and airplanes are factually incorrect, I tentatively accepted them to see if they constituted a coherent argument.

I: How do these differences matter?

R: Let me put it this way. We hear people say "My God—each nation has got the capacity to destroy the other one ten times over!" Sure, that's true if we could get the Soviets to bring all their forces together in downtown Moscow at a certain time under certain circumstances where they would not shoot back—there's no question we're going to destroy them. We'd destroy them ten times over.

Setting aside the issue of whether the Soviet capability to "shoot back" undermines an assured destruction capability, I focused on his idea that the Soviets would have to amass their forces in one place. He reiterated the idea that assured destruction would require that they can't retaliate and proceeded to outline the evolution of military force as a constant process of balancing, observing no discontinuity when he reached the nuclear level.

I: You question whether we have the capacity to destroy the Soviet Union several times over no matter where they are?

R: If they don't do anything. But that's the fallacy that so often enters the thinking capacity of man. If I developed a bow and arrow, and the other guy doesn't have any weapons, no question I've got an advantage. But now he develops a weapon against the bow and arrow. I develop a gun; he develops a better gun. And then we go on up to artillery; then we go to airplanes, go to nuclear, all the way up. There's always a balancing of those forces: I can take this one out; he can take that one out—like playing checkers or chess. And that's the way war works.

He then articulated the key idea that the balance of forces reflects the relative outcome of a battle, "You've got to see what is going to be left over when everybody else is through." But then, in response to a slight challenge to his rejection of the idea of overkill, he shifted to an argument based on the Soviets having defensive weapons.

And when you finally get through, in the analysis it isn't a matter of whether you've got ten times—sure you have . . . [But] there's no way we can take that ten-times capacity right now and heap them on them.

I: Why not?

R: Because they've got defensive weapons.

I: What defensive weapons?

R: They've got a defense against every weapon that we have against theirs.

Presuming that he meant antinuclear defenses, I challenged him on this point, which then led him to shift to questioning the viability of the ABM Treaty.

I: I don't understand. We have the ABM Treaty, which basically outlaws those kinds of weapons. They have one around Moscow, and we did have one around Grand Forks.

R: That's what I'm trying to say: It isn't likely to hold.

I: But right now we don't have an ABM system, and they don't have an ABM system to speak of, right?

R: That's correct.

Still undaunted, he shifted to the argument that ICBM vulnerability undermines assured destruction.

I: So we *can* wipe them out numerous times over?

R: If they don't destroy ours on the ground before we activate them. That's the thing that gets to me.

This concern did not, however, resolve into a coherent argument. In exasperation he gave up trying to rationalize his concern for the balance and explained his behavior as the most adequate response to an uncertain situation and as a course that gave him some means to act.

R: You're trying to ask me a question of how much is enough. My answer to you is I don't know how much is enough. But if I'm going to make an error I'm going to make it on the side that tells me that I can follow my philosophy of spending money for peace as opposed to not doing what we ought to do and paying for the mistake in blood. I'd rather spend dollars in peace than blood in war. If you ask me how many warheads will it take and so forth and so on, I can't tell you how many—I don't know if anybody can.

A second example of a challenge to assured destruction is from an interview with a prominent and well-informed strategic analyst who has been very influential in shaping the defense policy of the Reagan administration. His argument that the United States does not have an assured destruction capability was the most consistent encountered. Though he did ultimately abandon it, he never (and this was very unusual) explicitly agreed that the United States has a secure retaliatory capability that would deter a rational Soviet leader.

I: Are there important Soviet targets that are not presently covered by our survivable retaliatory capabilities?

R: Absolutely. Our problem today is that we don't have adequate target coverage with likely survivable strategic or theater forces—certainly not for a scenario in which there's a surprise attack . . .

He then clarified that he meant that the United States would not even have a minimum countervalue option in such a situation:

We've gotten ourselves in a situation where the Soviets have a first-strike capability and we don't. . . . The types of residual American warheads that are likely to survive a Soviet first strike were developed for assured destruction purposes—mostly soft targets—but they're very bad, really, for a lot of population damage. They're not going to cause fallout very heavily. Given the numbers and the yields, civil defense in the Soviet Union would be very effective against those types of warheads. . . . I would think that in the aftermath of a reasonably successful Soviet first strike on the United States the actual threats to the Soviet Union would not be awesome. . . . Let's just take the minimum deterrent thing. And let's go back to McNamara's minimum deterrence—four hundred megatons, reliably arriving and detonating on cities. . . . You're a strategic planner. You have to say, "Okay, what's the prelaunch survivability of those forces against a surprise attack? What if only 50 percent of them can survive?" And then I have to say, "Well, how many of them are going to work? What's the probable reliability of the system?" Let's say that the industry hasn't screwed us as much as they probably have and eight-tenths of them will work (instead of four-tenths, which is probably more likely). And then you say, "Well, how many of them are likely to arrive on the target?" The Soviets have rich defenses if they're bombers. The answer's going to be very few indeed. [And] the bombers are

probably as poorly survivable on base as the ICBMs. At least.
Then you say what's your probability of destruction of the target?
It may take two or three warheads to cause a particular level of
damage, and when you go through the multiplication here you end
up saying, "Well, I need a force ten times that to start with in
order to have that force at the end of all that logic."

Rather than dealing with this stream of information a piece at a
time, I shifted the discussion to an analysis of how many American
warheads would survive an all-out counterforce attack against ICBMs,
bombers, and submarines in port, pointing out that most people conclude that even by a worst-case analysis several thousand warheads
would survive. He first emphatically disputed the number and pulled
at a pencil and paper, saying, "You can figure it out exactly." After
going through computations based on the assumption that all ICBMs,
all bombers, and half the submarines would be lost, he seemed a little
surprised that he ended up with "two to three thousand." As we
continued talking, he rechecked his figures for a while and then put
down his pencil and brought up potential problems of communication
with the submarines and the possibility that the Soviets might be able
to find and destroy the submarines. Rather than arguing that there are
no indications that the Soviets have an antisubmarine capability and
that the Soviets could not rely on interfering with communication to
submarines, I said:

I: Let's even knock it down to fifteen hundred warheads. Can you
imagine a Soviet seeing that potential ragged retaliation and de-
ciding to make a move?
R: Sure.
I: Would that be in a crisis situation or something like that?
R: You can play that any way you want.

He then went back to reducing the number of submarine warheads that
would survive:

R: You've got these weapons at sea, which by the way are going
down in numbers as time goes on, I'd be willing to argue. So if

you wait forty-eight hours you're down below a thousand weapons in my viewpoint, and maybe even well below that.

Then, practically in midsentence, he paused for a thoughtful moment and recognized that the United States would not simply wait for forty-eight hours before retaliating while the Soviets were picking off submarines and would most likely fire them once a state of hostilities had been firmly established: "It does put more pressure on the president to use them while he has them." Immediately thereafter he completely abandoned his argument that the United States does not have an assured destruction capability. In the ensuing discussion he referred to the fifteen hundred to two thousand surviving weapons several times, apparently now accepting that at least the Soviets would have to assume that this number would survive. He shifted, instead, to entirely different arguments, saying that a countervalue retaliation was less *desirable* than counterforce retaliation for specific contingencies but not that American countervalue capabilities are inadequate to deter an all-out attack.

In a third example, a high-level official at the Arms Control and Disarmament Agency (ACDA) claimed that the Soviet Union had a "disarming first-strike capability" and that "the fact that they have one and we don't is destabilizing." This certainly gave the impression that he thought the United States does not have an assured destruction capability. The general definition of a "disarming first strike" is that it robs the victim of the ability to execute a second strike. However, when questioned further, it became clear that he did not really mean this.

I: Does that mean that we don't have a second-strike capability?
R: No, no. It means that we have a retaliatory capability.

He then went on to make the argument that if the United States lost its land-based ICBMs, it might *choose* not to retaliate for fear of a counter-retaliation. While this does present a potentially cogent argument (which will be discussed below), it does not support the notion that the Soviets have a disarming first-strike capability. Certainly if one chooses to redefine the term to mean simply a first-strike that disarms, then his argument makes sense. However, I tend to believe that this respondent knew this is not the correct definition. He also contradicted this definition by his statement that "they have one and we don't." I can only assume that he intentionally misused the term to dramatize his concern for the vulnerability of American ICBMs.

A fourth example is from an interview with a senator on a major defense-related committee. He expressed great concern about the size of the United States's arsenal. I tried to find out why this mattered to him.

> I: The original concept of deterrence was that we need a survivable retaliatory capacity to inflict unacceptable damage—going back to McNamara. Our arsenal has gone significantly beyond those requirements.

He used conventional analogies in his reply:

> Well, I don't conceive that we've gone beyond that; I think our deterring capability has been reduced because we have not modernized and replaced, while the Soviet Union has. You can talk about bows and arrows and say, "Hey! We have enough bows and arrows to kill everybody in the world ten times over!" But if the other side gets away from bows and arrows and gets to muskets, and so on, and [we] say, "Hell, we don't need muskets! We'll keep bows and arrows." I've got to stress modernization and replacement rather than buildup.

Still uncertain why this concerned him, I tried to find out if he was thinking in terms of war-fighting scenarios as distinguished from minimal deterrence. However, he did not pick up on this concept but continued to assert the need for improvements based simply on the need for greater numbers of surviving warheads.

> I: Do you regard [the MX or Pershing IIs] as essential for retaliatory capabilities by the traditional definition of deterrence? Most explanations that I have heard are that we need [these] to support escalation dominance or some relatively refined purposes within the scenario of a war. . . .

R: Not necessarily. . . . whatever percentage of kill you want to say—whether it's 80 percent or 90 percent, or whatever—[with the MX] you're going to have ten more heads survive for each three. So you get some marginal increase of deterrence with a ten-warhead missile compared to a three.

I then asked if his concern was derived from the idea, developed by those who promulgated the notion of a window of vulnerability, that if the United States lost its ICBM force, the president might not have the nerve to retaliate. But he rejected the idea.

R: Oh, I think if we were hit, we would retaliate. I can't imagine any American president saying, "Well, they'll hit us again, so." I just don't see an American president saying that.

When asked why, then, the vulnerability of land-based ICBMs is important, he pulled out small-scale models of American and Soviet ICBMs, emphasizing the relatively larger size of the Soviet ICBM. However, he offered no strategic rationale for this concern.

Once more, I steered the discussion back to the question of the purpose of the weapons. For the first time, he recognized, implicitly, that the United States does have an assured destruction capability but expressed his preference for striking counterforce targets rather than populations.

R: We must have a credible deterrent that tells them, "You simply cannot succeed with a first strike—the damage level will be unacceptable."

I: You don't think the damage level is unacceptable now?

R: Not in terms of what we can hit. That gets back to if you want to kill people. . . . Our retaliation will be not to kill people (in which you will accept the killing of large numbers of people), but we want to be able to eliminate—as much as possible—[Soviet] second, third, and fourth strike [forces].

SHIFTING BETWEEN MINDSETS

As discussed in the previous chapter, one of the patterns I watched for during the interviews was a tendency to shift between mindsets, in particular between a conventional mindset, which assumes that nuclear weapons have not fundamentally changed the character of military relations between the superpowers, and a nuclear mindset, which believes that there has been such a change. A critical factor in this distinction centers around whether the superpowers are or are not in a condition of mutual vulnerability. The cases, explored above, in which respondents initially asserted that the United States does not have an assured destruction capability and later abandoned this position are examples of this phenomenon of shifting between mindsets. In these cases, though, the shift only occurred after a series of fairly intensive questions. In other cases respondents shifted more spontaneously, often several times.

One of the more dramatic examples of this shifting took place in an interview with a specialist on Soviet strategy. For an extended period in the first part of the interview, he argued with great intensity that the Soviet Union was pulling way ahead of the United States in its strategic capabilities as part of a master plan for developing a "war-winning capability." As he became more agitated, he gradually took the position that the Soviets not only were already building toward such a war-winning capability but had already achieved it.

    I: Do you think they have that war-winning capability now?
    R: Yes!

I probed to find out whether the type of victory he had in mind was a traditional, conventional one or whether he was talking about the Soviets altering the ability for escalation dominance through a window-of-vulnerability scenario. He rejected the latter scenario as "a bunch of shit" and said that

> [The Soviet goal] is to destroy the United States—very simply . . . it's not a game. It's a pretty decisive conflict and once-and-for-all "who's gonna win?" . . . Their goal is clearly stated as a world socialist republic . . . they intend to win. . . . I don't know how else you can explain everything they're doing.

Gradually it became clear that he did not regard these war-winning goals as Soviet delusions but as being fairly realistic. Bit by bit, he explained how the Soviets could win a nuclear war. One of his key points was that the Soviets would attack by surprise, "while we're sleeping. . . . Given that there's going to be a war—accept that as a given—who in their right mind would attack without the most surprise possible? . . . It's the only way to go to war." American command and control could be easily destroyed. "It can't take more than half a dozen missiles to totally decimate the U. S. command, control, and communications." American retaliatory capabilities would be destroyed through a combination of counterforce and air defense missiles against incoming strategic warheads.

R: They have several thousand air defense missiles with a capability against Poseidon warheads.

I: Soviet air defenses can be used for ABM purposes?

R: You bet your ass they can. The SA-5, the SA-10, and the SA-12 have been tested in an ABM mode.

Furthermore, he said, many missiles would not even get off the ground because of domestic sabotage arising from ongoing Soviet efforts to "infiltrate" the American public.

He bewailed the effects of arms control treaties. In his mind, they had played a critical role in allowing the Soviet Union to get so dangerously ahead of the United States.

I: Why did [the Soviets] sign SALT I?

R: Look what they've gained from arms control over the past, say fifteen years.

I: You mean the slowing of the buildup on our side?

R: Slowing, shit—we stopped it! While they've increased their capability by over a factor of five!

A bit later, though, for no apparent reason, he changed his tune, both in content and tone of voice.

I: Let me ask the question in a direct way: How, as a Soviet, could you come to the conclusion that the U. S. wouldn't retaliate in some devastating way? That at least one hundred missiles wouldn't get through to targets—to countervalue targets, at least?

R: Well, that's what we're counting on.

I: Do you feel confident that—

R: I don't know.

I: It's an important question to come to a conclusion on. Maybe we need a lot more [weapons]. Maybe we don't need any more at all.

R: Oh, I agree. I think we've reached the point where the best we have is basically a minimum deterrent capability.

With the next sentence, though, he went back to making it a bit ambiguous.

R: We really should make a concerted effort to try and really ask, "What is the minimum that makes sense, and to what extent can we guarantee that the minimum will get through?"

I: Have you thought that through?

R: No, it's just a conclusion. It's struck me over the past eight or nine months that we do have the werewithal to stop them from being aggressive. . . . They would have to worry about [American] submarines, and I think that's what they do.

I: Could you describe a development that would alter that equation?

R: No, I don't see any risk over something like that at the present time.

I: But you're very pessimistic. I thought that you almost predicted that a war will happen.

R: No, I think we're at the point where there's still a minimum deterrent, and it's a very hefty deterrent.

He then described the apparent split with lucidity, "I'm extremely pessimistic on one side, but on the other side I think that the Soviets do things in a very sensible way." This recognition, however, was not stable. Shortly thereafter he reverted to an angry denunciation of present American strategic capabilities, asserting once again that because of asymmetries in the Soviets' favor, the Soviet Union could win a nuclear war with the United States.

Another example of such shifting came in an interview with a former Pentagon official when discussing Soviet plans for winning a nuclear war.

I: Do you think that's a realistic plan on their part?

R: It sure is. . . . The leadership is taking steps, making resolves for many many years, and there's zero of that on our side. So I think they'd just plain win it and survive.

I: Win? So that in an all-out nuclear war they would, as a society, survive?

R: Yeah. And I think we'd give up—hopefully, as soon as possible. Because it's not a war that we stand the remotest chance of winning or breaking even in.

He related this situation in part to American failure to maintain parity.

R: We haven't had parity (whatever it may mean), or even been close to it, for quite a few years now.

I: The Soviets have been ahead of us?

R: Because of all these things that the Soviets have been doing. . . . They have somewhat more ICBMs—right, more megatonage, more throw-weight, and all that nonsense, whatever it means. It *is* some crude measure of the force balance.

However, when questioned more specifically on this thinking, he abruptly shifted to saying that the balance was not relevant.

I: If they have 10 percent, 20 percent, whatever, more ICBMs, how does that matter? How would that be strategically useful for them?

R: It doesn't. Now, a lot of people who are on the hawkish side are yelling that it does matter.

I: I just want to understand what you think.

R: Whether it does or doesn't matter? . . . it's irrelevant. It's not an important factor.

I: It's not militarily relevant, strategically relevant?

R: Yeah.

At another point in the interview he even derided concern for the balance.

R: What we usually do is we say, "Okay, we have to have the same capability—a counter." Now, this is really nonsense. . . . The Soviets do something; we get all alarmed, and the politicians demand that we do the same thing.

I: This sort of centers around the notion of parity as a governing principle, right?

R: It's meaningless—it's absolutely meaningless.

He then told a story about having been on a panel at a prominent conservative institution where Soviet arms control violations were being discussed. "I said that it doesn't matter, that it's irrelevant. And I got this fellow hopping mad at me."

But then, momentarily, he changed his tone again, saying that he was seriously concerned that the Soviets might be concealing a substantial number of weapons, and portrayed himself as being quite alone in his concern, "What nuclear capabilities do the Soviets have that are unknown to us? Now, my gut feeling is that the bulk of their capabilities are unknown to us. . . . I have a great concern. Now, there aren't too many like me who have such a concern." When questioned further on reconciling this concern for concealed Soviet weapons with his stated attitude that relative capabilities are irrelevant, he became more entrenched in the view that an imbalance in the Soviets' favor would give them a war-winning capability. Asked why this is a problem if the Soviets are hiding some weapons, he answered:

Let's just suppose that we found out that 90 percent of the Soviet missile force has been mobile and hidden over the full extent of the USSR. And somehow or another we were able to figure this out. And we saw them all—some miraculous moment came when they were all bared, and at least we felt we saw everything. But what we saw was far in excess of what we thought they had. So instead of their having fifteen hundred ICBMs (or whatever these IISS numbers* are), we saw five or ten times that number. Now, that's relevant, and that's significant.

*He is referring to the International Institute of Strategic Studies, a London-based research institute that publishes *The Military Balance,* a highly respected report on the numbers of Soviet and American forces.

I: Why?

R: Because it represents an overwhelming capability on their part.

I: To?

R: To beat us in a war. Now, I think they have it already. I can't prove it to anybody's satisfaction, but that's my gut feeling.

I: So suppose they have ten times the number of ICBMs. How would they go about beating us? . . .

R: I think they'd go about beating us just about as easily or—pardon me, ten times more easily or x times more easily or something like that. And I think they can do that right now.

Throughout the remainder of the interview he continued to shift in a similar fashion. Never did he seem aware of the apparent inconsistencies in his positions, and he therefore made no effort to resolve them into a higher-order framework.

CHAPTER 4

Seeking Advantageous Termination

T HE IDEA of using military force to actively pursue certain advantages relative to the Soviet Union is perhaps the most vivid example of the perseverance of pre-nuclear thinking. Such ideas range from the notion of seeking a relatively advantageous outcome in a limited exchange to winning an all-out nuclear war. The goals specified are not to simply restore the status quo ante but to inflict greater relative damage, to actually cause a recession of Soviet power or even to seek its ultimate demise.

In an attempt to draw out respondents' concepts of war-termination, the key question asked was what the goal of American action should be in the event that deterrence fails and the Soviets take aggressive action either in central Europe or against the American homeland—either by purely conventional means or with nuclear weapons. A substantial number resisted the question: some simply by not answering, others by such a meaningless answer as "try to minimize damage"—meaningless because it did not define the central action that would be taken by the United States. As Karl von Clausewitz would have pointed out, to simply minimize damage the United States would probably do best not to respond at all—something these individuals were clearly not suggesting. Some respondents defined the destructive capabilities the United States should have in its arsenal but resisted specifying how these capabilities should be used in the event deterrence fails.

When pressed to be more explicit, not all respondents spoke in terms of advantage-seeking policies. Some articulated moderate symmetrical objectives, such as simply restoring the status quo ante (even if this meant accepting disproportionately greater casualties) or responding in a tit-for-tat fashion while vigorously using communication channels to end hostilities at the earliest possible point.

Others, however, did describe war aims that involved an advantageous termination. Some said flatly that the United States should aim to "win." Others used such terms as "prevailing" or seeking termination "favorable" to the United States. When asked for more definition of these terms, some spoke of generally being in a favorable position relative to the Soviet Union, for example: "Prevail means to stop on terms that place the aggressor in a position that is not as, uh, comfortable—that's not a good word—but is in a position that's not as, uh, strong, that's less favorable." Some spoke of relative damage—the war should "cost" them more. Others spoke of taking territory.

R: No war can really be won against a belligerent unless you not only hold your own land but also take some of theirs.

I: So it would be important to take some of it?

R: Oh, take a hell of a lot of it . . . obviously, you should march in . . . the only real answer is to take their land.

Sometimes the distinction between the traditional objectives of a conventional war and the objectives of a nuclear war were explicitly played down as, for example, in this exchange with a high-level Pentagon official:

R: The issue is, is nuclear war so essentially different from any other war that the terms for cessation would be different . . . is nuclear war so essentially different that [winning and losing] don't make any sense?

I: Was that a statement?

R: No. I'm saying, is it? A rhetorical question. And my view is that in more limited . . . use of nuclear weapons you *can* relate that more correctly to conventional use. When you begin to talk about massive use of nuclear weapons, that's when there's a breakdown.

However, he went on to say that it was not necessary to ultimately limit the United States to seeking advantageous termination in a limited war. Such goals could also be pursued in a general war if the United States takes "all the steps to ensure that the government will continue to exist, that the economy of the country can be reconstructed, that medical services will be [available]."

When such answers were given, I asked for specific scenarios. A recurrent one involved a conventional central European war that leads to the liberation of Eastern Europe. A Rand analyst said:

> If you really had a conventional war, we shouldn't mess around. We should try to win the war so we don't have another one . . . it would mean thoroughly defeating the Soviet army to the point where they could not even continue subjugating the Eastern European nations. . . . We would be building the buffer farther to the East and giving them more military disadvantage for the next war, giving us more warning time and giving them more hostile forces to move through before they get to Western Europe.

Another strategic analyst described a Central European war leading to the overthrow of the Soviet government, saying that the goal would be to:

R: . . .make it impossible for this kind of conflict to reoccur.
I: So you're talking about in some way breaking the military capabilities of the Soviet Union? So it's a real war-winning notion?
R: Yeah, the postbellum world will have to be profoundly different . . .
I: And how would you see that we could pursue these goals?
R: . . . Some of the planning that's going on is for decapitation strategies and for what is so delightfully known as ethnic targeting. . . . We have to generate a situation which tells the Soviet population that if they overthrow their government they have a possibility of terminating the war very quickly and on long-term terms that are extremely attractive to them. . . .
I: Do you have that second-echelon group identified in your mind? Do you have ideas about how we might communicate to them?
R: Yeah, I think you use extensive and massive radio broadcasts.

> . . . Even absolutely loyal supporters of the current government, if faced with a situation in which there was suddenly a very high possibility that military installations within their cities could become nuclear targets . . . the calculation of these political leaders is likely to change radically.

Several others described scenarios in which Eastern European nations would rise up against the Soviets, thus facilitating the ultimate occupation of Moscow by American troops.

Other scenarios involved an all-out war. Some asserted that if a war with the Soviet Union happened at all it would inevitably escalate to an intercontinental war. One analyst insisted it would definitely be a "big war" involving "thousands of warheads." A former member of the Joint Chiefs of Staff who explicitly embraced war-winning objectives said:

> I don't care what people say. If we attack 'em at all it's going to be a major attack. It's nonsense to think you'd shoot two or three missiles and get on the telephone and say, "How'd you like them apples?" Schlesinger thinks that, you see—well, that's bullshit. Most of the people who come up with these ideas have never been in a war.

A logical conclusion is that this confidence in the possibility of winning even a large-scale war indicates that some respondents did not perceive the American population as critically vulnerable to countervalue attacks. I had expected to hear arguments for the potential effectiveness of countersilo strikes, counter-command-and-control strikes, civil defense, and in the long run, of course, strategic defense. A few expressed the attitude that the apocalyptic character of nuclear war had been exaggerated. Others argued that damage to cities would be limited because the Soviets have a counterforce targeting doctrine. A fair number dismissed the nuclear winter theory, though their basis for doing so was not well articulated. Overall, though, there was very little effort to challenge the basic notion that the United States population would necessarily be vulnerable to massive attacks.

In one notable case, however, a respondent suggested that it might be possible to effectively decapitate the Soviet control structure and

thereby prevent Soviet missiles from being fired. Given the centraliza-
tion of the Soviet command, it might be possible to knock out the
leadership or at least cut the lines of communication to the missile silos.
When asked whether we knew if the Soviet command structure was
designed so that command authority would not devolve to a lower level,
he tilted his head to imply that the United States might have some
information to that effect. However, when asked whether we could
count on this assumption for our war planning, he made a hasty retreat
and clearly affirmed that we would have to plan on the basis of high
levels of vulnerability.

Interestingly, a number of individuals, while not professing such
views for themselves, attributed to other specific individuals the belief
that there was indeed a way to deal with the problem of vulnerability.
However, when I took their names and interviewed them, I got basically the same response—low-key efforts to downplay the certainty of
Armageddon but a strong recognition that vulnerability was certain for
the foreseeable future. Major efforts notwithstanding, I was never able
to find a real exponent of a point of view like that expressed by T. K.
Jones, a deputy undersecretary of defense, in his now-famous quote
about how Americans can protect themselves against a nuclear attack:
"Dig a hole, cover it with a couple of doors and then throw three feet
of dirt on top . . . if there are enough shovels to go around, everybody's
going to make it."[1]* Perhaps many of the people I spoke with really
did believe it was possible to deal with the problem of vulnerability but
did not express their beliefs for political reasons. At this point, though,
I am convinced that, perhaps with the exception of a few unique
individuals, the defense establishment as a whole does fully perceive the
American population as fundamentally vulnerable.

In trying to ascertain how respondents reconciled the aim of achieving an advantageous termination with this recognition of vulnerability,
four major types of responses emerged, of which some individuals gave

*I should note that I was not allowed to see T. K. Jones and two other government officials
who, I have been told, would have made such an argument. The two government officials verbally
agreed to see me. One official worked for an intelligence agency and I would need official
permission, which, he explained, was a simple formality, but which was denied. In the other case,
I arrived for the scheduled interview with a State Department official and was told at the front
desk that he would not be able to see me that day or any other day. When I requested an interview
with T. K. Jones, I was immediately told—and this was unusual—that it was unlikely that I would
be able to speak to him but that I would be able to speak to someone; however, I would have
to go through the public relations office—again, something I had not previously encountered.

more than one. The first, apparently derived from a conventional mindset, asserted that a victory strategy was logically imperative, that once war started military logic necessarily dictated the traditional objective of victory. The second type of response claimed that as long as the Soviets remain vulnerable, the United States can safely assume the Soviets will not escalate to intercontinental strikes—even if the survival of their government is at stake. The third modified the traditional concept of victory by incorporating the possibility of massive civilian losses. The fourth and most common response involved a shifting between a conventional and a nuclear mindset—serially recognizing the impossibility of achieving an advantageous termination when populations remained vulnerable and asserting the possibility of winning.

Imperative Traditional Logic

A Rand analyst explained that the United States should avoid war as long as possible but said that once war begins, the United States must pursue traditional war-fighting objectives.

R: . . . you would look at [a superpower war] the same way that military leaders have always looked at it . . . if we get into the situation, then we look at it "as a war."

I: What do you mean "as a war"?

R: After the war is over somebody occupies somebody else; somebody decrees to somebody else what the government will be like.

One congressman (on a major defense-related committee) began by making a distinction between principles of pre-nuclear and nuclear war but then said that once the Soviets attacked it would be imperative to pursue traditional goals.

R: See, in the olden days, well, the duke could take over the duchy next door, or the king could take over northern France or whatever it was. . . . Anyway, you could do that in the old days. . . . But that's not so attainable today.

I: So what does that mean our goals should be, then?

R: Well, I don't think the ultimate goals have really changed that much. We ought to try to reduce the chances of war, and once the war starts, to try to minimize its expansion. But if it's clear and determined that the other side is attempting to take land that doesn't belong to them, then the only real answer is to take their land.

Some respondents asserted a kind of dichotomous logic, saying that the only alternative to a victory strategy was to surrender. A Rand analyst said:

This may sound glib, but I'm quite serious about it. Either one surrenders, or one has a war-fighting strategy, which means that if deterrence fails you try to win the war. Now, winning the war may not be something that leaves you in a position that you would regard as very happy—there may be a lot of people dead. But the only alternative is to surrender.

A military official said, with a suppressed guffaw, "We're not going to say we're going to terminate to our disadvantage!"

With individuals who gave this kind of response, I eventually raised alternative concepts of termination—that is, in which the aim was not to achieve an advantage but to simply restore the status quo ante or to follow a tit-for-tat principle. These respondents discussed them seriously but were clearly uncomfortable with them. In some cases this seemed to be an emotional discomfort with the idea of not pursuing a climactic resolution, but a major root of the discomfort also seemed cognitive. The conventional mindset was so dominant that victory seemed like the only logical war-termination goal. Imagining anything else was like balancing on a greased ball. Without enough palpable images or ideas to support it, there was almost a magnetic pull back to the dichotomous logic of the win-lose model.

One key pattern was to put great emphasis on the inadequacy of the MAD doctrine. A substantial number of respondents referred to the MAD doctrine as if it constituted a targeting strategy similar to the massive retaliation strategy of the 1950s—that is, in the event of even minor Soviet aggression, the United States would launch a massive countervalue strike. However, such thinking all but disappeared from

American strategic thinking in the 1960s. In fact, the man who is most associated with MAD, Robert McNamara, is the individual most responsible for moving the United States away from a massive retaliation targeting strategy and replacing it with flexible response. MAD was formulated as a principle to describe the condition of mutual vulnerability and to set the context for strategic planning and to force sizing. It was never used to define a targeting strategy or war-fighting objectives. Criticisms of a latter-day massive retaliation strategy are largely against a straw man.

Nevertheless, I heard such criticisms on a regular basis; with numerous respondents this critique was the centerpiece of their general strategic argument. A number of individuals saliently argued that MAD had not adequately articulated war-fighting objectives in the event deterence fails. This was followed by an assertion that what necessarily follows from this is that American war-fighting objectives must necessarily be to achieve an advantageous termination. Sometimes when I raised problems with such objectives, the individual effectively refused to address the problems and simply reiterated the problems of MAD.

Others recognized that such objectives may be meaningless but were preferable to MAD (misinterpreted as massive retaliation). As one high-ranking military official said:

> Assured destruction is purely and simply revenge. You're not trying to get anything out of it. And I think the shift has been more toward using military forces for definable political or military objectives even if those tend to be meaningless in a nuclear war.

Arguing from an entirely different tack, others emphasized that if the Soviets initiate aggression, it is incumbent upon the United States to, in fact, punish the Soviet Union.* This punishment would generally

---

*This attitude can also be found in official statements. In his FY 1979 Report to Congress, Secretary of Defense Harold Brown wrote about a central European war:

> One mark of our seriousness is the determination not merely to stop an attack but to carry the war to the enemy and make him pay a long-term price for his transgression. To show that determination, we should acquire enough sustainability to indicate that we would and could charge an enemy heavily for having disturbed the peace. How far we should go in that direction awaits further analysis. However, I should point out that we already—and undoubtedly will continue to—maintain one major "long war" hedge. (U.S. Department of Defense, Harold Brown, *Annual Report to Congress FY 1979* [Washington, D.C.: GPO, 1978], 86). Such

involve an effort to extract some territory from Soviet control or inflict a relatively greater amount of damage on the Soviets. One analyst said:

> I think the desire is that in any crisis . . . you should not merely, you know, react to your opponent. You should be looking for ways to punish him for having caused this problem, and "punish" means to take advantage, to gain something. Chances are, crises will end, but someone will have won.

Another analyst explained the goals of a central European war to be:

> R: . . . in principle, war termination on terms that make the cost of the war . . . worthwhile. . . . Because when neither NATO or the East European countries will have initiated the conflict there cannot simply be restoration of the status quo ante. Because you will be talking about a pretty horrifying conflict. . . . We might have to include some penalties . . .
>
> I: Why?
>
> R: Because they have to start it—we can't. We have no interest in starting it.
>
> I: So it's a kind of punishment?
>
> R: Yeah . . . they should not assume they can, in effect, say, "Whoops—sorry. Let's all go back to the starting lines, and we're sorry we killed several hundred thousand of your people, and it's tough on our peasants, but what the heck—let's all go back to the start lines."

The rationale offered for this punishment was sometimes based on a crudely applied model of conditioning behavior. The Soviets would need to be punished in an effort to extinguish their aggressive behavior. A former member of the National Security Council said, "One may want to go marginally beyond restoring the status quo antebellum. . . . One of our objectives ought to be to tell the Soviets they can't—to punish them . . ."

The compelling question is how the United States could seek to

---

statements reveal how the countervailing strategy proposed by Brown can go beyond the more-emphasized "deterrence through denial" and seek to punish the transgressor even after an advance has been successfully denied and even if this requires substantially extending the war.

punish the Soviet Union when it would remain vulnerable to escalatory strikes. While some argued that under certain circumstances the Soviets might not escalate in response to a NATO advance into Eastern Europe, all agreed that it would be impossible to count on it. The dilemma was often spontaneously recognized. A former member of the National Security Council said that it would be desirable to

> make the Soviet Union pay a price, in a sense, for launching the war. But these are the sorts of things we have to judge in the circumstance. Nobody would be in favor of entering East Europe . . . if they thought they were going to lead to a Soviet first strike against West Europe or the United States.

However, he offered no principles that could guide United States decisions "in the circumstance." Even though the recognition of vulnerability did apparently put some theoretical constraints on the notion of seeking a punitive advantage, it apparently did not alter the basic principle.

Soviet Restraint

Several respondents stated that it was feasible to pursue advantageous objectives on the assumption that the Soviet Union would restrain itself from escalating to strikes against the American homeland for fear of a reciprocal response. A former member of the Joint Chiefs of Staff suggested that the United States could even pursue the overthrow of the Soviet government and the occupation of Moscow and still rely on Soviet restraint. He began by invoking imperative traditional logic.

I: Suppose the Soviets advanced into Western Germany, and we conventionally pushed them back and restored the status quo antebellum. Would we stop there?

R: Well, it depends on if you've got them on the run, so to speak. There's only one purpose of war. What do you think the purpose of war is?

I: What do I think it should be?

R: What it is, not what it should be. It's just one thing.

I: Well, I think a lot of people have a lot of different ideas of what the purpose of war should be under those circumstances [I mentioned several].

R: No! There's one reason for a war, and that's to remove the government that's doing something you don't like. . . . A war is nothing but a political confrontation, and the only purpose of a war—the *only* purpose of a war—

I: Of a conventional war in Europe?

R: Any kind of war! The only purpose of the war is to remove the government that started the war, that's doing something you don't like . . .

I: So we would advance past West Germany and try to go into Moscow?

R: There's all kinds of ways you could do that—you just mentioned one of them. I wouldn't be surprised if the so-called satellite nations didn't turn against Russia. I mean, do you think the Czechs are still happy about the way they came into Czechoslovakia and killed all those people? So you would try to remove the government . . . if I was succeeding in pushing them back, I would do what I could to continue to do just what I said—break up this present system they have of this very small group controlling and subjugating the whole country and continually trying to seek soft spots in the world and move in, like they've done all the way around the world. And they are the reason for this big arms buildup we have. . . . The first thing I'd aim to do [in response to a Soviet invasion of West Germany] is to get them out of West Germany. Then I would try to get them out of the satellites. Then, if I succeeded in that, then the third step is I would—either by fomenting a revolution, whatever I could do, or moving forces into Moscow, whatever—

Finally I raised the issue of American homeland vulnerability.

I assume that the reason that you wouldn't want to make any advances now is because the Soviets have the ability to knock us out with nuclear weapons.

R: No. You asked me—I think you said what would I do if they made progress going into Germany? What would I do if we drove them back? I don't think under any circumstances that the Soviets would make a major, full-scale attack against the United States as long as we had survivable forces. And that the difference between zero and few is far greater than [between] few and many. And they know that, and so if they are fighting a war and getting driven back, they are not going to commit what capacity they have for trying to stop this drive into Russia by risking getting completely eliminated by the nuclear weapons.

Incorporating Massive Civilian Losses

Most respondents dealt with the problem of population vulnerability by either avoiding it or downplaying it. They seemed to implicitly affirm that the notion of victory was not meaningful if it involved massive civilian losses. There were, however, a few respondents who did seem to incorporate such a possibility into their concept of an advantageous termination.

Such a perspective seemed to be implicit in the argument made by several respondents that the relative levels of damage after a general nuclear war would be the measure of victory. This argument was most clearly stated in a 1956 article by Paul Nitze. He recognized that nuclear weapons had invalidated traditional images of victory:

. . . No one could "win" a third world war, in the sense of being richer, happier, or better off after such a war than before it.

However, he proposed another "connotation" for the word *win* as suggesting

. . . a comparison of the post-war position of one of the adversaries with the post-war position of the other adversary. In this sense it is quite possible that in a general nuclear war one side or the other could "win" decisively.

Clearly, Nitze was speaking of a war involving very large-scale destruction. He even recognized that it was "conceivable" that the destruction "would be so great that nothing would remain, that life on this planet would be impossible," though he did not regard such complete destruction as "likely." He concluded that this redefinition of the concept of victory "brings out why it is also of the utmost importance that the West maintain a sufficient margin of superior capability so that it could 'win' in [this] sense."[2]

Such a concept of victory was reportedly articulated in an even more extreme form by General Tommy Powers, deputy to the commanding general of the Strategic Air Command in the late 1950s and early 1960s. Fred Kaplan writes that shortly into a December 1960 briefing on the possibility of restrained responses in a nuclear war, Powers burst out:

> Why do you want us to restrain ourselves? . . . Restraint! Why are you so concerned with saving *their* lives? The whole idea is to *kill* the bastards! . . . Look. At the end of the war, if there are two Americans and one Russian, we win![3]

In the interviews, this kind of thinking did not come up in such a raw arithmetic form. However, a few respondents rationalized the concern for relative postwar positions in terms of the ability to prevail in the long run. A high-level Pentagon official defined the victor as the side able to "reconstitute and recover more quickly." A strategic analyst emphasized that the goal would be, after a period of recovery, to "be in a better position to continue [the war] than the other side," until victory is fully attained. Nitze thought along similar lines.

> The victor will be in a position to issue orders to the loser and the loser will have to obey them or face complete chaos or extinction. The victor will then go on to organize what remains of the world as best he can.[4]

This attitude is apparently not simply in the netherworld of strategic thinking but has influenced official American war-fighting plans. Leon Sloss, director of a major nuclear targeting study during the Carter administration, has written that in 1975, with the Presidential National Security directive NSDM-242, it was

> specified that if escalation could not be controlled, the United States should target its remaining forces so as to *impede Soviet recovery*. . . . The goal of targeting . . . was to place the United States in a position, where even after

a general nuclear war, the latter could reconstitute itself as a viable national entity more rapidly than the Soviet Union [emphasis in original].[5]

Then Secretary of Defense Donald Rumsfeld in 1976 embraced "the effort to prevent or retard an enemy's military, political, and economic recovery from a nuclear exchange."[6] General David Jones, then Air Force chief of staff, said in a 1977 Senate Armed Services Committee hearing that "relative post-attack recovery capability is a critical factor in measuring national capacities for waging and surviving nuclear war."[7]

This kind of thinking becomes especially compelling if one assumes that in fact an all-out nuclear war is inevitable. The best outcome the United States can hope for, then, is to inflict greater damage, to recover more quickly, and then try again to prevail. Several respondents openly expressed the opinion, or implied, that a large-scale Soviet-American nuclear war is probably inevitable. One middle-level Pentagon official said several times that to understand American targeting policy, "You have to convince yourself that nuclear war is coming."*

Implicit in this line of thinking, though not necessarily fully realized, is a new way of defining the objectives of American defense policy. What is being defended is no longer limited to the state as something that exists in form, but, rather, a principle or an abstraction. To preserve the abstraction that the state embodies, it may even be necessary to sacrifice the greater part of the form of the state.†

---

*Interestingly, President Reagan has also confirmed that this kind of thinking is influential in policymaking circles. In December 1987, in response to critics of the INF Treaty, he said, "Now I think that some of the people who are objecting the most and just refusing even to accede to the idea of ever getting any understanding, whether they realize it or not, those people—basically down in their deepest thoughts—have accepted that war is inevitable and that there must come to be a war between the two superpowers." It is hard to say whether President Reagan was describing attitudes that he had heard expressed, giving a psychological analysis of his critics, or inadvertently revealing thoughts that he himself had had in the past when he was considerably more opposed to arms control treaties. (Steven U. Roberts, "President Assails Conservative Foes of New Arms Pact," *New York Times* [December 4, 1987], p 16)

†This is reminiscent of the theory of sociobiology, according to which a key determinant of biological behavior is the survival interest of genetic patterns. The genetic pattern, the genotype, directs its biological form to take actions to propagate the genotype even if this requires the sacrifice of the biological form of a particular individual.

In the case of the United States, though, what would be preserved is a kind of ideological type. Arguably, its preservation may require the sacrifice of the majority of the human expressions of this type so that the type can ultimately propagate itself and prevail. One is reminded of a statement by then Senator Richard Russell, who said that in the event of nuclear war, he wanted the only two survivors to be an American man and an American woman. (Robert Collison, "The New Threat of Nuclear War," *Saturday Night* [May 1980], 18)

This context sheds some perspective on statements such as General Alexander Haig's that "there are more important things than peace ... things we Americans should be willing to fight for."[8] The statement was not that Americans should be willing to accept the *risk* of war as a necessary price for freedom but that war itself was acceptable as a means for Americans to pursue certain values. If the consequence of such a war is to annihilate the majority of Americans and to disable American institutions for a substantial period of time, then the value being served is clearly of a very abstract nature. The goal is not to preserve the United States as an existing entity but to renew a socio-ideological pattern and perhaps to ultimately bring it to an even more powerful expression. When the value is placed in the pattern itself, the form being secondary, then it becomes logical to accept massive civilian losses in the service of the pattern.

Shifting Between Mindsets

Among those who argued for war-winning objectives, the most common pattern for dealing with the problem of population vulnerability was to shift between mindsets, one asserting traditional, conventional principles of warfare, the other dismissing them as inappropriate in light of the consequences of nuclear weapons.

One respondent, a strategic analyst at a private think tank, began the interview in a clearly conventional mindset. He described ambitious war-winning aims and emphatically rejected any concept of symmetrical war termination, saying that the Soviets must be punished for having initiated the aggression. He spoke of seeking to decapitate the Soviet control structure and of aiming for an ultimate restructuring of the Soviet government. When the critical question of population vulnerability was broached, he insisted that this was not a fundamental problem.

R: If we have survivable forces, we can probably limit damage to the civilian population by a threat of retaliation . . .

I: By saying that we won't strike populations we anticipate that they're going to be willing to not strike populations at the same

time that we have counterforce exchanges which could lead to
their government surrendering.

R: [nods]

When pressed, he began to equivocate:

I: So you would envision the Soviet government surrendering at the
same time that they have capabilities to strike the American
population?

R: I'd say there is at least a possibility.

He then tried to depict a scenario in which the pressure of war would
lead to a "reconstitution" of the Soviet government in which Soviet
leaders would be willing to accommodate a partial breakup of the Soviet
Union. The plausibility of his scenarios evidently stretched to the
breaking point, he then appeared to abruptly shift to another mindset:

R: Let me also add, as you spin through all of this, I always have
a strong feeling of unreality about it. I mean, you're asking me to
do my version of Herman Kahn's "thinking through the unthinkable." I'm not quite sure whether I would use the word "happy,"
but I'm certainly prepared to follow it through. . . . If you ask me
how seriously I take it, the margin between this and the George
Lucas *Star Wars* I regard as fairly limited . . . I really regard this
as being heavily into the speculative side of the discipline.

I: So if you were to try to apply realism to such scenarios and war
aims, what would you—

R: What would I say? It'll all be absolutely bloody chaos and we'll
end up improvising. And I'm not at all confident of our ability to
get war termination.

He then went on to say, in sharp contradistinction to his earlier comments, that the only hope the United States could have would be to
try to keep the exchange at very low levels by aiming to restore the
status quo ante, not trying to change the Soviet government, and
following a tit-for-tat exchange principle.

When I asked a ranking congressman on the Armed Services Committee what the United States's goals should be in response to a Soviet

counterforce strike, he applied imperative conventional logic, saying that if a war starts, the United States must seek victory. "Well, we ought to do everything we can to see if we don't have a war and if we have a war it'd be the least possible war, and if we have to go into any kind of war, to win it." He paused a moment, thinking, and then added, "It's a difficult thing to straddle because how do you win a war that you want to reduce in size? So that's difficult but that doesn't evade the objective." However, later in the interview when I brought up the concept of prevailing in a nuclear war, he said flatly, "Well, I don't think anybody can prevail in a nuclear war."

A former member of the National Security Council staff said that the NATO goal should be "to win" a central European war, and that in response to Soviet aggression NATO should not only advance to the Elbe River but should attempt to invade Eastern Europe as well. However, when asked whether NATO efforts to invade Eastern Europe should be constrained by the vulnerability of European capitals and the American homeland, he responded that we should only go as far into Eastern Europe as we could with reasonable confidence that they would not be pushed to the point of retaliating with countervalue strikes. When asked how far we could push with this confidence, he equivocated for a moment and then said, "Probably not very far." When asked whether it was likely that we could, with confidence, push "at all beyond the status quo ante," he thought for a moment and answered, "Probably not." He spoke with an air of forgetfulness, as if he felt that he knew a stronger answer to the question but at that moment was unable to retrieve it.

Later in the interview his general strategy goals began to shift toward symmetrical concepts. He began to speak of restoring the status quo ante and using tit-for-tat principles. Eventually, when, I asked him, perhaps too aggressively, if these outcomes were what he had meant earlier when he said the United States should aim "to win," he stiffened and said, "Well, I suppose the Soviets could win too."

A Rand analyst shifted so facilely and so often it was hard to keep up with him. Initially he said, "You do have to think about [war-fighting] objectives like who occupies whom, who is free to decide." In response to queries about specific scenarios, he said that in a central European war an objective would be "At a minimum to restore the boundaries of the pre-war situation and, if possible, take more."

I: And how would you decide whether or not to take more and how much more to take?

R: At the time that would be a decision primarily determined by the nuclear war. If it were a conventional war and political leaders did not think that the Soviet Union would go to nuclear war merely because NATO managed to recover some of Eastern Europe, I'd imagine we'd go ahead and try to do it.

He then shifted as he began to consider the problem of vulnerability:

On the other hand, being more realistic, I think it would be most surprising to see a real strategic counteroffensive by NATO because I think that there would be tremendous fear of a Soviet nuclear response, and one doesn't know where that would go.

However, soon afterward it appeared that the problem, in his mind, was not vulnerability but lack of conventional capability:

R: If we had . . . a lot more conventional capability, then if the Soviets invaded Western Europe, it would be a much greater potential to not only trim them back but to keep on going for a while.

But consideration of the Soviet response once again led him to some pause.

I: And how do you anticipate the Soviet Union would respond to that?

R: The attempt to change the boundary unfavorably? Conventional wisdom is they'd "go berserk and unleash a nuclear war."

But this perspective did not hold, so he momentarily discounted it:

R: But I think, in fact, if things were going slowly enough so that they were not trying to make decisions in hours, that rather than a nuclear war—this is just a guess, I could be wrong—I think that they would accommodate reality if we were defeating them conventionally.

I: Do you think that they would begin using tacticals against the front lines?

R: No.

Once again, he began to equivocate, saying,

I would say there's a 50 percent chance that they would actually be willing to lose some territory conventionally rather than start a nuclear war that they would not be confident that they could control.

When asked what level of certainty he would require, he only gradually returned to the vulnerability problem.

I: What kind of certainty would you need that the Soviets would not go nuclear?

R: First, I'd have to have a real belief that we were doing good, that we were going to be liberating somebody in some sense. Secondly, I'd have to be quite confident that as a result of the counteroffensive we weren't going to risk having a disaster conventionally. If those criteria were met, then the nuclear problem would come up and I suppose—[Stopping in mid-sentence, he paused at length and then seemed to shift.] I don't know. I think national leaders would tend to stop and they would have to be almost positive the Soviets would not use nuclear weapons before they would go on.

A bit later he made a statement that encapsulated the inconsistency of his position. Because he had firmly identified himself as being from the countervailing school ("I would associate myself with the attitudes of the most vigorous countervailing-strategy people"), I asked him to distinguish this strategy from the more recent strategy for prevailing. His response was remarkably jumbled.

The difference between countervailing strategy and what is talked about now [i.e., prevailing] is that the countervailing-strategy people do not really talk about counteroffensives in Eastern Europe.

On the other hand, the same people who talk about countervailing strategy, if these events actually arose, I think would consider such counteroffensives as if they were practical, which they probably are not.

As the interview unfolded he continued to shift. On several occasions he flatly asserted that it would be impossible to seek an advantage, after which he appeared to be uncomfortable and said, "Well, let me back off that a little bit," and tried to resurrect the concept. Near the end of the interview, as his frustration grew, he directed a minor outburst at himself: "I'm describing this badly! I'm not doing a good job on this!" I felt sorry that he seemed to blame his failure on his own intellectual inadequacies and was also struck by his persistent faith that, indeed, there was a logically consistent explanation for the apparent inconsistencies of which he seemed to be so painfully aware.

While in the above cases there was a general movement from a conventional mindset toward a nuclear mindset, in some cases the movement was in the opposite direction. In at least one case—the foreign policy aide to a prominent prodefense senator—the process appeared to be, in part, an adaptation to the respondent's political environment. Initially he said, "I think if you actually got into [war] you would definitely want to go tit-for-tat and be negotiating like fucking bandits." When asked what he thought of the notion of prevailing, he avoided the question ("I will confess that its meaning eludes me"). When pressed, he answered in an agitated tone:

> I think it's the ultimate extension of the deterrent notion . . . it's like saying you're going to walk into a bar and beat up every goddamned person in the bar to convince the last big guy in the bar not to mess with you. . . . The president of the United States was told he had to have the nuclear weapons, command and control, surveillance, etcetera, plus survivable everythings such that he could engage in global protracted nuclear war with the Soviet Union and come out on net with more military assets—or being able to do more things around the world. And that that is what he's going to have to buy in order to deter the Soviets.

Because his tone was so consistently emphatic, it was a little unclear where he stood. When asked what he thought about that, he replied, "I think it's madness. I think it's absolute fucking madness. But it's the only game in town right now. It's the only goddamned game in town." It appeared that the "town" he referred to was Washington, D.C., suggesting that it was the only politically viable position at that time. But though he may have meant this initially, he gradually seemed to take on that position, saying, for example, "In a world of offensive-based deterrence . . . you've got to be superior."

While many individuals found it difficult and even upsetting to wrestle with these inconsistencies or simply shifted in a fairly uncon-scious way, some seemed to have a fairly good grasp of the dynamics and even commented on it in a philosophical way. In the following excerpt, a member of the Joint Chiefs of Staff appears to shift between mindsets, but he simultaneously refers to the process and even specu-lates on the roots of the inconsistency as he sees it operating in the defense establishment.

R: I don't see using nuclear war to gain an advantage. I see that if you ended up in a nuclear war, there would be great efforts to seek an advantage . . .

I: Can you characterize what those advantages we would pursue would be?

R: I don't know if there are any advantages. I think it's minimize the loss since everybody will lose in a nuclear war.

I: Is that what you mean by advantage?

R: Advantage is to minimize your loss since everybody will lose. And I don't mean by that capitulation. . . . If you said minimize loss, then you could say capitulation—I don't mean that. But very little thought has been given to how to fight a nuclear war. I don't mean targeting and war-planning, but what you would do once the war started. And there's very little debate in this government or in any administration.

I: Why do you think that is?

R: I think for a number of reasons. One is it is thought that a major nuclear war is so remote that people don't tend to address it as happening. Two, . . . nobody really can come up with any realistic situation as to what would happen during a nuclear war. So you're kind of groping in the unknown . . . it's such oppressive business . . . I don't think anybody really knows what we would do. Obviously, an objective would be to displace the government in the Soviet Union. But there would be a whole bunch of objectives, and some of them may be contradictory.

CHAPTER 5

The Military Value of Hard-Target Kill Capability

THE MAJORITY of nuclear weapons that have recently been or are currently being deployed have as a critical feature their capability to destroy hardened targets such as missile silos or command and control centers. One purpose of the interviews was to elicit explanations of how this capability is useful. The first "layer" in such rationales seemed to be based on traditional, pre-nuclear concepts of warfare. Respondents seemed to regard it as self-evident that the military should strike at the enemy's "military assets" and that the United States should develop weapons with ever-improving accuracy.

A rather curious widespread attitude was that the United States "might as well" improve its hard-target kill capability given that it had the technological ability, as if the effort to improve such capabilities was virtually costless. Even respondents who understood and were actually sympathetic to concerns about the instabilities engendered by hard-target kill capability often shook their heads as if to say that only an overwhelming logical argument could stop such technological developments. There was a pervasive feeling that despite multibillion-dollar costs, building new weapons with greater accuracy was virtually effortless, while refraining from doing so was a gargantuan effort. Some simply asserted that the weapon in question was a good weapon in a technical sense and therefore should be built. In a few cases, respondents even seemed surprised when pushed for a stronger rationale based on strategic considerations.

The rationales offered fell into several categories. The most common involved concerns for perceptions, which will be discussed in chapters 6 and 8. Some, however, were based on military force considerations. One was that hard-target kill capability would be useful in the event of a war for limiting damage to the United States by directly reducing the number of Soviet missiles. The second, and most common, was that hard-target kill capability is important for filling in the ladder of escalation, and it, therefore, increased the probability, in the event of a war, of keeping the process of escalation under control.

Limiting Damage

A popular idea in strategic thinking is that it would be desirable in the event of war for the United States to use its nuclear weapons against Soviet nuclear weapons and command and control centers as a means of reducing the number of weapons that would reach American soil. This idea was particularly popular until the early 1960s, when it became apparent that the Soviets had or would soon have a secure second-strike capability. With the emergence of this condition the Soviets had gained the option of inflicting unacceptable damage on the United States, even after a major counterforce attack by the United States. Then Secretary of Defense Robert McNamara stressed that as a result deterrence should take priority over damage limitation and that to maximize deterrence it was important for the Soviet Union to feel confident that its second-strike capability was secure.* Otherwise, in the event of a crisis, they might feel pressed to strike first.

Nevertheless the idea of trying to limit damage through countersilo targeting has persisted in strategic thought. At first, this seemed to be another example of conventionalized thinking. It implies that the side with a greater damage-limiting counterforce capability might achieve

*McNamara reached this position only after flirting with damage limitation concepts and even originating the term *damage limitation*.

a relatively advantageous outcome. It does not explain how the United States could hope to reduce damage to itself as long as the Soviet Union retained the option to strike again. And it seems to ignore the fact that an effort to destroy Soviet silos might only prompt the Soviets to launch out from under the incoming warheads, thus effectively increasing the certainty of damage to the United States.

In the interviews it was very difficult to find respondents who would defend the position. When asked about the need for hard-target weapons, a few respondents did say that they considered it the responsibility of the American military to minimize the number of warheads that would land on American soil in the event of a war. When asked whether the United States could destroy enough Soviet warheads to prevent them from inflicting unacceptable damage, no one felt the United States could do so, even with greatly increased hard-target capability. When they were asked whether targeting Soviet silos might encourage them to launch out from under, there was some question as to whether the Soviets would, in fact, do so but nonetheless easy agreement that they would have such an option. However, these answers did not seem to shake the original conviction that damage limitation would be the appropriate goal for American forces to pursue in the event of war. The argument had the character of imperative logic—as if such an effort was intrinsically necessary given the existence of American armed forces.

This perspective was confirmed by a nonmilitary individual working for the Joint Chiefs of Staff who explained that the prevailing attitude in the military is that if political leaders decide to go to war they should relinquish control over American forces and allow the military command to do what is "militarily efficient." When I asked what this latter phrase meant, I was told "to limit damage to the United States" to whatever extent possible. When I raised the point that given Soviet military power, the best hope for limiting damage might be through political, not military, means, there was no counter-explanation—just a shrug, as if to say, "Well that's the military."

FIRST STRIKE

Logically, the most persuasive argument for hard-target kill capability for damage limitation would be based on the United States being the first to use nuclear weapons. If the United States could make a massive surprise attack against Soviet ICBMs, command and control centers, and other soft military targets, such as airfields and submarine ports, the number of deliverable Soviet warheads would be greatly reduced. It is still doubtful whether the number of deliverable warheads would be reduced enough to significantly diminish the amount of damage the Soviet Union could inflict. Nevertheless, if one were to make a damage-limiting argument, such a scenario would be the most promising context.

However, I found extremely little argumentation along these lines. Even though the first-strike option is formally part of American defense policy, nearly all respondents refrained from using first-strike reasoning. Instead, they generally justified arsenal requirements in terms of a second-strike scenario.

Nevertheless, there are indications that such thinking does play a role in defense planning. In a 1980 Senate Foreign Relations Committee hearing, there was some reference to the United States's plans for striking pre-emptively. Making comparisons to a pre-nuclear situation, Senator Charles Percy made inquiries to then Secretary of Defense Harold Brown:

> Senator Percy: Certainly if we had had intelligence that we were going to be attacked at Pearl Harbor, we would have done something about it then, rather than waiting to retaliate.
> Do we have a plan? If our intelligence, for instance, gave us 100 per cent assurance that there was an intended strike on us unless we did something about it, what would we do? Do we have such a plan to deal with such a hypothetical situation?
> Secretary Brown: There are options that cover that situation.[1]

His further comments, however, were deleted from the public record.

Daniel Ford, author of the book *The Button,* did succeed in eliciting this kind of thinking from some defense planners. A "Pentagon official who worked on the Reagan Administration's Nuclear Weapons Employment and Acquisition Master Plan" told Ford:

> In a real situation you don't compare going first to going second. . . . You compare going first with not going at all. If you're going to get into a nuclear war, that's big-time. When you go, go. Do it. Finish the job. Launching under attack just means you've missed the moment.[2]

An "Air Force strategist who has worked on the United States war plan" said, "If there is a nuclear war, the United States will be the one to start it."[3]

Although no respondent referred to first-strike scenarios as a direct justification for hard-target-capable weapons, a former member of the Joint Chiefs of Staff (JCS) did say that the United States would attack first in a pre-emptive fashion.

> Regardless of what people suppose, though if we . . . have warning that we're going to get attacked I'm confident that the decision would be to [make] a very major response. Ridiculous. I mean no president is going to sit there and wait for all these weapons to strike the United States and destroy his weapons.

First-strike thinking is not difficult to understand. Traditionally the military is charged with planning to fight a war as well as it can should the political leadership decide to enter into one. Within this logic it would be advantageous for the United States to go first rather than to wait for the other side to attack. It would also follow that hard-target-capable weapons might be useful.

However, while this line of reasoning may well be operative at an institutional level, no respondents espoused it in its pure form. Most argued in terms of simply assuring American survival through some form of mutual restraint or intrawar deterrence.

Nevertheless, I was still concerned that perhaps some argument was missing. Numerous attributions have been made that United States defense planners are seeking a disarming first-strike capability through a combination of SDI, civil defense, and an improved hard-target kill capability that could decapitate the Soviet control structure and draw down its strategic forces. But, when interviewed, individuals to whom this view was attributed would tend to discount it and stress escalation control or perceptual arguments.

However, a cogent argument for a first-strike capability came in a second-hand form from an individual who worked on war-planning in the Pentagon in the 1960s but eventually became disaffected. Based on his past experience and his current observations, he gave a kind of surrogate interview articulating what he thought Pentagon planners are presently trying to achieve. According to his argument, they are seeking the ability to carry out a surprise pre-emptive strategic strike, primarily through decapitating Soviet command and control centers. There is an assumption that then Soviet command authority would not devolve automatically, thus delaying the launching of Soviet weapons and allowing more time for United States missiles and bombers to knock out many Soviet missiles. With a strategic defense program and civil defense, American civilian losses would be minimized.

When asked how much confidence there was that such a scenario would lead to minimal population damage, he said, "No one says you can get off lightly. Any system leaves you with a real possibility of total obliteration." The "likelihood" was that the United States would "probably suffer very heavy damage" but "one hundred warheads is a lot less than one thousand." He then began to shift the nature of his argument to a more perceptual rationale. Independent of what would actually happen in a strategic war, if the United States is perceived as having an incentive to go first, this enhances the credibility of its threat to use nuclear weapons even at the tactical level. This surrogate interview left some uncertainty about whether the goal of the policy was simply the perceptual effect or whether some strategists genuinely felt they were meaningfully pursuing a damage-limiting first-strike capability. One result of this surrogate interview was the name of an active strategic analyst with a first-strike, damage-limiting orientation.

When I interviewed this second strategic analyst, he at first recounted the key elements of ideas that he had developed in the past. Basically the argument was that the United States needed to have the capability to comprehensively destroy the entire Soviet counterforce-capable arsenal in a first strike. This would deter the Soviets from exercising its advantage at the conventional level because the United States would have such a dominant escalatory response. The Soviet Union would not be prevented from launching a countervalue attack against American cities, but they would be deterred for fear of a reciprocal response. When asked whether the United States can presently pursue such an option, he said that it can do so by adding radio guidance to its warheads, thus improving accuracies to such a level that only one warhead would be necessary for each Soviet target.

However, when asked if the Soviet Union could employ counter-measures to such efforts, he began to change his tenor. The Soviets, he said, could easily undermine these efforts by making their systems mobile and increasing their number of warheads. He then said that this would actually be good because it would enhance stability by reducing Soviet incentives to strike first. It was surprising that he embraced this possible outcome, because such a Soviet move would also undermine American efforts to achieve a first-strike capability against Soviet counterforce. When this was pointed out, he said, "Let me back up one level and tell you what I was up to" when developing these first-strike ideas. He explained that they were presented "a little bit tongue in cheek" to "shake up conventional thinking"; at the time the United States was so dedicated to offensive second-strike thinking that they needed a "psychotherapeutic" intervention. The idea was to "introduce a laxative in order to clear the system rather than being a proponent of the laxative." He also used the metaphor of an "intellectual hand-grenade." His ultimate goal was to get more people interested in thinking about defensive systems. (He did recognize the irony of proposing that the United States pursue major improvements in its offensive capabilities as a means for increasing interest in defensive systems.)

When asked whether it is possible for the United States to pursue such a first-strike capability, he shifted his tone again and returned briefly to some technical arguments to explain how the United States could in fact pursue such a capability by improving accuracy. However, shortly he said doing so was not politically feasible and he never really thought the United States would adopt such a policy. Furthermore, he did not really think it should. He then voluntarily pointed to a major flaw in his central argument, saying that in response to a completely successful American counterforce first strike the Soviets could simply use seven countervalue-type weapons against some soft military targets, such as naval bases located in residential areas. In this way the Soviets would be able to restrict their response to the counterforce level but possibly even kill more civilians than the United States would from its massive counterforce strike. He implied that he had seen this flaw even when he had been actively promoting his first-strike arguments and reiterated that their real purpose was simply "intellectual gymnastics."

Controlling Escalation

During the 1950s, the United States had a policy of "massive retalia-tion," calling for a major countervalue response to Soviet aggression. As the United States became vulnerable to a similar counter-retaliation against its cities, nuclear strategists became dissatisfied with the all-or-nothing character of this response. Ever since, there has been a search for more flexible options. In particular, there has been a desire to find responses that, if posed as a threat, would deter and, if executed, might not force the confrontation to automatically escalate to an all-out exchange. While it has rarely been specified just how the conflict that prompted aggression would necessarily be resolved after a limited ex-change, the desire has been to create openings during which the Sovi-ets, in response to the awesome potential of further escalation, might choose to desist.

This line of thinking was frequently used to support the deployment of hard-target-capable weapons. Because hard-target-capable weapons can destroy military targets, such as silos and command and control centers, it was argued, such weapons supply the limited options that might improve the chances for keeping a war from escalating out of control.

A common scenario involved the Soviets taking some aggressive action short of an all-out attack on the American mainland but major enough to require a nuclear response on the part of the United States. The president, not wanting to surrender Soviet gains or launch a major countervalue attack that would lead to retaliation against American cities, would still want to be able to strike something. Hard-target-capable weapons would offer just such an option. The Soviets, noting the president's restraint, might then show similar restraint and refrain from escalating to a countervalue attack. Furthermore, by withholding an attack on Soviet cities, an American president would preserve a threat that might be used for intrawar deterrence. As a Rand analyst explained, "The longer you keep the cities relatively unscathed, the more you can use cities to say, 'If you don't stop, we'll blast your cities!'"

This kind of thinking is derived from a larger theory about the "ladder of escalation" that was developed in the 1960s. According to this theory, there are a number of generally recognized dividing lines (sometimes called "saliencies") in the escalatory process, which differentiate it into "rungs." The assumption is that, in an exchange, if either party attacks the other in an indiscriminate fashion, it would most likely lead to an all-out nuclear war. However, if one party limits its actions to a certain level (or rung) on the escalatory ladder, the other party will have an opportunity to limit itself as well. Through such a process of mutual inhibition, a conflict may ultimately stay limited.

There has always been considerable debate about how many rungs on the ladder of escalation would actually be recognized in the midst of conflict. Herman Kahn, in a seminal piece, articulated forty-four rungs.[4] The Soviets have consistently asserted there are only two, conventional and all-out nuclear (though they stress that in the latter they will put a priority on military targets). American policy has formulated several rungs in between the conventional and all-out nuclear levels. It has been argued that an exchange involving tactical weapons, such as in a central European war, might stay limited to that level because both sides would have an interest in keeping the war away from their soil (a homeland sanctuary policy). It has also been argued that, in the interests of escalation control, the United States should be able to respond to attacks against Europe using only missiles based in Europe. Forward-based systems currently deployed in European waters have been deemed inadequate; because they are not based directly on European soil, they muddle the saliency between strategic and intermediate-range weapons. Finally, it has been suggested that there is an escalatory rung that involves limited strategic strikes against counterforce targets but refrains from countervalue strikes. Some strategic analysts have envisioned large-scale intercontinental counterforce exchanges that do not escalate to the countervalue level.[5]

As the concept of the escalation ladder has become deeply imbedded in strategic thinking, it has led to concern that the Soviets might find a way to use the dynamics of the escalation process to achieve an advantageous outcome in the event of war. In particular, if the Soviets are able to pre-emptively destroy a rung in the ladder of American capabilities, the United States, out of a wish to keep the exchange limited, might refrain from escalating to the next higher rung. This might leave the Soviets in a relatively advantageous position. It is this kind of concern that has led to the concept of a window of vulnerability—that is, the idea that the Soviets might make such a powerful strike against American counterforce weapons that the United States would be left with only the option of escalating to countervalue strikes. To thwart such Soviet designs, it is argued, the United States must improve its counterforce weaponry so as to preserve its option to respond in a limited way.*

There is clearly a compelling logic to the concept of escalation control. It is quite plausible that in the circumstances of the outbreak of hostilities an American president would seek some limitation on the escalation process, presumably by demonstrating restraint according to some recognizable saliencies. Even if the probabilities of limiting conflict are very low, certainly the president should make some effort in this direction.

However, there are some problems with using escalation-control concepts in support of hard-target-capable weapons. The most obvious problem is with the argument that hard-target-capable weapons are intrinsically necessary for a limited response. A very common argument was that without new hard-target-capable weapons, the president would be faced with "the old surrender-or-Götterdämmerung choice" in the face of Soviet aggression. However, James Schlesinger, as part of his original formulations of the concept of limited options, asserted unambiguously that no new weapons would be required for the policy being proposed.[6] Harold Brown offered a long list of intermediate options that were already in existence when he was secretary of defense.[7]

In the interviews, when people made the "surrender-or-Götterdämmerung" argument, I pointed to some of the intermediate options available even with soft-target-only weapons (for example, military bases, airfields, rail lines, shipyards). This elicited little counterargument. One respondent questioned whether Soviet air bases would still have enough bombers left to make them worthwhile targets. Implicitly,

*It is my impression that as this kind of thinking has gradually worked its way into the level of nonexpert debate, it has to some extent merged with other conventionalized lines of thinking. The idea that the United States is at a disadvantage in a certain hypothetical scenario because of certain asymmetries in force capabilities has merged with the conventional concern that a relatively larger arsenal would give the Soviets an advantage in an all-out war in which all weapons are used. When some respondents (especially nonexperts) referred to the window of vulnerability, they seemed to have the impression that the conventional type of vulnerability to losing an all-out war was of concern, not the inability to exercise a specific option in the interest of keeping a conflict limited.

everyone seemed to agree that there would be numerous options. But they generally shrugged it off with surprising ease and shifted to another argument. Why the argument—that without hard-target-capable weapons, surrender or massive countervalue strikes would be the only options—still has so much currency in defense thinking is somewhat perplexing.

A second problem has to do with whether the options would in fact be valuable for the goal of keeping an exchange limited. Even a limited countersilo attack might provoke the Soviets into an escalatory response. In a scenario in which the Soviet Union takes a major aggressive action against the West, it is reasonable to assume that they would put their strategic forces on high alert. Furthermore, in all probability the Soviets would, in the midst of hostilities, adopt a launch-on-warning policy as there would be little ambiguity about whether the incoming missiles had been fired intentionally. If the Soviets did not launch their missiles, they would surely be destroyed—that is, they would be in a use-them-or-lose-them position. The net effect of an American counter-silo response, then, might well be to greatly decrease the probability of controlling escalation and to press the Soviets into launching their missiles in a precipitate fashion.

When this issue was raised in the interviews, once again the responses were weak. Some individuals simply ignored the issues by changing the subject; one stressed that we could not be "sure" that they would launch out from under. This was surprising because his tone of voice was the same when he had earlier stressed the need for worst-case thinking—thinking that would presumably lead to the working assumption that they *would* launch out from under.

Others recognized the problem but asserted that the Soviets would refrain from firing some of their missiles while under attack. When I raised this issue with a senator, even in an aggressive fashion, he persisted.

R: No, I do not think that any country is going to launch all their assets on warning.

I: After [they make] a first strike, you don't think they will fire their missiles seeing our missiles coming at their silos? Why not?

R: I don't think any country is going to risk everything they've got.

I: But if missiles are coming at them, they won't be risking their

> missiles by firing them. . . . maybe we're wasting our weapons
> . . . [if] they are going to fire them . . .
>
> R: You're using a term that answers your own question—"maybe."

A few respondents insisted that it would be worthwhile to strike at silos even if the Soviets would launch out from under. When I raised the possibility that the Soviets might launch out from under with a Pentagon analyst, he said, "Uh-huh. True. That's right." Then he looked at me as if he failed to see the problem.

> I: So isn't it questionable whether or not, under the circumstances, we would want to do that?
>
> R: No, no. I don't agree at all. I think you got the problem at the wrong stage. . . . Just as a factual point, Soviet silos can be reloaded—they practice reloading—so you would want to destroy silos even if they were empty.

Speaking along similar lines, one Rand analyst agreed that some missiles would be launched out from under but also said that because of technical failure "some of them wouldn't get out."

What was striking about the above cases was that their concern became so heavily focused on destroying Soviet missiles. The answers— "maybe" some of the Soviet missiles would not be fired, it would be desirable to prevent the Soviets from reloading, or "some" would technically fail to "get out"—did not really address the fact that the chances were exceedingly high that a substantial number of missiles would reach American soil. There was little indication that the destruction of some Soviet missiles and the consequent firing of other Soviet missiles against the U.S. had been considered together in a cost/benefit analysis. Even more important, the respondents tended to lose sight of their earlier concern with controlling escalation.

In a curious way, even when respondents recognized that countersilo targeting was problematic, this conclusion did not always stay firm. Countersilo rationales would sometimes creep back into the discussion. For example, a strategic analyst seemed to initially embrace countersilo targeting. He said that hard-target-capable deployments would make "a great big difference. The president then has an option to not go against countervalue targets. And then the retaliation goes into a more elegant form. It goes in the terms of counterforce." When I raised the problem of launching out from under a countersilo attack, he unhesitatingly agreed: "No. [Silos] are not an optimum target, right. Command structure—that's the main target." However, when asked what the offensive requirements would be for this target set, he thought they were actually quite low. He said: "They probably have in the order of fifty to one hundred, maybe, key command posts for their strategic forces," and that these would be "not too demanding in terms of warheads." When the discussion turned to what weapons would fulfill this mission, he felt that the Mark-12A warheads on the Minutemen III were adequate. However, when I tried to raise the question of whether enough of these nine hundred Mark-12A warheads would survive a Soviet first strike, he resurrected his argument for countersilo targeting.

R: We have three hundred Minutemen III with the Mark-12A. Nine hundred warheads—three warheads on each missile.

I: So that if we lost—

R: But you need those for other targets too. Even Minutemen III, if you believe the new estimates of Soviet silo hardness.

When reminded that he had said that silos were not such a good target, he concurred but then gave a muddled explanation, so that it was unclear whether he was interested in having a countersilo capability.

I: But I thought we were just saying that, in a way, silos really are not a good target.

R: Right, but I'm speaking of even silos that are not that hardened compared to the equivalent of a Soviet Cheyenne Mountain, let's say, which will be a very hard target to destroy, a lot of the command post buried quite deep and that sort of thing—well protected.

Shortly thereafter, he dropped his arguments based on military concerns and shifted to an argument based on political perceptions.

Sometimes when the problem of launching out from under was raised, even highly sophisticated strategists reverted to a very conventionalized assertion that hard-target-capable weapons are simply good weapons. For example, a prominent strategist and high-level government official started by arguing that hard-target kill capability is important for taking out Soviet missiles.

> If you don't have a hard-target kill capability, you are giving a sanctuary, really, to all their hard targets . . . they can use those systems when they want to—there's nothing you can do about it.

When I raised the possibility that the Soviets might launch out from under, he completely concurred, saying:

> Whether you want to [strike at Soviet missiles] or not . . . whether you want to attack a bunch of holes, most of which are empty and others are probably launched under attack, that is problematical for them and for us. It clearly is a problem for a country that has absorbed a first strike. It's one hell of a problem. What the hell does he hit? It is a big problem, sure.

Shortly, though, he made the argument that striking at hard targets is important as a controlled response, the only alternative being countervalue targets. Without a hard-target capability, he asked rhetorically:

> Then what do you have to go after? You have to go after industry and population. You don't want to go after industry and population because if you go after industry and population, then that's worse for us than it is for them because we don't have any civil defense or evacuation programs of any kind that are worth a damn, and they do. Therefore you go down a hopeless path.

When I once again raised the possibility that the Soviets might launch out from under, he became a bit agitated and asserted in a more simplistic fashion that it would still be good to have the option.

> I: So we want to strike at them, but if they're going to launch out from under, then we still don't have anything to strike at, right?
> R: It may be! You're better off having that capability than not having it!

Then, as I started to formulate another question, he interrupted me with an outburst.

> I don't understand the purpose of this conversation! I really don't, because this is all conjured stuff. I don't want to talk about this at all. Strike all this! I don't understand the purpose of this!

Soon after, he stopped arguing for hard-target weapons in terms of escalation control and simply asserted the military value of the capability in simplistic terms:

> [The Pershing II offers] the military capability . . . to take out a hell of a lot of military targets . . . I think the Pershing II's a hell of a good weapon system. If you want to take something out, it's the way.

A third key problem with escalation control arguments used in support of hard-target kill capability has to do with the wisdom of targeting command and control centers and leadership, given that the goal is to keep an exchange limited. The option for negotiation at critical junctures plays an important part in attempts to forestall escalation. Destroying the leadership on the other side or disrupting its ability to control its forces would undermine this option.

This problem was a familiar one to most respondents. One analyst said that the United States would probably not want to knock out all their leadership and command and control—just some of it. The most common response, however, was that it was important for deterrence that the Soviet leadership feel itself and its forces to be at risk. While this is a cogent argument (which will be discussed in chapter 8) in terms of the goal of controlling escalation, there is still a problem. If Soviet leaders believe that they and their control systems will be attacked, they will have an incentive to escalate to a pre-emptive attack against the American control structure and its hard-target weaponry. Also, Soviet leaders would have an incentive to set up some system in advance for devoluting launch authority (that is, passing authority to a lower level) for their strategic forces in the event of war. Both of these incentives would clearly work against the potential for escalation control. When this problem was raised, no counter-argument in terms of the goal of keeping a war limited was offered.

The fourth major problem with hard-target-capable weapons centers on the question of whether a major counterforce retaliation would truly be distinguishable from a countervalue attack. There seemed to be a general recognition that such an assumption was highly questionable. The few individuals who insisted that there was a significant possibility did so in a tone suggesting that they felt they were swimming upstream. As one Pentagon analyst explained,

> Maybe these are distinctions which are sufficiently strange that only military planners and strategists think of them. . . . Maybe the difference would not be discernible to the fabric of [the society being attacked].

More common was the dubious tone of an official at ACDA:

> A lot of this is a sort of academic discussion because if you look at the map and look at where the pins are, you may not be trying to target populations, but obviously there's not much left of Moscow after you hit all these targets.

It was not uncommon to hear that even a small counterforce strike would produce so much collateral damage that it would be hard to distinguish it from a countervalue strike. A strategic analyst said:

> Once you start detonating, I would think over a hundred or so warheads, even against military installations, whether they be here or in the Soviet Union, you're going to have a tremendous amount of collateral damage. And at that point you are hitting a gray area, where you don't know whether the strike has sort of creeped into the countervalue area.

Even active proponents of escalation control concepts sometimes blithely dismissed the possibility of limiting a nuclear war. For example, one respondent, who played a significant role in developing the countervailing strategy under the Carter administration, said:

I don't think we should be under any illusions that once a nuclear war gets launched that we can have much chance of controlling it. I happened to be in a discussion of this yesterday with several very senior retired generals who were expressing as much skepticism about escalation control as you'd find in a liberal university.*

Another respondent, who worked under Schlesinger during the Nixon administration and currently serves in the Reagan administration, also dismissed the possibility of controlling escalation (at the same time that he argued in favor of developing plans and building the corresponding capabilities).

I: Do you see stability as arising primarily from the assured destruction capability, or do you see it as depending on having each rung on the ladder of escalation pretty robustly covered?

R: I think it's the end of the ladder that worries people . . . it's the feeling that you have no idea that either will stop when you get into it . . . I don't believe in limited nuclear. It's up there with limited pregnancy. Pregnancy is a fact—you are or you are not. I don't think there is going to be such a thing as a limited nuclear war.

He later elaborated a psychological explanation for this impossibility, explaining that at a certain point the traditional concept of all-out war would simply take over even though it would be irrational. I asked:

I: So what is the purpose of developing the plans, capabilities, posture—

R: [interrupting] Oh, you've got to do that. . . . As long as you've got the things [nuclear weapons] you want to have a plan to use them in some sort of controlled way.

*This comment is not really surprising since it echoes a statement that Harold Brown made in 1980: "In adopting and implementing this policy we have no more illusions than our predecessors that a nuclear war could be closely and surgically controlled." (U.S. Department of Defense, Harold Brown, *Annual Report to Congress FY 1981* [Washington, D.C.: GPO, 1980], 67.) This was a bold statement, given that the policy being proposed was actually a plan for controlling nuclear war in the way Brown was saying was virtually impossible.

In some cases respondents abandoned their position at even the slightest challenge. For example, a current member of the START (Strategic Arms Reductions Talks in Geneva) negotiating team initially articulated a concern that the Soviets have an advantage at one rung of the ladder of escalation—a concern that presumably shapes the positions he is involved in putting forward in arms control negotiations.

> I: Can you say what the military value of a hard-target kill capability is? What role it might play?
>
> R: Well, I think it is viewed as taking away a Soviet advantage which exists today, where they conceivably could destroy a high percentage of our land-based force and we could not do the same.

However, when asked to "say a little bit more about the scenarios that call for these kinds of capabilities," he smiled and said, "Well, I must say I don't think very much myself about actual war-fighting scenarios."

Some respondents, however, seemed to feel a need to put up a stronger defense of escalation-type arguments even when they did not appear to put much stock in them. This sometimes produced emotionally awkward moments, as in an interview with a middle-to-high-level official in the Pentagon. From the beginning he showed signs of unease with the interview, requesting that I not tape record, thus limiting me to scribbling key phrases as they were spoken. Nevertheless, as he started explaining why it was important that the United States match Soviet hard-target kill capability, he began to find his stride and relax. He explained that if the Soviets initiated a first strike against land-based ICBMs, the United States, for lack of an appropriate hard-target response, might be deterred from responding. I asked him if he thought the United States would not respond. He looked at me quizzically, as if he didn't understand the question, and then said, nodding with apparent effort, "Many people think we might not respond." I then asked, "But what do you think?" At this he became visibly agitated, broke eye contact, and said, "That scenario is not obviously ridiculous." He then glanced back at me, restraining a smile.

He went on to explain that the Soviets, if they were able to execute such a strike against American ICBMs and still hold significant force in reserve, might feel that they had met their "definition of success."

When asked if he could imagine feeling that way if he were a Soviet, he said, in a deliberate fashion, accentuating each word with a nod, "It's a plausible way they could think." When asked if he assumed a rational adversary in his calculations, he refused to answer.

Frustrated, he said that he did not think this way about these issues. His job was to analyze the ladder of escalation in an objective, mathematical fashion, and then try to "plug the holes." And one of the problems he saw was that American inadequacies in counterforce capability might jeopardize the "firebreak" between counterforce and countervalue targeting.* When I asked him if he thought about this in a purely abstract way or if he tried to relate his analysis to what would actually happen in a war-fighting situation, he repeated, this time a bit more comfortable with the statement, "I think there's a nugget there that's not obviously ridiculous."

I then asked him what would stop the Soviets from launching out from under if we fired at their silos; surprisingly, he said flatly, "Nothing would stop them," and that "it would force them to attack full scale." A bit confused, I pointed out that some people saw this as an argument against having countersilo capabilities, to which he replied in a cavalier tone, "It doesn't affect me what the arguments are."

Within a few moments, however, he threw up his hands, and with some real anger said, "What do you expect me to do, argue against hard-target kill capability?!" I said I just wanted to know what he thought. This made him even more agitated, and he said, "Don't ask me what I think or feel!" His job, he said, was simply to explain administration policy, and he would not continue the interview if I insisted on probing into his "personal" views. Naturally, I immediately backed off, and for the rest of the interview simply accepted his answers, which led him to calm down and relax.

In conclusion, very few respondents consistently argued the need for hard-target kill capability on purely military grounds while still accounting for such problems as the possibility that the Soviets might launch out from under incoming warheads. Respondents who simply insisted that the Soviets might not launch out from under, to my mind, gave the most cogent rationale, if not an entirely plausible one. The first-strike rationale given in the surrogate interview with the former strate-

*Firebreak refers to differentiations of the ladder of escalation that might become agreed-on stopping points during a war.

gic analyst had a convincing logic to it, but I have yet to find more definite empirical evidence that defense planners carry their logic to such far-flung heights.

I must admit, though, that I still feel uneasy about the extent to which respondents so easily relinquished their military arguments for hard-target kill capability. It is disquieting to think that somewhere there are individuals who have worked out a line of military logic that they, at least, find consistently persuasive. Many people in defense circles whom I have spoken with believe that such people exist. Either I have failed to locate them, the interviews have failed to fully draw out their thinking, or the belief that such people exist is a potent myth in the policymaking community.

Given the evidence, the most compelling general conclusion is that the desire to deploy hard-target kill capability is an expression of a wish to in some way make nuclear war controllable. In other words, it is an expression of the urge to assimilate nuclear war into a conventional war paradigm. The thrust of my questions has been to find out why defense planners think that hard-target kill capability increases the probability of exerting this control when, in a variety of ways, it looks like it might do just the opposite. In short, deploying hard-target kill capability has apparently become associated with the effort to exert this control, and this association is stronger and more compelling than the logical processes that, in most cases, do recognize the questionability of the association.

CHAPTER 6

Maintaining the Perception

of Balance

I N THE previous three chapters rationales for American defense policies based on objective considerations of military force have been explored. In the next four chapters we will explore rationales that recognize that from a military perspective, the policies in question are unnecessary or invalid; nevertheless, these rationales assert that such policies are necessary or important as a means of strategically manipulating perceptions. Sometimes in the interviews these rationales arose as the first offered. In some cases they emerged only after the respondent attempted rationales based on military considerations but encountered logical problems with them. Overall such perceptual rationales were the most dominant offered.

When I raised questions about the policy of maintaining a balance of nuclear forces relative to the Soviet Union, many respondents recognized that given the condition of secure, flexible, and redundant second-strike capabilities (that is, overkill) on both sides, from a military point of view the United States need not maintain a balance relative to the Soviet Union. Nevertheless they argued that a variety of key audiences still perceive the balance as having military significance and reflecting the potential outcome of a military conflict. Such perceptions shape political reality in critical ways. Therefore, they argued, it is

Portions of this chapter are based on an article entitled "Nuclear Nonsense" that originally appeared in *Foreign Policy* 58 (Spring 1985). Copyright 1985 by the Carnegie Endowment for International Peace.

essential for the United States to build weapons that, at a minimum, sustain the perception of United States equality with the Soviet Union. In other words, although the respondents themselves, in their concern for the balance, say they are not conventionalizing, they attribute this tendency to others. They then conclude that the United States should, in effect, "play along" with such mistaken perceptions. The net effect is that these respondents support the United States's behaving in a conventionalized fashion even though they know that such behavior is inconsistent with military reality.

A prototypical expression of this concept appeared in an interview with a former member of the Joint Chiefs of Staff:

R: I'm not really concerned about the military aspect of the nuclear balance, because the effect of exchanges would be so catastrophic to the Soviets—regardless of whether they chose to shoot first. . . . That being the case, though, it's necessary for us to maintain modern systems that are perceived not just in the mind of the Soviets but in third-world nations. That's why I say it's political. The other nations are sitting there watching this balance—

I: Why do they have that concern about the strategic balance if the balance isn't so important from a military point of view?

R: I don't think they get into that depth. I think they just count. And if the Russians say that they've got fifteen hundred missiles and the United States has only got one thousand—[throws up hands]

I: So what does that mean to them?

R: Well, then they think, "The Soviets must be more powerful and maybe we'd better not oppose them in any way." . . . All they do is measure the amount of your numbers.

I: Why do you think they do that?

R: You know, there's not a hundred people that really understand the whole nuclear problem. . . . And so I think that many nations—and particularly the public (and that's what really counts) count. They just count! In other words, if you've got fifteen hundred missiles and the other side's got one thousand; if you've got two-hundred-fifty submarines and they only got ninety-five; and it goes on . . . I mean it!

I: Would you say that they tend to view nuclear weapons as basically not that different from conventional weapons?

R: I think they just look at 'em as weapons of varying damage effect.

When I asked a former staff member of the Senate Foreign Relations Committee why it was necessary to add to American hard-target kill capabilities, he answered:

We need 'em 'cause they got 'em. That's the only reason for having 'em. One should match them point for point for every weapon they have. They aren't useful for military purposes. They're only useful for psychological and political purposes.

In some cases these concepts were presented in more abstract and theoretical terms. A prominent strategic analyst explained:

Strategic weapons are political artifacts first. And when they cease to be political artifacts, then they're entirely irrelevant, entirely without a purpose. . . . The only existence that these weapons have that has any meaning is in political terms. And perceptions is the only relevant category. The only question is to debate how people, in fact, see them—what these perceptions really are.

It was particularly striking how easily many individuals, even members of the current administration, would blithely dismiss the military value of weapons proposed or currently being deployed, as in the following exchange with a high-level spokesman for the present administration.

I: What about the military purpose of the Pershings and GLCMs?

R: Well, that's sort of a phony issue. . . . I think it's fairly well known that if we did not have the Pershings and we did not have GLCMs we would target those targets some other way.

Several individuals who played a key role in developing the window-of-vulnerability concept also clarified that their real concern was not military vulnerability but political perceptions. One of these individuals explained the emergence of the window-of-vulnerability concept:

R: The indicators showed there was a strong possibility that if they decided to attack with, let's say, the SS-18 force . . . a substantial portion of the U. S. ICBM force would have probably been destroyed. So what it said to me was that there was definitely a window of vulnerability there coming up.

I: So that window of vulnerability only applied to our land-based ICBMs—it wasn't to American deterrent capability or American retaliatory capability?

R: Right. It didn't address the question of a sane approach. . . . It's invalid when one takes into consideration the other survivable forces in terms of the triad—the SLBMs and the bomber force. If you take those things into consideration, then you say no, there is no such thing as a complete vulnerability because there's always the capability for retaliation with what's left.

He then clarified that his real concern was for perceptions of relative capabilities.

R: The window of vulnerability then comes to bear only in terms of the perception that one gives it, the importance that one gives it.

I: These are perceptions that the Soviets are having?

R: The Soviets. And we're also giving them perceptions in the international arena. If the world—third world particularly, and everybody else, even our own allies—perceive that the Soviets are inferior to us, they're more likely to acquiesce to us. Whereas if they feel that the Soviets have strategic forces that are equivalent to ours, they may be a little bit more careful [about] their policy in relationship to them.

I: So the concern is that somehow there's this perception that the Soviets have this superiority?

R: Perception, right.

While many respondents elucidated such perceptual rationales easily or with enthusiasm, others seemed to arrive at them with reluctance when other lines of thinking were exhausted. For example, when I first contacted an official of the Arms Control and Disarmament Agency and said that one subject to be discussed was the role of perception in nuclear strategy, he indicated that he did not regard it as a very relevant issue. During the interview he offered a rationale for current weapons procurements based entirely on military considerations using an analogy from a conventional context:

R: We have nuclear weapons to assure ourselves that we have whatever the state of the art permits—

I: Why?

R: Very simply, advanced technology is the difference, in many cases, between winning and losing. If you look, for example, at why countries like Great Britain were able, with one hundred thousand soldiers, to own India for more than one hundred years . . .

However, when pressed, he seemed to dismiss these military concerns and recognized a key feature of the nuclear revolution.

I: Do you conceptualize certain technological breakthroughs that the Soviets could achieve that would grant them a capability to, say, launch a first strike?

R: Oh, people think about this all the time. I don't believe in any of the propositions that have been advanced. My own personal belief is that a disarming first strike is not feasible.

I: Even with some kind of technological breakthrough?

R: . . . I can't see it on either side.

I: If you put yourself in the shoes of a Soviet, do you see certain variations in the strategic balance that are possible in the near future that would alter your conclusion about whether or not to take aggressive action?

R: What do you mean by that?

I: . . . Imagine the United States does not enhance its hard-target kill capability. Imagine that the United States removes the INF forces. Imagine that the U. S. doesn't build the D-5. Imagine that the Soviets continue a general expansion and put in more SS-20s, build some more big ICBMs, maybe improve some of their accuracies. Could you imagine any of those kinds of developments modifying your attitudes about whether or not to take aggressive action in a particular theater?

R: Generally speaking, I think that we and the Soviets have such a profound shared interest in not using nuclear weapons that all of the things that you've just talked about are not going to change that situation fundamentally. . . . We're not talking about the prospect of holocaust or cataclysm because of the kinds of changes that you're suggesting.

I: Or even a limited conventional attack of some sort, against allies?

R: . . . I think that we could fail to make that unattractive, but it wouldn't be because of changes in the nuclear balance—or imbalance, as the case may be. It is my view that there is not a nuclear balance; there is a nuclear imbalance, and it is presently not in our favor.

I: In that case, why is it important for us to rectify that imbalance, if it's not going to have any—

nterrupting, he began to shift his argument, with apparent uneasiness, oward a perceptual argument.

R: Okay, this begins to get to your perceptual concerns. I'm not a big fan of perceptual approaches to this. Having been trained as a historian, I've always been wary of some of the political science approaches . . . [but] here we begin to get into the potentially interesting part of the perceptual problem . . . I believe that there are lots of people in the world—in governments, out of governments—who are trying to estimate the power relationships in part based on things like relative nuclear forces (as best they understand them). . . . A lot of important states around the world—some of them allies, some of them are not allies—want to be sure they pick the winner. And their political behavior is going to be conditioned in part by their judgment as to who is holding the relative advantage—who is doing the most to retain or to acquire a relative advantage . . .

Historical Background

The concern for perceptions of the superpowers' strategic arsenals has been a prevailing concept in the American policymaking community for quite some time. For example, shortly after the Cuban missile crisis, then President John F. Kennedy said, "[The missiles in Cuba] would have politically changed the balance of power. It would have appeared to, and appearances contribute to reality."[1] However, it was in the early 1970s that this kind of thinking became particularly prominent.* During the debate about the SALT I Interim Agreement, there was a distinct uneasiness that the Soviets were allowed a greater number of ICBMs and SLBMs than the United States.† During the Senate's ratification hearings, virtually all the strategic experts agreed that from a military point of view these numerical disparities were more than offset by American technological superiority and numerical superiority in bombers. The general consensus was that the SALT agreements were beneficial to American military interests. However, as the *Congressional Record* explains:

> Several witnesses, including Dr. [Donald] Brennan [of the Hudson Institute], addressed themselves to the question of whether possible imbalances might not affect political perspectives. Dr. Brennan said that, with ratification of the treaty and approval of the agreement, the Soviets will think of themselves as very much in the ascendant, that an image of American inferiority will be established in American conventional circles, that the new imbalance will perhaps cause allies to become unduly responsive to Soviet diplomatic pressures and initiatives, and that the enshrinement of a Soviet superiority will have adverse consequences in any serious crises that develop.[2]

Ultimately SALT I was approved but only after the Senate included an amendment by the late Senator Henry Jackson that requested "the President to seek a future treaty that, *inter alia*, would not limit the United States to levels of intercontinental strategic forces inferior to

---

*This argument was identified as early as 1976 by former CIA official Arthur Macy Cox, who, in a critical vein, termed it *perception theory*. (Cox, *The Dynamics of Détente: How to End the Arms Race* [New York: W. W. Norton, 1976])

†ICBMs are land-based intercontinental ballistic missiles; SLBMs are submarine-launched ballistic missiles.

the limits for the Soviet Union." Although the wording of the amendment was a bit vague, the intent of the amendment was not only to achieve rough parity, or essential equivalence, but to bring about numerical equality in virtually every dimension of the strategic arsenals. Senator Jackson clarified in subsequent speeches that the goals for SALT II should be to achieve equal numbers of delivery vehicles and throw-weights.[3]

The passage of this measure represented a significant development in official American defense thinking. Hitherto the American defense posture had been at least ostensibly rooted in military reality. Traditional deterrence theory recognized the importance of perceptions in nuclear matters but primarily stressed the need for an adversary correctly to recognize American retaliatory capabilities and intentions. But the Jackson Amendment demanded equality regardless of its military relevance. Hereafter *perceptions* began to drive weapons procurement in a manner increasingly independent of military considerations.

In 1972, during the SALT I debate, the Georgetown University Center for Strategic and International Studies (CSIS) released a report by strategist Edward Luttwak, *The Strategic Balance,* that articulated the key tenets of this perceptual rationale. Luttwak recognized that a "near consensus of strategic experts would undoubtedly answer that the United States has in fact conceded nothing" of military significance in SALT I. Yet such thinking, he argued, "totally discounted" the "prestige effects deriving from the possession of strategic weapons" that are "psychologically by far the most impressive of all instruments of power." He claimed that "with informed public opinion the world over" there is a "definite awareness that one side or the other has more. And 'more' is widely regarded as implying greater power." Luttwak recognized not only that this balance is essentially a misdirected measure of political power but also that the balance is correctly assessed: "Outside the narrow circle of the technical experts the balance of strategic power is not measured in operational terms. Gross numbers and crude qualitative factors provide the only indices of strategic power which are widely recognized."[4]

Such thinking quickly moved into policy circles. Former Secretary of Defense James Schlesinger enshrined it as official U. S. policy in his annual reports to Congress for fiscal years 1975 and 1976. Schlesinger began the fiscal 1975 report by expressing concern about the improvements the Soviets had made in their nuclear arsenal during the 1960s, and he called for appropriate U. S. countermeasures. He recognized that this situation did not create an immediate military threat because the Soviet Union did not and could not hope to be able to launch a disarming first strike. But he added that "there must be essential equivalence between the strategic forces of the United States and the USSR—an equivalence perceived not only by ourselves, but by the Soviet Union and third audiences as well."[5]

Schlesinger elaborated that there is "an important relationship between the political behavior of many leaders of other nations and what they perceive the strategic nuclear balance to be." Rather than correctly perceiving this balance, he said, many leaders "react to the static measures of relative force size, number of warheads, equivalent megatonnage, and so forth." He concluded, therefore, that "to the degree that we wish to influence the perceptions of others, we must take appropriate steps (by their lights) in the design of the strategic forces."[6] Using a pre-nuclear analogy, he warned that this perceived imbalance might trigger serious miscalculations:

> Opponents may feel that they can exploit a favorable imbalance by means of political pressure, as Hitler did so skillfully in the 1930s. . . . Friends may believe that a willingness on our part to accept less than equality indicates a lack of resolve to uphold our end of the competition and a certain deficiency in staying power. Our own citizens may doubt our capacity to guard the nation's interest.[7]

Of course, Schlesinger also argued that in addition to the perceptual requirements of its arsenals, America must have the capability for flexibility and selectivity should deterrence fail. However, Schlesinger explained that flexible response "does not imply major new strategic weapon systems and expenditures. We are simply ensuring that in our doctrine, our plans, and our command and control we have—and are seen to have—the selectivity and flexibility to respond to aggression in an appropriate manner."[8] In other words, Schlesinger implied that the United States already had the hardware necessary for flexible response. The rationale for the proposed improvements in American military capabilities then fell primarily on perceptual arguments.

These statements did not go unnoticed by Congress. A 1975 report prepared for the Senate Committee on Foreign Relations observed:

> The discussion of the issue of "essential equivalence" found in the current DoD Report is unique in four ways:
>   a) it makes the achievement of "perceived" equality with the Soviet Union the first objective of our strategic forces . . .
>   b) the need for equality is defined in such a way that it seems independent of military requirements;
>   c) it notes that the "perceptions" of "non-superpower" nations are also of central importance; and
>   d) it is much more specific than previous statements about how to define "essential equivalence."[9]

During this period such perceptual rationales also began to appear in the annual statements on United States Military Posture from the chairman of the Joint Chiefs of Staff. Admiral Thomas Moorer embraced the principles of the Jackson Amendment, terming it "unacceptable" that "the numerical ICBM and SLBM force levels authorized for the Soviet Union by the [SALT I] Interim Agreement are larger than those authorized for the United States." He insisted, "If we are to maintain a credible strategic deterrent . . . the appearance of military strength cannot be neglected," and then, in somber tones, referred to "essential equivalency" as "necessary to the preservation of peace."[10] General George Brown stressed the importance of preserving "the perception of equilibrium, which in the long run may be as important as equilibrium itself and is essential for stability." Failure to do so could even "jeopardize our survival as a nation." Gradually the concept of maintaining perceived equality became fused with the concept of deterrence.

> [O]ur nuclear strategy is to maintain nuclear stability through a clearly *perceived* essential equivalence in strategic nuclear forces. *By this equivalence* we expect to deter the use, or the threat of use, of nuclear forces against the United States, our deployed forces, our allies and other nations considered essential to our security [emphasis added].[11]

Such thinking was also not limited to Pentagon-based advocates of expanding defense budgets. Then Secretary of State Henry Kissinger, in 1974, discussing the strategic arms race, said, "While a decisive advantage is hard to calculate, the *appearance* of inferiority—whatever its actual significance—can have serious political consequences."[12]

Meanwhile, analysts at the Center for Strategic and International Studies were adding new twists to this line of thinking. In the 1975 study *World Power Assessment,* CSIS Executive Director Ray Cline argued that "a growing and innovative arsenal will be perceived as more powerful than one which is static—even if the latter still retains an advantage in purely technical terms."[13] This argument is explained by concern that as the Soviet Union strove to catch up with the United States, it was improving its arsenal at a faster rate. Even though in absolute terms the United States was still ahead, the fact that its forces were growing more slowly than the Soviets' could be perceptually problematic and presumably would need to be remedied. Similarly, Luttwak has argued that in the realm of perceptions, "time is discounted," and that "the most direct consequence of discounting time is that in determining perceptions of military capabilities the impact of rates of change may equal or outweigh the impact of current capabilities."[14]

To deal with such perceptual complexities, Luttwak proposed that the United States carry out "perceptual-impact analyses," with an eye to "enhancing the images of power they generate." He even argued that a cosmetic restructuring of American ground units to make them appear larger in number should not be ruled out and expressed concern that bombers—a dimension the United States was superior in—"may be discounted because of a tendency to regard them as 'old fashioned.' " Luttwak reiterated, "Objective reality, whatever that may be, is simply irrelevant; only the subjective phenomena of perception and value judgment count."[15]

After Schlesinger left the Pentagon, concerns for perceptions remained a major rationale for weapons deployment. In his fiscal 1978 report to Congress, Schlesinger's successor at the Pentagon, Donald Rumsfeld, recognized that not even the Soviet ICBM buildup posed the threat of a disarming first strike. But like Schlesinger and others, he feared the dangerous international miscalculations these asymmetries might produce. Rumsfeld also reiterated the view that the balance was incorrectly assessed because of failure to make "detailed analyses." Rather than attempting to clarify that asymmetries do not necessarily constitute a military threat, however, he called for "actions to create the necessary perception of equivalence." Accordingly, he wrote, "U. S. plans and programs for future U.S. offensive capabilities must be geared to those of the USSR."[16]

Despite President Jimmy Carter's public recognition that the U. S. arsenal far exceeded the requirements of deterrence, his secretary of defense, Harold Brown, was a major proponent of perceptual rationales. He dismissed any concern that the Soviet Union might gain the ability to launch a disarming first strike. In strong terms, he even discounted the widely discussed concern for the vulnerability of Minuteman ICBMs to a Soviet counterforce strike.

> In short, the vulnerability of MINUTEMAN is a problem, but even if we did nothing about it, it would not be synonymous with the vulnerability of the United States, or even of the strategic deterrent. It would not mean that we could not satisfy our strategic objectives. It would not by itself even mean that the United States would lack a survivable hard target capability or that we would necessarily be in a worse post-exchange position in terms of numbers of weapons, payload, or destructiveness.

Nevertheless he did express concern for this imbalance on the basis of perceptions. "All this is by no means to say that we can or should ignore the problem. There would be political costs were the Soviets to appear to us, to our friends, or to themselves to have such an imbalanced or unmatched capability against a key element of the U.S. force." He repeatedly stressed the need for "essential equivalence," which, he wrote, "guards against any dangers that the Soviets might be seen as superior—even if the perception is not technically justified." He warned about the "coercion and intimidation that could result from perceptions of an overall imbalance or particular asymmetries in nuclear forces."[17]

Members of the Reagan administration have, on the whole, made less use of perceptual rationales and have, instead, implied that the weapons being deployed fulfilled significant military needs. Nevertheless, perceptual rationales have also been employed. Alexander Haig, when secretary of state, argued that "perceptions of the military balance . . . affect the psychological attitude of both American and Soviet leaders, as they respond to events around the globe."[18] Secretary of Defense Weinberger has said: "Our military strength must not be, *nor appear to be,* inferior to that of the Soviet Union [emphasis in original]." Weinberger has worried about "the longterm consequences if our allies and friends perceive us waning in military strength" and warns, "Many would notice the subtle erosion of our security as once-friendly nations drifted toward neutralism, or worse, accommodation to the pressures of our adversary." He has also stressed that American force posture must "take into account our adversaries' perceptions and calculations." Brushing off arguments that the American arsenal is adequate, he writes:

> The issue for a deterrent strategy that incorporates perception seriously, however, is whether the Soviet leadership shares the judgment that additional capability is pointless. The fact that for the past decade Soviet investment in strategic forces (as measured in dollars), has been two to three times the size of our own investment, strongly suggests that they do not.[19]

There are also good reasons to believe that some major weapon systems deployed during the Reagan administration were seen as primarily serving perceptual purposes. When Richard Burt, then undersecretary of defense, was told that the Pershing II deployment might need to be delayed because of continuing technical problems, he reportedly said, "We don't care if the goddamn things work or not. After all, that doesn't matter unless there's a war. What we care about is getting them in."[20]

The Reagan administration also fully embraced the Report of the President's Commission on Strategic Forces (the Scowcroft Commission), which employed perceptual rationales as its major argument for the MX. The commission rejected the primary strategic argument for deployment (the "window of vulnerability") but argued that the MX was necessary for political perceptions. They argued that the Soviet counterforce superiority constituted a "serious imbalance" that "must be redressed promptly." They recognized that "in a world in which the balance of strategic nuclear forces could be isolated from [political considerations], a nuclear imbalance would have little importance." But with an air of philosophical regret they supported building the MX because "the overall perception of strategic imbalance . . . has been reasonably regarded as destabilizing and as a weakness in the overall fabric of deterrence."[21]

Interview Findings

Although perceptual rationales in support of maintaining the balance appear with frequency in official government writings and in defense literature, no writer has really developed them in a systematic fashion. The interviews afforded the opportunity to discover how these ideas emerged and to amplify them.

One individual involved in the original formulation of such thinking in the early 1970s explained how he and others had been

> . . . very interested in the science of ethology, in which people look at and examine the behavior of animals and primitive tribes and so forth. Since one was not going to fight with nuclear weapons, presumably, and one is primarily interested in the political utility of a nuclear force—and this was primary in terms of nuclear forces, as you may recall. But one has no way of gauging the military utility in actual combat, and therefore it was all based upon impressionism. And so we tended to think increasingly that the other fellow's impression of what you might have is far more important than what you might actually have. It was for this reason that we altered our way of behaving in regard to the elimination of obsolescent weapon systems. But anyhow, the game between the United States and the Soviet Union tended to be two frogs in a pond, each one of them blowing one's self up larger than the other and wanting to be more impressive. And the impression that was made was not only on the other frog but on third audiences—particularly so in the case of the United States because we had acquired, one way or another, the responsibility of holding a nuclear umbrella over the heads of other people. . . .

> Now, similarly, in the SALT negotiations, we used to keep B-52Ds that we had decommissioned, we would keep them around and in a position so that the Soviets could see them—so that the Soviet's intelligence officers would consider them to be part of our force structure and that we would be viewed, therefore, as having a higher number of strategic nuclear delivery vehicles. . . .

I don't resent spending some money—small sums—on blowing ourselves up as a frog, as long as it's going to be cheap. For example, I was all in favor of redeploying the Minuteman I, which was cheap since we had the Minuteman I, as the Soviets broke through that one thousand-ICBM barrier, just to tell them, let them know: You've deployed an additional one, we're deploying an additional one.

Two main streams of thought emerged as the discussion became more detailed. According to the dominant stream, there are critical audiences who, not really understanding nuclear reality, continue to view military power in conventional terms and therefore regard the strategic balance as reflecting the potential outcome in the event of war. A second, and much more minor, stream emphasizes that maintaining the balance continues to be a critical means for signaling the resolve to retaliate or escalate against aggression.

THE GREATER-FOOL ARGUMENT

The first major argument is, in some ways, similar to a phenomenon that has been described by economists as a greater-fool market. Such a market emerges when individuals invest in things at prices significantly higher than what they perceive as the real value, that is, they act like a "fool," on the assumption that somewhere there is a "greater fool" who is willing to pay an even higher price. In some cases the objects invested in are of no real value from the investors' point of view—for example, speculative stamp collecting—while in other cases the value is simply inflated by the greater-fool market dynamic—for example, speculative real estate investments or the tulip craze in Holland. Although a greater-fool market often arises from the belief that somewhere there is an actual fool who misestimates the value of an object, it is not really necessary for such a party to exist. The market can continue its momentum with every participant believing that someone else is the greater fool.*

*Because I will use the term *greater-fool argument* in subsequent chapters, it may be valuable to clear up any potential misunderstandings. Although individuals who seek to follow a greater-fool rationale intentionally act like "fools," this does not necessarily mean they are really foolish. Rather, they are following a conscious strategy which, if successful, may bring substantial rewards. Stock market investors follow such strategies on a daily basis. They will pay a higher price than they perceive a stock to be worth on the assumption that the price will continue to rise long

According to the greater-fool perceptual rationale, the United States should invest in weapons that do not really have significant strategic value because some important audiences perceive that they do have such value. Such deployments will lead these audiences to behave in a manner consistent with their misperceptions and to the benefit of the United States. In terms of the tendency to conventionalize, respondents basically said, "It's not that *I* believe nuclear weapons are fundamentally the same as conventional weapons, but *other* people do. Therefore, it is to the benefit of the U. S. to play along with this illusion and invest in weapons accordingly."

The audience most readily identified as holding these misconceptions were third parties—either allies or nonaligned third world countries. The concern expressed was that these third parties might perceive the Soviet Union as gaining an advantage in usable military power and therefore they would be more accommodating to Soviet wishes and would distance themselves from the United States. In the parlance of political science, the concern was that nations would "bandwagon"— that is, they would jump on the Soviet bandwagon because they perceive it as waxing in power.* A prominent Rand analyst explained such thinking:

I: Why is that important—that perception of balance?

R: Because, for example, an Italian government might take a move unfriendly to the U. S. if they thought the U. S. was substantially outclassed by Soviet nuclear weapons—just to give an example; I don't mean the Italians necessarily.

I: And why would they do that?

R: Because statesmen typically don't go through complicated calculations about war games and scenarios; they just look at the basic balance—pull out the IISS *Military Balance* [see page 70] and say,

_____

enough to give them the opportunity to sell at profit before the general market realizes that the stock is being overvalued. Naturally such a strategy (like all strategies) can backfire terribly, but this does not mean that the strategy per se is inherently faulty. As we will see, though, it does have some problems when used as a rationale for certain defense policies.

* It should be noted that this view that smaller states will gravitate, or bandwagon, toward dominant states that are waxing in power runs contrary to the more prevalent view in the field of international relations theory. According to the more prevalent view, smaller states are more apt to try to "balance" the waxing power of the rising state by aligning themselves with an opposing power.

"Oh—the Soviets now have three times as many nuclear weapons that can hit my country as the U. S. has that can do the opposite thing. So I have got to be accommodating, to induce a sort of Finland-like approach to Soviet demands." . . . They don't make careful calculations, even if somebody does and presents it to them. Experienced statesmen know they'd better not trust expert witnesses all that much.

I: But they do trust the notions of balance, of parity, or the numerical terms? Those things they respond to?

R: Yeah . . . I think something like only ten percent of the world's leading statesmen really have thought very hard about nuclear weapons in a quantitative sort of way.

A former member of the Joint Chiefs of Staff explained why these perceptions by third parties were so important:

R: The other nations are sitting there watching this balance. And the minute they perceive that the Soviets have a significant majority you will see that impact on the economy. They'll, to use Kissinger's term, "tilt" towards the Soviets. In the same way they'll vote for the Soviets in the United Nations—and many of them do that now.

I: Do you know about some correlations between the balance and those patterns—economic patterns and voting patterns?

R: Yes. As the Soviets have built up their missile inventory, their positions have been supported more frequently in the United Nations. . . . And then it'll do the same thing in the economic and trade side: they're more inclined to welcome Soviet ships into their ports.

I: . . . [Because] they assume that difference, that advantage would work out to a military advantage in a war-fighting situation?

R: Yeah.

I: . . . That perceptual response is based on a misunderstanding of what nuclear weapons can do? Is that right?

R: I think they've got a pretty good idea of what *one* will do, but I think it's a misunderstanding of the balance between what the Soviets have and we have. The point is that, speaking in terms of damage, the difference between zero and a few is far greater than the difference between a few and many.

The concern for third-party perceptions has also appeared in published literature. Using gangland analogies, Harold Brown writes, "Nuclear capabilities, however, are not solely instruments of deterrence . . . [they] can play a role . . . as an inducement (to change camps, for example, so as to receive better 'protection')."[22] A publication from the National Strategy Information Center warned:

> Even in the absence of a specific crisis, general awareness of an adversary's military superiority can encourage the development of policies consistent with that country's goals. Moscow's military buildup has fostered perceptions, in Europe and elsewhere, of growing Soviet strength at a time of American weakness and decline. *These perceptions have led some Europeans to urge their governments to reduce ties with the United States and NATO, in recognition of the new "objective realities" of power.* Soviet leaders understand full well the fear and political paralysis which can derive from the recognition of a neighbor's overwhelming military edge. By promoting and manipulating these anxieties within the NATO countries, Moscow hopes to weaken the unity and resolve of the Western alliance and extend Soviet influence without incurring the dangers and costs of a major war [emphasis added].[23]

The second key audience for critical perceptions was the American public. A few respondents argued that because the American public does not really grasp nuclear reality, they will be impressed by a Soviet advantage in some of the more visible areas of the nuclear arsenals. This might intimidate the public to the extent of not supporting a vigorous foreign policy, thus giving the Soviets tacit permission to extend their influence. As will be discussed, the Soviets were generally attributed with the active intention of evoking such intimidation. Balancing Soviet developments was seen as a way to counteract these efforts.

Several secretaries of defense have voiced similar concerns. Harold Brown explained, "We plan this [strategic] capability increase . . . to offset growing Soviet strategic armaments in order to ensure that there is no doubt as to our capability . . . even in our own minds."[24] James Schlesinger warned that if the Soviets are perceived as "having the probable capacity to inflict damage on our ICBM fields—and we lack the capacity to do the same to them—then perceptions will have been altered in such a way that the political will of both the U. S. and our allies may be less firm. We may be more willing to yield to pressure."[25]

When I probed into the makeup of this misperceiving public there was some ambiguity. Some respondents clearly distinguished between the general public and a sophisticated elite; some saw the elite as divided or itself ambiguous about the military necessity of the weapons being built. Others felt that only a rarefied few really grasped the military irrelevance of the weapons and even included in the misperceiving public not only high-level Pentagon officials but also, in some cases, the American president. Concern was even expressed that, should a nuclear imbalance emerge, the Soviets might correctly sense that the American president might underestimate the strength of his capabilities, thus undermining an American threat of escalation to nuclear weapons in response to a conventional invasion.

R: If we are far weaker than the Soviets, then the perception of escalation is weakened if they make a conventional attack in Europe, and so forth.

I: The perception that we will escalate would weaken, even though technically it shouldn't be weakened?

R: Technically it shouldn't be, but if the perception is that we are weak and therefore the president feels weak—

I: But in a sense it's not a correct perception; it's not a necessary perception from the technical facts.

R: Well, it may not be . . . [but] it's realistic if you think you're weak, you're going to act differently than if you think you're strong.

Sometimes the intimidating response was depicted as something that would not occur immediately but would evolve across generations. A staff member of the Committee on the Present Danger explained:

I put it in terms of a generational change more than psychologically—in terms of the change, not so much the people (individuals change their minds), but over generations, as, for instance, people my own age—who were not really involved in things, Vietnam or that, but are more politically aware only fairly recently—grew up with the idea that the Soviets are at least equal to us militarily and strategically. And for instance, the next generation, they grow up with the idea that the Soviets are superior. And all of their other assumptions begin with that. . . .

My fear—and it is a fear that I'm trying to combat—is that a generation that grows up with an inferiority complex, I guess you could call it, in terms of the strategic relationship, may be more obliged to act in such a way to keep, to maintain that inferiority. Let me see if I can describe it: well, we can't, we're number two and we'll always be number two, and therefore we shouldn't do anything to upset the Soviets. I think that continuing attitudes such as that lead to even a further deterioration.

Consistent with the primary focus of deterrence theory, the audience that was seen as most important was the Soviets. There was a strong concern that if the Soviets believe the strategic balance is in their favor, they will assume they can win an all-out war with the United States. This apprehension was based on the judgment that the Soviets do not grasp nuclear reality nor the condition of mutual vulnerability.

R: I have no feeling that the Soviets take assured destruction seriously.

I: How come?

R: Because I think, unlike the United States, the Soviets do not think that nuclear weapons have necessarily transformed the nature of warfare.

A former CIA employee worried that the Soviets were getting ahead in the strategic competition: "I think we still have a minimal retaliatory capacity. I'm not so sure in my own mind that the Soviets recognize that or continue to recognize that." The assumption that the Soviets conventionalize nuclear weapons was quite explicit. A presidential advisor said that the Soviets are "animated by very conventional ideas of what war is all about." A Pentagon official asserted, "What we think of as strategic forces are seen [by the Soviets] far more as almost a superior form of artillery."

The recurrent conclusion was that to counteract these Soviet misperceptions, the United States needs to maintain a strategic balance (not just a secure second-strike capability). A congressman explained:

> In the real game you get back to perception: does the other guy think he has better than parity . . . and bring himself to an unacceptable conclusion? . . . What I'm talking about is to make him psychologically lean to the psychological conclusion that war is unwinnable on his part.

This line of thought is distinct from a traditional approach to deterrence because it is not predicated on a rational adversary. If so, the argument would be based on whether the Soviets *in fact* could gain a war-winning capability through marginal advantages. To base the argument for maintaining the balance on the notion that the Soviets greatly misperceive the significance of that balance is to use the greater-fool argument.

When these respondents were asked to explain how the Soviets could acquire such mistaken beliefs, they equivocated. A firm answer was sometimes very elusive. When asked whether they believed a marginal advantage could be decisive, some respondents implied that they did not but the Soviets might. But when asked how the Soviets could have such a mistaken belief, they implied that the Soviets were correct. When asked to explain how it is correct, no answers were forthcoming, but once again the idea was attributed to the Soviets.

In another, much more overt, example of equivocation, the Soviets were first attributed with a tendency to conventionalize based on their historical experience.

> If you look at the history of Soviet Russia, they've somehow worked themselves into the state of mind where they feel by virtue of historical experience that they're kind of paranoid over the thought that they're going to get attacked. And they feel that the way to prevent that, of course, is to outnumber the other side.

The same respondent went on to explain how this kind of thinking might lead the Soviets to believe that their ICBM superiority gives them a disarming first-strike capability or that at least "they could have perceived they did [in the late '70s] if we didn't do anything [that is, redress the balance]." Nevertheless, in the same interview the respondent on several occasions contradicted this view, saying that there was no ambiguity in the minds of Soviets about American retaliatory capabilities and that "both sides are certain about the other side's capability to do damage they don't want to accept."

In sharp contrast to those who depicted the Soviets as a key audience because of their failure to grasp nuclear reality, an even larger group depicted the Soviets as consciously manipulating perceptions in much the same way as they proposed that the United States should.* Some credited the Soviets with thinking along these lines as early as the 1960s, when Nikita Khrushchev actively sought to enhance perceptions of Soviet strength through exaggeration and disinformation. As a former high-level Pentagon official explained,

> I think the Soviet military tends to brood about the military significance, just the same as the American military would. [But] the Soviets as a whole are much less interested in the military quantities than they are in the political significance of it—that's solidly Leninist of them, if I may put it that way. It got a little out of hand with Khrushchev when he was hitting flies in outer space with the military equipment that didn't exist, and he was running a total bluff. And Russians don't abhor bluffing, but they like to have something there to build on, and Khrushchev was running a total bluff.

Several respondents went further to bewail American ineptitude in dealing with such perceptions relative to the Soviets' ability, as seen in this example:

> This [Soviet] elite is defective from many points of view, but not in its understanding of power. For them, a conscious, deliberate understanding of how you use perception, and so on, is just integral to them. They would never have dreamed of publishing the

---

*Interestingly, some of the same individuals who cited the Soviets as being the greater-fool audience also cited the Soviets as consciously manipulating perceptions. One individual, who first said that the Soviets mistakenly fail to grasp assured destruction, later made the argument that Soviet behavior is more influenced by changes in the balance *because* they are more sophisticated in their "political use of force."

[SALT II] interim numbers to their disfavor. It never occurred to them. They would rather give away half their power.

When I asked at whom Soviet efforts were directed, the audiences were largely the same as for American efforts—Japan, China, the third world in general, and especially the NATO allies. There was also an assumption that the Soviets believed that relative capabilities would affect NATO behavior in a crisis.

> [The Soviets] have pursued a form of nuclear superiority which from my point of view just looks kind of kooky. How much is enough? Well, they seem to be buying ten times more than what is enough. And I think there's a reason for that. They find it useful to have this kind of superiority because, in my view, they think that should events degenerate and a crisis becomes a test, this kind of nuclear offensive superiority will be in the backs of the minds of all the people they're facing and will have some effect on their behavior.

More common, though, was the attitude that the Soviets were trying to change perceptions of relative nuclear strength as a means of exerting a subtle coercion to make the West more accommodating to Soviet wishes. A Pentagon official explained:

> R: I think [the Soviet buildup] is for coercive purposes.
> I: To coerce?
> R: The West—particularly West Germany.
> I: Specifically to?
> R: To make them more malleable. . . . It's this combination of that overt military power, not always admitted to and yet not explicitly denied when Western sources leak its existence, coupled with this sort of seductive, "It's really in your interest to accommodate me" kind of line. "It's really best not to jeopardize the future of the world—let alone future generations of Germans or Brits or Americans—by provoking me. And let's find some sort of reasonable terms. And I'll tell you what my reasonable terms are. . . ." Somewhere in the world, someone—some public body, some influential organization, some statesman or other, some political

party—is being, usually, given the carrot and the stick in varying degrees.

The conclusion of this line of thinking was that by maintaining a balance such coercion could be neutralized.*

Choosing to Play Along with the Illusion   The most critical feature of the greater-fool argument for maintaining the balance is not the idea that there is this widespread illusion about the military significance of the balance. The most critical feature is the prescription to play along with the illusion as if it were real. Logically, this is not a necessary conclusion. It is possible for policymakers to actively work to neutralize the illusion. Furthermore, playing along with the illusion is more than a passive response. Behaving consistently with the illusion implicitly confirms and thereby effectively promotes it.

In interviews with proponents of perception theory, I asked why they chose to play along, attempting to pose the question in a nonprovocative way. Nonetheless sometimes the response was mildly defensive. An ACDA official appeared visibly uncomfortable and attempted to obfuscate the issue by creating epistemological confusion.

To me the only question is: Do people think this way and act this way? And the answer is yes. Do you want to know whether it's

---

*There was an interesting disparity between several secretaries of defense in their perspectives on such potential coercion. Donald Rumsfeld seemed to suggest that Soviet superiority *would*, in fact, give the Soviets "peacetime and crisis leverage over the United States and its allies." (*Annual Report to Congress FY 1978* [Washington, D.C.: GPO, 1977], 32.) Harold Brown made a similar point: "Essential equivalence . . . minimizes the probability that strategic forces will be used to seek any diplomatic advantage over us. . . . We owe it to our allies as well as to ourselves to assure that both explicit and implicit pressures can be confidently resisted." (*Annual Report to Congress FY 1979* [Washington, D.C.: GPO, 1978], 56)

However, James Schlesinger suggested that such capabilities would not, in fact, give the Soviets such coercive options but might make them think it would, thus leading them to take risky actions. He writes that because of emerging static measures

> in favor of the USSR. . . we cannot exclude the possibility that future Soviet leaders might be misled into believing that such apparently favorable asymmetries could, at the very least, be exploited for diplomatic advantage. Pressure, confrontation, and crisis could easily follow from a miscalculation of this nature.
>
> It is well and good to assert that the Soviet leaders, faced by an adamant and unified America, would come to their senses in time to avoid fatal mistakes in such a situation and would recognize the illusory nature of their advantages. But a crisis might already be too late for such an awakening. *It is worth a price in research and development hedges to prevent such illusions* from arising in the first place [emphasis added]. (*Annual Report to Congress FY 1975* [Washington, D.C.: GPO, 1974], 43)

right? I mean, if you're just talking about validity, I don't know what that means.

Nevertheless, when I reiterated some of the original questions, he once again seemed to revert to a concept of validity.

I: Are the imbalances in the strategic balance necessarily a reflection of how things would look after the termination of a war?
R: No.
I: So, intellectually, it's not a valid way to assess—
R: No.

Others sometimes deflected responsibility to *other* people who have told them that a failure to compete in the realm of perceptions has negative effects. A member of the Scowcroft Commission explained:

I: And what negative effects does that have?
R: I don't know [smiles].
I: What's the smile?
R: [pause] It's hard for me to go through these things in detail. I just believe that [pause] people more knowledgeable than I inform me that it has a bad influence over the long run.

Overall, though, the most common response was an argument that conformity with the illusion is necessary, inevitable, and not really a choice. Harold Brown has also written, "I do not see how, to be on the safe side, we can do otherwise than insist on and maintain essential equivalence."[26] Respondents depicted themselves as not really playing a causal role but as simply maneuvering in the midst of powerful political forces. As one Rand analyst said, almost plaintively, "Look, I didn't make up the music. So when they play the waltz, what can I do but waltz along?"

Particularly striking was how certain some respondents were that there were really no other options. I asked a former member of the Joint Chiefs of Staff,

I: Is there anything we can do to correct that misperception [re: the balance] other than building weapons according to it?

R: I think Mr. Reagan's already corrected it.

I: How so? How do you think he's corrected it?

R: By taking the decision he has about building up the defense.

I: But is there anything we can do other than that?

R: No!

I: Why is that? It's just that people don't respond to anything other than arms building?

R: They only respond to real things that they can count and see. And they respond either up or down depending on the figures.

Some respondents expressed ambivalence and even some regret about going along with the illusion. One Rand analyst explained that it was an unfortunate necessity because of the features of a democratic system.

You have to distinguish between what you think, you know, "if I were czar," and what you would as a policy analyst advise. And as a policy analyst, I came to the conclusion some years ago that, like it or not, it was probably appropriate to have a very stable policy based on strategic equivalence, which would mean balancing these perceptions out, as opposed to saying they're not very important. If you had a strong president, a strong secretary of defense, they could temporarily, if you will, go to Congress and say, "We're only going to build what we need, and we're not going to spend a penny more on it; we're going to cancel this, we're going to cancel that, and if the Russians build twice as many, tough!" And if President Reagan did that, it might go whipping through, and people would feel great. But I personally think that that kind of situation is unstable politically, and that five years hence—maybe less—there would be a political scandal. The political elections would be dominated by foolish considerations. And it's therefore better for our own domestic stability, as well as international perceptions—it's not only more conservative, it's a lot more conservative—to insist that we remain good competitors, even if the objective significance of the competition is—uh—dubious.

To go a little farther, I would *personally* prefer that we be good competitors in conventional forces and in things like peaceful use of space, and that within the strategic realm we do only that which we thought was really smart and forget about matching weapon with weapon, completely forget about counting numbers of missiles and launchers as points of comparison, and just build a good force structure, to our objectives. But I have a profound skepticism that that kind of thing can be made to work over a period of time politically.

What was particularly striking was that this respondent was not too concerned about the potential responses of the Soviets or third parties or even the spontaneous responses of the American public. Instead, he felt it was necessary to play along with the illusion because a failure to do so would give other American opinion leaders the ability to consciously take advantage of the misperceiving public.

I: So the key perceivers in this case seem to be the American public. The American public needs to perceive that equivalence, and if they don't, then they're going to get upset.

R: Well, the American public believes what they're told in all these matters. So I think the problem is the fairly high-level—they're the influence makers, they're the ex-government officials, they're the columnists, and so forth. An example here would be SALT II . . . I thought the quality of the debate was just absolutely spurious. People—especially on the anti-SALT II side—raised lots of arguments that were just pure baloney, and I thought frequently they knew it . . . I think it's hopeless; I think that equivalence is the only stable solution. And strategic equivalence is a very vigorous competition. I think we truly have to be vigorous competitors, or these people will be very critical—sometimes correctly, and sometimes not very correctly—but they will make an awful lot of stink, and then there will be political problems.

This ambivalent feeling was also expressed by an individual who had played a role in the original formulating of the concern for perceptions. He explained that the emphasis on the significance of the military balance "*is* a distortion of reality. It is probably a necessary distortion of reality." Soon after he looked at me and said, "You know, I kind of envy you academics. You get to tell the truth." He then explained how "it's different" when one is a "public person"—betraying a degree of self-doubt by the intensity of his apparent concern that I might not understand.

THE BALANCE AS A SIGNALING DEVICE

Naturally, since so much thinking seems predicated on the assumption that there are key audiences that perceive the strategic balance as militarily significant, a critical question arises: Do such audiences in fact misperceive in the ways attributed to them by the greater-fool argument? In a greater-fool market it is not necessary for a real greater fool to exist. The market can continue its momentum with every participant believing that someone else is the greater fool.

In the late 1970s, as the perceptual rationales described above were gaining increasing currency in the Pentagon, the Department of Defense commissioned a series of studies that referred to the ideas of Schlesinger and Luttwak on the political significance of perceptions and sought to find out how, in fact, the superpower balance was perceived. The studies, published in the 1978 book *International Perceptions of the Superpower Military Balance*, focused on audiences in Europe, Japan, the Middle East, the Soviet Union, and the United States. One of the key questions addressed was whether "perceivers tend to think in terms of numerical comparisons of superpower military strength." Based on a variety of evidence, the conclusion was that "it is generally felt that both sides have more than enough." The researchers found that some groups even stated directly that it is "moot to ask, 'Who is ahead' in a situation of mutual nuclear overkill." The authors also observed that Soviet officials have recognized that numerical superiority has no real value in the face of mutual assured destruction, and that "parity is not the issue at hand."[27]

Yet the authors argued implicitly that it is still important to build arms in light of international perceptions. They suggested that although America's allies and the Soviet Union apparently attach no military importance to the strategic balance in an environment of overkill and do not consider themselves to be affected by whatever shifts they perceive in the balance, some countries nevertheless keep a close eye on the balance and look for signs of U. S. resolve to maintain it. As the authors point out, if the "U. S. resolve to match Soviet military strength" is perceived as weakening, "the end result would be very significant for the United States, whatever its actual or perceived strength compared with the Soviet Union."[28] The argument seems to suggest that in international power relations, perceptions of the super-power military balance are the coinage of the realm even though all the key parties involved seem to recognize that from a military point of view the coins are counterfeit.

These studies apparently had little direct impact on defense thinking. No one I interviewed made any reference to them. And indeed, the dominant view seemed to be based on the assumption that somewhere there is a greater-fool audience having critical misperceptions. Nevertheless a substantial minority did develop a rationale for current defense policies that does not require a misperceiving audience and still recognizes nuclear reality.

According to this view, the act of maintaining a balance with the Soviet Union serves to function as a device for sending certain signals. In a conventional context, matching the other side's capabilities sends key signals because by doing so one preserves the option to take certain military actions. In a nuclear context, such capabilities may not have any significant effect on the range of military options available. Nevertheless, it can be argued, the act of maintaining the balance has persevered as a means of sending the same kinds of signals that they did in a conventional context. Although, perhaps, all key parties recognize the military irrelevance of the capabilities, maintenance of the balance has become a consensually validated mode of communication.

A political analyst articulated this line of thinking, saying that it was very important for the United States to follow "standardized calculations" of force capabilities—which are "widely believed" when planning the American force structure—as part of this consensual symbolic competition. He explained:

> [The Soviets] regard [these calculations] in about the same way that I think U. S. decisionmakers regard them, which is to say that . . . you take these calculations very seriously because these are the established ways of answering the question of how much is enough.

He went on to explain that these considerations have little relationship to a real military situation:

If you asked a different question, how are these calculations likely to be regarded in the kind of crisis in which there is even a small possibility of nuclear weapons being used, then I will suspect the answer is that on both sides the political leadership will be extremely skeptical of these calculations in terms of (a) their own forces working as advertised, and (b) any of these more esoteric scenarios playing out.

Several respondents recognized the nonrational character of these processes. Nevertheless, they argued, a failure to sustain signals of strength can have major repercussions. A former staff member of the National Security Council pointed to how John Kennedy was perceived as weak by Nikita Khrushchev, based largely on their personal encounter in Vienna. This led, he believed, to Khrushchev's decision to try to deploy missiles in Cuba. The respondent argued that presently the critical measure of strength is whether we are going to match Soviet hard-target kill capability.

As for the signals to be sent by such methods, the most frequently cited had to do with the credibility of the threat to retaliate or to escalate with nuclear weapons. A recurrent theme was that to support the credibility of American threats, it was necessary to maintain a balance. Although balance was not seen as a real measure of American options, it has come to symbolize American resolve to use nuclear weapons. A former member of the Senate Foreign Relations Committee staff said that a failure to match Soviet capabilities would "lower the image of U. S. resolve to respond in kind" and would weaken the perception of America's "general will to defense."

This kind of thinking has been clearly (and sometimes in the interviews explicitly) influenced by the concept of the paradox of deterrence. During the 1950s and 1960s, a major topic of discussion in strategic circles was based on the recognition that a logical flaw emerged when the theory of deterrence was applied to two or more powers with secure second-strike capabilities. The threat to retaliate against aggression, while eminently sensible as a deterrent before aggression occurred, had the potential for losing credibility after aggression had occurred. If the Soviet Union were to make a limited attack against the United States or its allies, the United States, while perhaps desiring to make good on its original threat, might in the event actually prefer not to retaliate for fear of the consequences of counter-retaliation. The motive for executing the threat would, to a certain extent, have evaporated once the originally-to-be-deterred aggression actually occurred. The concern was that the Soviet Union might feel that it could undertake such aggression and be confident that the United States would lose its nerve and refrain from retaliation.

To solve this problem, strategists have looked for ways to "enhance the credibility of American threats" by indicating United States "resolve" to retaliate. One such solution (others will be explored in later chapters) is for the United States to maintain a strategic balance as an indicator of resolve. Implicit in this line of thinking is the existence of some consensus that maintaining this balance is a generally understood and respected signal.

Robert Jervis has written, "Lacking objective and reliable indicators of resolve, . . . states are forced to do many odd things to convince others that they will stand firm in a major crisis." He goes on to say that to show resolve, there is a tendency to look for actions that are difficult, such as building militarily "unnecessary capability."[29] In a published discussion of a paper I presented at the Center for the Study of Democratic Institutions, Dagobert Brito, an economist and strategic analyst, described the superpower arms competition as a "push-up contest" to signal the willingness to use nuclear weapons.[30]

Closely related to this kind of thinking is the idea that the measure of resolve is the balance of residual capabilities after a hypothetical Soviet first strike. An informal presidential advisor said,

> The reserves on each side become tremendously material in deciding whether they would make a first strike. A reckless Soviet leader may bet (and there may be a reckless Soviet leader) if he made such a strike and he had more in reserve than the United States did, then we would not counter. But if we had still more in reserve—for instance, if we had forty Trident submarines at sea— he wouldn't make the first strike at all.

This argument is almost directly derived from one made by Paul Nitze in 1976. He argued that if the United States, after suffering a Soviet first strike, had a relative disadvantage in the throw-weight of its residual forces, the credibility of its threat to retaliate would be weakened even if the absolute levels of its remaining capabilities were adequate.[31]

Several respondents emphasized that the balance was particularly important for signaling to European allies (as well as the Soviets) American willingness to uphold its commitment to respond to aggression even to the point of using nuclear weapons first.* Sometimes the state of the balance and the strength of the guarantees almost became fused into a single concept. A high-level Pentagon official explained:

> We have given, in effect, nuclear guarantees in Europe. . . . And the U. S. nuclear posture relative to that of the Soviets is an essential feature of that issue of how the allies see the state of the balance or the adequacy of those guarantees.

The purely symbolic nature of these gestures was well recognized. For example, an influential political analyst said:

> I: What's the purpose of the Pershings? . . .
> R: Let's take one step back. What's the point of keeping all those troops in Europe? . . . We have these troops there not because so many are needed in some military sense, but because that was the number we once had and any diminution is regarded as a loss of commitment, right? . . . Well, it's the same with the Pershings. I can't see any effect of the Pershings on our position—none, zero!

Some expressed frustration with the cumbersome effects of this numerical thinking, as in this comment from a former high-level Pentagon official: "One of the problems I always had was that Bob McNamara had made such a fuss about having seven thousand nuclear weapons in Europe . . . because the number itself had become symbolic of the American commitment."

Sometimes symbolic acts were not tied to a clear logical structure. For example, one strategic analyst felt that deploying the MX was a

---

*An article in the *Washington Quarterly* states that "Soviet success in matching Western nuclear arsenals from the strategic to the artillery level reduces the belief that a conventional Soviet attack on NATO Europe will be met by a nuclear response." (Thomas Hirschfield, "Tactical Nuclear Weapons in Europe," *Washington Quarterly* 10:1 [Winter 1987], 101)

good way to send the Soviets a "political message" that it was unaccept-able for them to "pull their targets out from under the forces we have deployed" by putting their ICBMs on mobile bases. It was not clear how deploying the MX would send this specific message since even in a war-fighting situation the MX would not impinge on the mobility of these ICBMs. It was also not simply a symmetrical response because the proposal for the MX he supported did not call for the MX to be mobile. Nevertheless, it was felt that deploying the MX sent the political message, "Hey—you're not going to be able to get away with that."

In some cases the symbolic message was of a more general nature. The resolve to maintain the strategic balance was sometimes seen as symbolizing America's willingness to maintain itself as a superpower.

R: . . . and so you'd better deploy the [MX] . . . so that you demonstrate that you are prepared to go and deploy your ICBMs. . . . The U. S. does need a new strategic bomber for both nuclear and conventional roles because it's a superpower. But you also probably need to deploy B-1s to send some kind of signals to the Soviets, who are deploying their Blackjack on top of their Back-fires, and say, "Look, you guys had better realize the U.S. is not, despite attacks of terminal silliness, going to abdicate as a super-power . . . You guys have got to realize that we're not going to fold; correlation of forces is not moving irrevocably in your favor. In fact, it may be rolling back."

I: And building these weapons makes those signals?

R: That's right.*

In this symbolic context, the value of nuclear weapons lies as much in the act of building the weapons as in actually having them. The act of building is a gesture that sends certain signals. Several respondents

*In 1957, the Gaither Committee, appointed by President Eisenhower, used a similar argu-ment to support the construction of bomb shelters. Recognizing that shelters would not signifi-cantly limit damage, they nevertheless argued that building them would "demonstrate to the world our appraisal of the [cold-war] situation and our willingness to cope with it in strength. It would symbolize our *will to survive,* and our understanding of our responsibilities in a nuclear age [emphasis added]." ("Deterrence and Survival in the Nuclear Age," Report to the President by the Security Resources Panel of the Science Advisory Committee [November 7, 1957], 22. Quoted in Robert Jervis, "The Symbolic Nature of Nuclear Politics," The Edmund Jones James Lecture [Department of Political Science, University of Illinois of Urbana-Champaign, 1987], 35) pointed out that since Reagan has taken office, no major improvements to our arsenal have been completed (the INF weapons had only begun to go in at the time). The window of vulnerability was as wide open as always. Nevertheless, they argued, the act of deciding to build the weapons and to commit the necessary funds created a certain positive perception in the present. Of course, the other side of this thinking is that once weapons are completed they lose their symbolic saliency. One congressman explained that the weapons the United States built in the 1960s made it clear that the United States was willing to use them then.

> Our planners, our thinkers were not only planning to use [nuclear weapons], but geared up our factories to produce them. And the will was pretty clear in all the intelligence the Soviets came by in the past. We had the will to use them.

But later, as American nuclear weapons programs tapered off, this perceived resolve was weakened. "It became clearer and clearer that we would not use it except as an absolute last resort. So they could see it psychologically."

This line of reasoning encourages a dichotomous approach to weapons procurement decisions. Without an established military criterion for evaluating the necessity of a certain weapon system, the choice tends to become focused on whether the United States will or will not symbolically show its resolve in the arena of a particular decision. There is no way to choose against a proposed weapon system and then not suffer some political loss. A negative choice symbolizes weakness.

Furthermore, having a large arsenal only partly mitigates this effect—last year's weapons are indeed last year's gestures. The intention to use nuclear weapons (being so incredible) requires constant reiteration. And as the number of weapons in the American arsenal has grown, presumably so have the additional increments required to make the desired perceptual impact. Obviously, this line of thinking logically leads to an ongoing arms race.

The Tendency to Assume Beliefs

The perceptual rationale for maintaining the balance suggests that policymakers, as a means of managing perceptions, should behave in ways consistent with the incorrect belief that the balance is militarily significant. A substantial amount of psychological research suggests that it is quite stressful for people to behave in ways contrary to the beliefs they hold. They experience a dissonance which they tend to want to reduce by either modifying their behavior or their attitudes. In the interviews I found evidence that when individuals' behavior is consistent with the conventional belief that the balance is militarily significant, they tend to assume that belief even though a persisting intellectual awareness remains about its lack of validity.

A respondent involved in developing the window-of-vulnerability idea described this process with remarkable lucidity. Earlier in the interview he had dismissed military rationales for weapons deployments, emphasizing instead the concern for perceptions. In describing how he became involved in the window-of-vulnerability idea, he told of increasingly accepting a belief he had not originally taken seriously. Speaking of the call for a strategic buildup in the late 1970s, he said,

> It did make sense then. . . . Those were the good old days of the window of vulnerability until we wished it out of existence. Having wished it into existence we wished it out of existence with the Scowcroft Commission . . .
>
> I: Did you buy the window-of-vulnerability idea?
>
> R: No, not entirely. It was invented in part in my office. . . . [We] discovered it in 1975, I distinctly remember it—
>
> I: You don't seem to think the problem you focused on was a real problem.
>
> R: [nods]
>
> I: Do you think most of the people involved with that thinking also recognize that it wasn't really a problem?
>
> R: I think for a while I did believe it. I think for a while a lot of us believed it . . . I think that we probably ended up scaring ourselves a bit more. Sort of like the tales children tell themselves,

"Hey, let's really get scared"—and then you do your old "Geez, it's terrible."

I: Did you know you were doing that?

R: [under breath] Did we know we were doing that? In part, probably, yes. The trouble with intellectuals is that they get seized by the power of their idea and then say, "Gee, this is fun," or you play "what-if" and the what-if becomes—you forget at a certain point that you're playing what-if.

Given this phenomenon, it is not surprising that some respondents appeared somewhat confused or uncertain when they tried to explain their concern for marginal asymmetries. At times they explained their concerns in terms of misperceiving audiences and then at other points apparently took on those beliefs previously labeled as misperceptions. An example of this behavior appeared in an interview with a member of the Scowcroft Commission.

R: I don't believe that it is politically stable or politically good with us, our allies, with the Soviets, for us to be in a situation where even a part of the triad has such an imbalance as the land-based portion of the system does now.

I: Why is that?

R: Because it affects what you would call political perceptions. . . . I don't like a political world where . . . [there is] that big of an imbalance in the ICBM force in terms of the relative strength of the ICBM forces.

He then made a statement that seemed to shift between the military and political significance of the ICBM force, leading me to probe for a more precise statement.

R: I do believe that it is such a usable force because it is seen as a symbol of nuclear power by so many people and because it is the most controllable, usable part of the force, that such an imbalance is unhealthy.

I: Politically?

R: It influences the reactions of countries all over the world in how they react to the perceived relative strength of the Soviet Union to us. If you're going to try to take me through the scenarios of five thousand-megaton exchanges, I know that it doesn't matter, okay? And that view is probably . . . the general view of members of the [Scowcroft] Commission.

Although it appeared that he was espousing a classic perception theory argument, immediately afterward he seemed to shift to believing that these imbalances have military significance.

I: Now, do you think that perception—
R: [interrupting] I think it's true.
I: That what's true?
R: That it does adversely affect strength.
I: . . . you think it's a correct perception on the part of those audiences?
R: Yes.
I: Militarily correct?
R: Yes.

Sometimes the dissonance pressed respondents in the opposite direction. They would start by trying to affirm the correctness of the military concern for marginal asymmetries but would gradually move toward a perceptual rationale that discounted the original concern. For example, a State Department official initially described himself as having a "traditional" concern for maintaining the balance. "I'm old-fashioned in this, I'll admit it, sort of a traditional. . . . What you need is probably peacetime parity or essential equivalence or call-it-what-you-will." However, when pressed for his rationale for this concern for parity, he shifted to a not-so-traditional perceptual argument, saying that parity is necessary "so when the rest of the world looks at the arsenals, it doesn't draw tremendous conclusions that the Soviets are way ahead." Soon after, he directly contradicted his traditional concern for parity, "Parity, to me, is almost meaningless."

Some respondents shifted their position when I explicitly pointed to their strategy based on manipulating perceptions. For example, a congressman argued that having nuclear superiority would give greater credibility to the threat to use nuclear weapons.

> If [the Soviets] think that even if we are inferior conventionally, but if we have the superiority in the nuclear, that we would use it, it will deter them.
>
> I: What is the relationship to our superiority or inferiority if we have something well beyond a minimal deterrent?
>
> R: [pause] Well, now we come to . . . the psychological thing. What, given the Russian-Soviet mind, what would it take to make them believe that we would use nuclear arms?

He then cited the Vietnam War as an example of a situation in which the Soviets were deterred from entering the conflict because American superiority created the perception that we would use nuclear weapons. However, when I articulated the implicit assumption, he partially retreated from his position.

> I: There's an assumption here that our having superiority is a way of indicating that we are willing to use the weapons?
>
> R: I don't think your having superiority at all necessarily means you're willing to use them.

He then tried to reconstruct his original argument, saying, "Psychologically, it isn't so much what we would do as so much what they perceive we would do." Shortly thereafter, however, he abandoned the argument: "Well, let me start all over again. I don't think there's necessarily any correlation between having superiority and deterring the other guy from acting," contradicting his first statement that if the Soviets think "if we have the superiority in the nuclear, that we would use it, it will deter them."

The Circularity Problem

Even if policymakers have a strong enough self-awareness to enable them to execute perceptual manipulations without assuming the beliefs they express, there is yet another problem with the general approach. When policymakers decide to promote a new round of arms building, they cannot simply state publicly that the weapons are necessary for perceptual purposes. A former member of the Joint Chiefs of Staff explained, "If [an American leader] said, 'We're playing catch-up,' which we are (for some of us), the Congress would never support doing a thing." Instead, an American leader must create the impression that a real military requirement for the weapon exists and that in some way American security would be threatened by a failure to build the new weapon. As a former high-level Pentagon official explained, policymakers have to "concentrate on our weaknesses" and stress that "the Soviets have [such weaknesses] to a lesser degree."

Obviously, making the Soviet Union look stronger than the United States runs counter to a key objective of the entire perceptual rationale—to promote the perception of America as strong. Logically, the concern for perceptions should make American leaders brag publicly about the extraordinary power and invincibility of the American deterrent, augmenting their claims, of course, with extensive documentation. However, the concern for perceptions of the imbalance has instead led policymakers to publicly stress how inferior the United States is to the Soviet Union. Many of the key proponents of perceptual rationales were, in fact, some of the loudest public voices of alarm about American weaknesses.*

James Schlesinger, in an August 1981 *Time* article, sought to explain this apparent contradiction. He recognized that the emphasis on American weakness "is a self-inflicted wound" but went on to say that "one of the penalties of a democracy is that we have to call public attention to the problem in order to get the necessary remedies."[32]

As Arthur Macy Cox noted in his 1982 book *Russian Roulette,* this kind of thinking leads to a Catch-22. According to this concern for perceptions, the original problem that needs to be remedied is the perception of inadequacy, not inadequate weaponry. The purpose of

---

*This effort to depict the adversary as stronger has been noted in the press. An article in *U.S. News and World Report* titled "Is the U. S. Really No. 2?" noted with irony the "curious" and "bizarre" situation in which American and Soviet leaders are "poor-mouthing their might—each conceding an edge to the other." (Jan. 10, 1983, 16)

At times, President Reagan's efforts to play up Soviet arms building has reached extraordinary proportions. The *New York Times* reported on May 22, 1986, that in a public statement "The President said that in the last five years the Soviet Union had outbuilt the United States and other members of the North Atlantic Treaty Organization by '50 times' in such military hardware as fighter planes, bombers, tanks and ballistic missiles." (Gerald M. Boyd, "Reagan, Defending Budget, Says Lack of Knowledge Hurts Hungry," *New York Times,* May 22, 1986, A1) This suggests that Soviet spending on these items alone is approximately ten times greater than the entire U. S. defense budget.

new weaponry is to modify this misperception. But in order to galvanize support for expenditures meant to modify the misperception, the misperception is intentionally enhanced. Remedying the problem thus requires making the problem worse.

THE DOUBLE IMAGE

In the interviews, I tried to get respondents to account for this circular reasoning. One former high-level Pentagon official had clearly thought about the problem and had a kind of answer. First he described the problem lucidly:

> [There is a] fundamental dilemma. In order to get any change in your force structure in this society, you've got to go to the Congress. And you've got to persuade them that it's worrisome. If you can persuade them that it's worrisome, then you've got an international problem of perception.

He then formulated a strategy for dealing with it. He suggested that a leader should have at his disposal two very different postures or images in relation to the question of the significance of the balance. When he wishes to promote a weapon system that he deems important for perceptions of the balance, he should assess in advance the likelihood of succeeding in winning approval for the weapon system. If he thinks it is possible, he should project a conventional mindset image that asserts the military necessity for the weapons. If he thinks it is impossible to win the necessary support, he should try to defuse the potential perceptual effects by projecting a nuclear mindset image that discounts the significance of the imbalance on the basis of the high levels of overkill.

> If you know in advance that we were not going to deploy MX in counterforce, the secretary of defense probably shouldn't run around saying, "Hey! Look at that Soviet advantage in throw-weight counterforce," because that calls the attention of third audiences to the very thing that you're worried about—the Soviet possibility of political exploitation. When you call attention to that problem here in a political democracy, you're assuming that your democracy will respond and Congress will give you the

money to cure the problem. If you know damn well that that's not going to happen, it is a disadvantage in terms of perception to even raise the issue in the first place. Let the Soviets raise the issue, and then you say, "Aw, come on—we've got ten thousand warheads, and don't talk about this counterforce crap, you know—lookit!" That's what you should do if you know that you can't even up.

THE PROBLEM OF SIDE EFFECTS

This double-image solution, even if it could be perfectly executed, nevertheless has significant problems. First, it does not address the possibility that, even when the effort to redress the balance is successful, the problem of perceptions of weakness may actually be derived in significant part from the very effort to solve the problem. The study *International Perceptions of the Superpower Military Balance* found that American government statements were the primary source of information on the condition of the balance. It also noted that "the tendency of many U. S. spokesmen (particularly government officials at budget time) to emphasize Soviet strengths and U. S. weaknesses often had a negative impact on the perceived U. S. standing."[33] The effort to solve the problem of perceived weakness may actually produce side effects whose magnitude may be as great as the countering effects of the sought-after deployments. In other words, the entire effort of calling attention to an imbalance and then ameliorating the condition through new deployments may actually produce a net gain of zero.

Furthermore, the general double-image strategy produces corollary side effects that cannot be easily controlled. When one plays out the conventional mindset image of stressing imbalances as significant, this might lead to public support for a specific weapon system. However, a corollary result may be that the public (and not just the American public) might become alerted to other imbalances that the United States may not be in a position to redress. If one attempts to neutralize perceptions of inferiority by projecting a nuclear mindset image that downplays the significance of the balance, a corollary effect may be a weakening of the perceived significance of—and thus concern for—inferiorities that policymakers do wish to redress.

Finally, persisting with pre-nuclear policies in a nuclear context has costs that respondents rarely recognized. If in arms control negotiations

Maintaining the Perception of Balance

both sides give more weight to arsenal weapon categories in which they are at a disadvantage, and deemphasize categories in which they have the advantage, negotiations can quickly bog down in a mire of valid accusations that the other side is trying to gain an advantage. Even if both sides are negotiating in good faith, an excessively precise concern for equality can turn a minor disparity in judgment into a major stumbling block. Ultimately, then, this concern can interfere with the attainment of security-related benefits that may accrue from arms reductions. Overall, the balance of costs and benefits in terms of security interests makes it seem highly questionable whether the policy of maintaining a balance, even with the extra flourish of the perceptual rationale, serves security interests.

CHAPTER 7

Appearing to
Seek Advantageous
Termination

I N CHAPTER 4 we explored a variety of rationales for advantage-seeking war objectives based on traditional military arguments. In this chapter we will explore rationales for such objectives based on the strategic manipulation of perceptions. Respondents who gave such perceptual rationales readily recognized that the Soviet Union would always have the option to escalate to higher rungs on the ladder of escalation, up to and including countervalue targets. Therefore it would not be a prudent policy to hope to use force to achieve such an advantageous outcome. Nevertheless, they argued, it is strategically valuable for the United States to be *perceived* as having such advantage-seeking objectives.

One way this thinking was elicited from respondents was by asking to what extent advantage-seeking (or war-winning, or prevailing) policies are *action policies* (that is, what the United States would actually *do* in the event of a war) and to what extent they are only *declaratory policies* (what the United States says it would do in the event of a war). For example, an interview with a State Department official went as follows:

I: To what extent do you regard [the goal of prevailing in a nuclear war] as a kind of declaratory policy, and how much do you regard it as an action policy?

R: I think it's more the former . . . there was a growing consensus in the strategic community that that's what was necessary for our deterrent to attain its credibility.

A Pentagon official said, "The idea of prevailing is something you have to understand as a useful device in declaratory policy." Even an official who was involved in writing the 1982 Defense Guidance Statement that set out plans for prevailing in a nuclear war (including a protracted one) said that such plans are not primarily action policies but "mainly what people believe will enhance deterrence."

However, to project such a declaratory policy, it was explained, requires more than simply making an official policy decision. It requires that, to a certain extent, leaders believe in it and feel a desire to execute it. A Rand analyst explained:

I think the extent to which it is more than just declaratory is the notion that military leaders and even political leaders should operate with an attitude that says [changing voice], "If deterrence fails, then by God we ought to try to win." Now, if the circumstances are such that the significance of living afterwards would be pretty marginal because devastation is pretty great, then the practical attitude should be that under all circumstances we have the visceral desire.

It also requires building an arsenal that corresponds to this belief, with weapons that project what was called "war-fighting images." Virtually all respondents who argued for the perceptual value of such a policy bewailed the woeful inadequacy of the American arsenal, and most supported strategic defense. There was a strong feeling that the Soviets had gained great political advantages by projecting a war-winning strategy buttressed by a vigorous arms-building program, though they did not feel that the Soviets, in fact, had gained or could gain a real war-winning capability.

When asked who are the key audiences of such American policies and what are the desired effects, the respondents gave varied responses. The two dominant answers were: to strengthen NATO and to intimidate the Soviets.

Strengthening NATO

Several respondents expressed the argument that it is important to project war-winning ideas because members of NATO respond to such rhetoric. In some cases this was based on the greater-fool theory, that within the alliance there is a widespread tendency to conventionalize nuclear war. A staff member of the Senate Armed Services Committee said that the idea that nuclear war is not simply "an extension of conventional war . . . is something that I think is very, very hard in coming." A State Department official explained that the idea of prevailing "is much easier mentally" than any alternative. Sometimes the emphasis was on the need to show resolve to fight a war in Europe should it become necessary. A State Department official explained that the war-winning rhetoric of the Reagan administration was "a signal to the allies . . . [that] reflected a new determination."

A recurring part of this argument was that projecting such an image was also necessary to offset the political advantages the Soviets have derived from projecting their war-winning image. The basic argument was that Soviet confidence would produce a bandwagoning effect. The logical conclusion, then, sometimes implied and sometimes explicitly stated, was that the United States should answer this challenge by following suit.

Senator Jacob Javits, during the Senate Foreign Relations Committee hearings on Presidential Directive-59 (PD-59),* also expressed such thinking.

If Ogarkov will not admit that a nuclear war cannot be won, we are in a position where we have to adopt a doctrine to meet that; that can't just be left, that we are decent people and he is a roughneck, because the world perceives that statement standing beside our statement. We, ourselves, say

*PD-59 was a directive issued in 1980 by then President Carter calling for more ambitious war-fighting objectives with greater emphasis on counterforce targeting.

a nuclear war cannot be won; the Russians say it can . . . this is a fact of world life, and . . . this has weakened us; and I will tell you why, if I may. Because the Soviet Union has the right to assume that because we have not won the debate that our allies will peel away because of their confident assertion they can win a nuclear war; and believe me, that is not far-fetched. I believe, and I will state unilaterally, that 10 percent of the thinking of every chancellory in Europe is that maybe the Russians will win and Europe has survived for centuries because it has always tried to pick the winner.

Although in these hearings then Secretary of Defense Harold Brown emphasized the importance of disabusing the Soviets of their possible illusion that they could win, Javits seemed convinced that the Soviets did not really hold this belief. He said that "the Russian strategy, *not the belief but their strategy*, is that a nuclear war can be won" [emphasis added]. In other words, Javits perceived the Soviets as also trying to manipulate misperceiving parties. He perceived the Soviets as gaining advantages through such actions and was concerned that PD-59, though a nuclear war-fighting doctrine, was perhaps not strong enough to match the Soviets' doctrine.[1]

Intimidating the Soviets

The most frequently cited reason for projecting a belief in victory was that the Soviets would be intimidated by the impression that American leaders hold such beliefs. Many respondents felt that simply having an assured destruction capability was not adequately intimidating and was, therefore, a precarious deterrent.

When I asked respondents why they felt that the Soviets might not be deterred, their explanations centered on the fact that retaliation would actually be an irrational act. One former high-level official of the present administration said in a hushed tone, "An American president is never going to launch a nuclear attack knowing that sixty million Americans are going to die." When asked whether he thought the president *should* retaliate under such circumstances, somewhat surprisingly this respondent, a prominent hard-liner, replied that he did not. Another respondent exclaimed, throwing up his hands, "Retaliation would not be rational!" There was an implied concern that the Soviets might come to the conclusion that the United States would behave rationally when attacked, leading the Soviets to either launch an attack with aplomb or at least go to greater lengths in risking war. In fact, some seemed to feel that this latter possibility was already occurring.

The logical problem being identified here is, once again, "the paradox of deterrence." The credibility of the threat to retaliate is weakened by the fact that, for fear of counter-retaliation, one would rather not execute the threat. The threat to retaliate makes sense as long as deterrence holds. But once deterrence fails, there is no real benefit in making good on the threat. In fact, it is exceedingly probable that it will only lead to greater losses. The potential for paralysis under such circumstances has sometimes been called self-deterrence.

The concern for self-deterrence does not apply only to the threat to retaliate with nuclear weapons after a nuclear strike—it applies also to the credibility of American guarantees to escalate to the first use of nuclear weapons in the event of a conventional attack on Western Europe. The cohesion of the NATO alliance is sometimes seen as threatened by the incredibility of the American threat to "go nuclear" knowing that it might lead to nuclear attacks on American cities. Furthermore, the potential for bringing American nuclear capabilities to bear as a point of leverage in any local theater is greatly undermined by the perception that the United States would be self-deterred.

To counteract such a perception, the United States would benefit by projecting a belief that a nuclear war would not be Armageddon and that the country could, in fact, emerge from it in an advantageous position. Of course, that the Soviets can see this is not a rational belief remains a problem. Therefore, it becomes necessary to convince the Soviets that American leaders are a bit irrational.

In the late 1950s and early 1960s, this kind of thinking first emerged in defense circles. In 1959, Daniel Ellsberg, who would become an analyst at Rand and later at the Pentagon, presented a paper, "The Political Use of Madness," in which he said,

> [A leader] may refuse to believe that the objective consequences of "conflict" would be as bad as his opponent indicates. If nuclear war is at stake, he may reveal immense ("mad") confidence in his air defenses, or the effectiveness of his civil defense, or his ability to lessen the opponent's

attack by a counterforce strike. If the physical devastation is too predictable to be denied, he can diminish its significance.[2]

Thomas Schelling and Herman Kahn are most noted for developing this idea under the rubric of "the rationality of irrationality" strategy. They illustrated their point by comparing superpower relations to the game of chicken, in which teenagers drive their cars toward each other—the loser being the first to lose his nerve and veer away. In such a game, the advantage goes to the player who is perceived as, in Kahn's words, "totally reckless, oblivious to the danger or out of control."[3] The other player, convinced that his opponent will keep on a straight course no matter what, will have no choice but to veer out of the way first and lose the game.

Evidently, this kind of thinking did reach into higher levels. Robert Haldeman has described how then President Richard Nixon tried to appear irrational in an effort to give credibility to his threat to use nuclear weapons in Vietnam.

> We were walking along a foggy beach after a long day of speechwriting. He said, "I call it the Madman Theory, Bob. I want the North Vietnamese to believe I've reached the point where I might do *anything* to stop the war. We'll just slip the word to them that, 'for God's sake, you know Nixon is obsessed about Communism. We can't restrain him when he's angry—and he has his hand on the nuclear button.' "[4]

Nixon also reportedly wrote in his diary: "The North Vietnamese really thought that the President was off his rocker. . . . [I]t was absolutely essential for them to think that."[5] Later, in his book *The Real War*, Nixon explained:

> international relations are a lot like poker—stud poker with the hole card. The hole card is all-important because without it your opponent—the Soviet leader, for instance—has perfect knowledge of whether or not he can beat you. . . . The United States is an open society. We have all but one of our cards face up, on the table. Our only covered card is the will, nerve, and unpredictability of the President. . . . If the adversary feels that you are unpredictable, even rash, he will be deterred from pressing you too far. The odds that he will fold increase greatly, and the unpredictable President will win another hand.[6]

Based on my interviews, it appears that such thinking has continued in defense circles. Numerous individuals explained the value of war-winning policies in just such terms. One Pentagon analyst said:

> You might want them to think we are a little bit crazy. . . . Deterrence is enhanced by saying [changing voice], "We can achieve our objectives. We would survive, and we're not sure whether they would." . . . Because then they don't know what these crazy Americans would do.

One Rand analyst emphasized the need to appear determined to persevere whatever the consequences, using metaphors from childhood fist-fights:

> If you reduce it to crude proportions, talking about an individual in a tough neighborhood, he could go through some analysis and say, "Gee, if I really get in a fight, chances are I'm gonna get killed so I might as well not go out of my house." Or he can take the attitude that, "If anybody comes after me, I'm going to do the best I can, and by God I'm going to try to win!" Now, he still may not think the odds are very good if it really comes down to that, but if he has that attitude, he will act differently, people will act differently toward him, and the whole thing may never arise.*

Some analysts or former officials explicitly described how they would actively work to create these irrational images. One analyst described his goal of making Americans appear "wild and crazy" and imagined— with apparent delight—the effect of articles about winning nuclear wars on Soviet analysts at the Moscow Institute for the Study of the U.S.A. and Canada. He then affected a controlled, sinister tone, as if he were speaking to the Soviets, saying:

---

*Interestingly, I heard almost the exact same story from another respondent. Such stories are presumably autobiographical and offer some insight into the experiences that shape some strategic perspectives. What is striking is that when these metaphors were used, there was no attempt to address the issue of whether principles that may have been appropriate in a neighborhood of children armed with their fists could be applied to nation-states armed with nuclear weapons. However, it is not unusual for the effects of crucial, formative experiences to be immune to fundamental changes in the environment.

Over time we want to move to acquire a selective decapitation capability. We regret the necessity for using undiplomatic words like that, but hey, you guys gotta understand—there are possibilities in this world.

Near the end of the interview, he even explained how earlier he had been playing his irrational role with me when talking about the possibility of winning nuclear wars. He also credited some of his well-known hawkish friends with intentionally appearing irrational as part of an unofficial role they had designed for themselves in the service of the United States Government.

Several individuals evaluated various administrations as to how effectively they could project such an intimidating image. There was some consensus that Eisenhower was particularly effective, as in the following excerpt:

I think Eisenhower was a very shrewd president, and it's partly the Eisenhower plus the Dulles and Curtis LeMay technique—do you know what I'm saying? You point at Curtis LeMay and you wanna say, "Look, hey—listen—you know this is really a mad dog, but I keep him for those situations where I might be reluctantly compelled to unchain him. Now, you don't ever want to get me into a situation where I'm even thinking of unchaining him, but at the same time you understand that it might be necessary."

Nixon was frequently cited as playing the irrational role, but one official in his administration criticized him for this: "[Nixon was playing the] wrong role as president. He should have had a tough hombre around to play the role of the man of menace."

A recurring variation of the argument for a war-winning strategy was that it was necessary because the Soviets have such a strategy. One current Pentagon official explained that the United States must focus

. . . attention on Soviet assessments, Soviet ways of looking at things . . . that forces you directly into developing what people think of as war-fighting capabilities because that's the way the Soviets are scoring the game. . . . You have to begin thinking of wholly

163

different kinds of scenarios . . . almost situations like World War II, in the sense of early defeats, prolonged war of some sort. . . .

When I probed into why it was important to emulate the Soviets in this way, some respondents used a greater-fool argument, saying that the Soviets mistakenly believe it is possible to win and it is necessary for the United States to accommodate this misperception by projecting the same belief.

I: Do you feel we need to have a war-fighting strategy or war-fighting capability?

R: Yeah, deterrence is creating that uncertainty and doubt in the adversary. We are going to be a mirror image, our goal is to be a mirror image of what we perceive to be their doctrine and their force posture. I think we are taking steps to be that mirror image.

I: Why?

R: It comes back to deterrence . . . I think they have to perceive that we are prepared just as they are. That our goal is to prevail . . . their [nuclear weapons'] whole purpose is to create this perception that, hey, we've got to stay away from that stuff, 'cause we can't lick 'em.

I: Do you think we can lick 'em?

R: No, and I don't think they can lick us. I agree it's a self-defeating goddamn thing. . . . [But] I think that this is one of their illusions that they believe.

I: So what you're saying is that we've got to act like we've got that illusion too?

R: Or we've got to act to create that perception in their minds.

I: And we do that by acting as if we do?

R: Right. [laughter]

I: But you don't really believe we can prevail in a war?

R: I agree with you, it is senseless. I mean, what is there that's going to be left that really has any value or that is recognizable to us or to them? I mean, I'm not sure there is anything of value in what will remain.

I: But we should do what we can to develop the hardware that makes it look like we are getting ready to fight a war in which we

think we could prevail. Because that's going to have the right
psychological effect on them. Is that right?

R: As crazy as it sounds, I think so. I think so.

Oddly, he had not considered that the Soviets might also be manipula-
tively projecting such an image.

I: How do you know that the Soviets are not doing the same thing?

R: I don't [surprised laughter] . . . I don't! . . . But if that's all it
is, it sure is a waste of GNP on both sides!

A more subtle argument was that the Soviets are also consciously
projecting the intimidating image of believing in the possibility of
winning. An analyst from the Center for Strategic and International
Studies elaborated this view with some complexity:

I: Do you take it seriously when [the Soviets] talk about winning?

R: It's hard to describe the level . . . it's probably their second-level
generals and industrialists and technicians and design bureaus who
say, "Hey, look, the best way to guarantee that we have a superior
psychological exchange of pressures with the capitalists is to have
a [war-winning strategy]." . . . I would guess both sides are bluffing,
but simply the secrecy and the top-level control structure there
makes it possible to make this talk seem more plausible to a lot
of people.

Several respondents expressed some concern that the Soviets might
be able to more credibly project war-winning objectives because they
can more believably imply that they are more willing to accept damage
to populations resulting from a nuclear war. A former high-level Pentagon official stressed that the essence of the Soviet-American competition was each side's ability to project such willingness—a competition
he was not confident the United States was particularly successful in.
Whatever is in fact the case, the Soviets are perceived as more willing
to accept losses because they have a dictatorship and because under
Stalin they showed a willingness to sacrifice large portions of their
population. Herman Kahn, in his original writings on the game of
chicken, depicted the Soviets as particularly adroit in this competition:

The Soviets seem to fully appreciate the advantages of a greater willingness to risk war. For example, the reader should consider Stalin's remark to our then Ambassador Walter Bedell Smith: "We do not want war any more than the West does, but we are less interested in peace than the West, and therein lies the strength of our position."[7]

One analyst specifically credited Khrushchev with being particularly masterful at the game of chicken—something he almost admired.

There may be occasions when, indeed, it's appropriate to pull a Khrushchev line and take your shoe off, bang on the podium, and then let off a sixty-megaton bomb . . . you knew Khrushchev understood, "I've got a problem of strategic nuclear inferiority." . . . That means you've really got to get wild and crazy—but in a controlled, careful manner. You may say, "Look! I've thrown the steering wheel out the window."*

The Double Image

Projecting the image that one believes in the possibility of winning a nuclear war presents some distinct problems. While one may want to present this intimidating image to the Soviets, it was simultaneously seen as important not to terrorize the American public or the European allies with the impression that American leaders might be too willing to launch a nuclear war.

This problem was raised spontaneously by several individuals. They pointed out that it was necessary to present a kind of double image— one for each audience. One analyst referred to this as a "two-track" approach. A former high-level Pentagon official explained:

You're always dealing with contradictory audiences. At the same time you want to persuade the Soviets that there's an absolute certainty that if they cross the Elbe that they are going to get caught, you want to persuade the American and the European

*This is a reference to an idea developed by Herman Kahn, in which he suggested that one could improve one's chances in the game of chicken by throwing one's steering wheel out the window.

audience that war with nuclear weapons will never be waged
. . . there are inherent contradictions if you want to appear gentle
and thoughtful to your own public, and tough—and just a touch
irrational—to your adversary.

He went on to say, "You usually do that with two personalities, and
you kind of move them forward or back depending on the circumstances." When another former Pentagon official was asked about the
United States having such inconsistencies in its war aims, he said
emphatically, "We have to! I've never heard of a nation that didn't.
Can you imagine one that doesn't have a discrepancy of that sort? I
can't. [laughter] Everybody—come on!"

Making the problem even more complex, it is also seen as necessary
to present a double image to the American audience. To maintain the
favor of the more hard-line constituency, leaders must project the belief
that they can win. A former high-level Pentagon official explained that
there is "a basic constituency" that "want[s] to know that in the event
of a nuclear war that America would prevail." At the same time, there
is a major constituency that wants to be assured that leaders do not even
contemplate such possibilities. Another former Pentagon official respondent explained, "Politicians play to various audiences and they're
always saying things for effect—all kinds of things. They speak with
forked tongue so they say all sorts of inconsistent things."

This object of presenting a dual image may have been what led
George Bush into making a flap in the 1980 election campaign. An
interview with Bush by Robert Scheer, which was published in the *Los
Angeles Times*, included the following segment:

SCHEER: Don't you reach a point with these strategic weapons
where we can wipe each other out so many times, and no one
wants to use them or be willing to use them, that it doesn't really
matter whether you're 10 percent or 2 percent lower or higher?

BUSH: Yes, if you believe there is no such thing as a winner in a
nuclear exchange, that argument makes a little sense. I don't
believe that.

SCHEER: How do you win a nuclear exchange?

BUSH: You have a survivability of command and control, survivability of industrial potential, protection of a percentage of your

citizens, and you have a capability that inflicts more damage on the opposition than it can inflict upon you. That's the way you can have a winner, and the Soviets' planning is based on the ugly concept of a winner in a nuclear exchange.[8]

When this interview was published in the *Los Angeles Times* with a headline to the effect that Bush believed in the possibility of winning a nuclear war, it created an uproar. Bush, however, immediately called a press conference and explained that he had not said that *he* believed that a nuclear war could be won but that the *Soviets* did. In a rereading of the interview passage, it becomes immediately clear that Bush did say that he believed a nuclear war could be won. Why did he then deny it? It is possible that in a moment of inattention he revealed his deeper beliefs and then tried to cover them up later. It is also possible that he was trying to project a double image—each for a different constituency. After the uproar, those who believe that nuclear war can be won are left believing that Bush inwardly really does believe this too (otherwise why would he have said it in the first place?), while those who do not believe a nuclear war can be won place more credence in his later denial because they see that as the only sensible view he could possibly hold (after all, Bush isn't crazy).

Going a step further, it is possible that this double-image approach also addresses internal "constituencies" within each individual. Just as defense analysts and policymakers at times seem to have two semi-autonomous mindsets—one conventional, the other nuclear—so may members of the public. There may also be different motivations associated with each mindset—for example, one more oriented to security, the other to competition. As people in the advertising industry know well, it is very possible to simultaneously speak to and even gratify highly disparate parts of the personality. If effectively done, each sub-personality will respond to the messages that it finds gratifying and that confirm its world view.

Apparent Confusion

In a variety of cases, when respondents discussed the concept of advantageous termination, they appeared confused about what they were trying to say. This may have arisen from genuine confusion or a failure to think through the subject. It may be part of the desired effect of the double-image approach just described. It may also have been derived from the psychological effects on the policymaker of the double-image approach. As discussed in the previous chapter, when people express attitudes, they tend to take them on even if they did not originally hold them. This can become quite problematic when the individual is called on to project a subtle double image consisting of contrary beliefs. In the course of executing such a double image, an individual may become confused about what he actually believes.

Such apparent confusion appeared regularly when I asked members of the present administration to explain the policy of seeking to prevail in a nuclear war. To account for it, they shifted between presenting perceptual rationales in support of it, drastically redefining the word *prevail* to mean something quite different from its standard meaning, and denying that the word was ever used to describe American objectives.

In one interview, the respondent—a high-level START negotiator—initially defined *prevail* as not using force, practically inverting its real meaning.

 I: We've talked about aiming to terminate on terms favorable to the United States; we've talked about prevailing in a nuclear war. What do those terms mean to you?

 R: The terms mean that we want to try to relegate negotiations to peaceful means, and particularly nuclear force—that we'd want to stop that. And we want to try to negotiate settlements which are acceptable to both sides.

I then pressed him:

 I: But don't we have war-fighting plans in the event that deterrence fails?

R: We've got all sorts of contingency plans. Those are plans which have to look at what happens if deterrence fails, but their primary object is to be sure that we have capabilities and plans to use those capabilities so that deterrence doesn't fail. It all comes back to deterrence.

Assuming that he was now talking about a perception-management rationale, I asked:

Given that everything comes back to deterrence, does that mean that when we talk about prevailing that we are in some way trying to enhance deterrence?
R: Sure—

But then, in midsentence, he abruptly denied that we ever even use the term:

—I don't know if we ever talk about prevailing. As a matter of fact, we say that a nuclear war should never be fought because it can't be won.

When I reminded him of statements by Secretary Weinberger, he went back to trying to modify the definition:

I: Caspar Weinberger said any secretary of defense who didn't have the intention of prevailing in a nuclear war should be impeached.
R: Well, I guess it's a question of how you interpret *prevailing*—what's *prevailing* mean?
I: The dictionary says it means winning.
R: Well, maybe, but if you say the opposite—that it's not losing, then that's a definition that you want to succeed. And if you've had some perjorative or extreme view of *prevailing*, that we want to put these people under the heel or bomb them into submission or bomb them back in the Stone Age or something, that's not so, and that's not prevailing if somebody wants to look at that as an interpretation.

A presidential advisor also asserted his right to define the term in his own way:

> R: What it means to prevail is to have the ability to protect our most cherished values and political objectives and goals. And that includes at least our own territorial and political integrity, and our sovereignty, and to the extent possible that of areas over which we feel we have a vital interest.
>
> I: That's not quite the dictionary definition of *prevail*. *Prevail* refers to a certain impact that you have on the aggressor as well, in the sense that you—
>
> R: [sharply] You asked for my definition; you didn't ask me for a dictionary definition.

Weinberger has also used this method of blurring meanings to smooth over an apparent contradiction. Some months after the 1982 Defense Guidance Statement was leaked to the *New York Times,* in a published exchange of letters with Theodore Draper, he wrote, "[There is no] contradiction between our view that there could be no winners in a nuclear war and our planning to prevail, if war is forced upon us, in denying victory to the Soviet Union."[9] This apparent contradiction is momentarily offset by defining *prevail* as meaning simply denying victory to the Soviets—a definition that does not accord with the plans described in the Defense Guidance Statement or the dictionary.

A high-level Pentagon official in the present administration initially candidly described the double-image strategy of projecting to the Soviets a belief in the possibility of prevailing and to the public a denial of such a belief. Discussing Secretary Weinberger's use of the term *prevailing* to describe United States nuclear war-time objectives, he said:

> I think the term was not a wrong term to use. It was an appropriate term because it's a term that . . . will contribute more to deterrence and never having to use these weapons than being vague about what your goals would be . . . it's a reflection of strength.

At the same time, though, it's necessary to project a different image to the Western public:

> Frankly, I think [Weinberger] has to be first and foremost concerned about public interpretation of what he says, and no administration wants to be thought of as trying to make nuclear wars as opposed to making deterrence because everyone gets upset—our allies in particular get upset.

However, at another point in the discussion he seemed to be confused about whether such objectives were militarily feasible or simply useful as declaratory policy. When he spoke of an advantageous outcome within a vaguely defined scenario, it was not clear whether he was saying that this would be derived from actual battlefield events or the political leverage derived from more ambitious war objectives.

I: So when you say "an advantage," you're not referring to a military advantage or militarily derived advantage?

R: Oh, no—not necessarily. Right—a militarily derived advantage, right. No, not necessarily militarily derived.

I: Could it be militarily derived?

R: It could be, but we're talking about things that are so—

I: I know, but—

R: I know, I know!

Somewhat frazzled, he changed course abruptly, denying that the United States has a policy of seeking to prevail: "But we don't have such a policy!" At other points in the interview, though, he did speak of the goal of "prevailing," and described the United States warfighting objective as one that leaves the adversary in "a less favorable" position.

Sometimes this double image came up in response to the question of whether the United States should pursue superiority in its nuclear arsenal. Respondents who advocated war-winning objectives sometimes made statements that the United States should pursue arms control agreements based on the principle of parity. In the interviews I tried to point out that pursuing equality was not entirely consistent with the goal of prevailing in a conflict. This sometimes produced apparent confusion. For example, a foreign policy aide to a prominent prode-fense senator first embraced the goal of prevailing in a nuclear war. I then asked:

> So we need to have the armaments to prevail, which means we need superiority?
> R: Not necessarily.
> I: How would we prevail then?
> R: By superiority. We need to have that one last remaining pill.

When a former Rand analyst described the goal of prevailing, I said,

> So you're saying that we have to choose superiority in our arsenal?
> R: Well, it's not superiority.
> I: But if after an exchange we come out ahead, that's superior.
> R: . . . Okay, if you include better, smarter, quicker, blah-blah-blah, not necessarily more—you've got to be superior. That's right.
> I: Now, do you think the Soviets are going to accept that?
> R: Hell, no . . .
> I: Are you supportive of the idea of us having treaties based on parity?
> R: Sure, I think it's very important . . . equality is the way to go. There's no question.

But when I tried to find out how the United States could prevail without superiority, he implicitly dismissed the whole concept of pre-vailing.

In some cases, it seemed that perception-management rationales created substantial confusion as to what the United States should actually do in the event of a war. For example, a former member of the National Security Council began a statement with the apparent intention of answering what the United States should do if deterrence fails and nuclear war begins. However, before he reached the end of the sentence, he illogically shifted to talking about making a certain impact on Soviet thinking before a war.

> If you actually get down to using nuclear weapons, God help us, it seems that everything we try to do . . . ought to be designed to

convince the Soviets never to do anything which might result in [a nuclear war].

When I pressed him, he did say that the United States does have advantage-seeking war-fighting objectives. But here again he showed confusion, this time quite openly, about the real meaning of these policies. I asked him: "How much are these war-winning policies declaratory and how much are they action policies?" His answer was remarkably candid and summarizes what is perhaps the most central problem with perception-management approaches. After a long pause, he said slowly and somewhat quizzically, "I don't even know if we know that ourselves, really. I'm really not sure." It is worth noting that this individual is quite prominent and from the highest levels of government. If there is any certain knowledge about what United States policy "really is," presumably he would have it. His uncertainty, then, may not only reflect his individual uncertainty but rather general confusion even at the highest levels—a confusion that is apparently enhanced by strategies ostensibly designed to manipulate perceptions.*

The Problem of Side Effects

Setting aside the question of what American war aims in fact are and even assuming that policymakers have enough self-awareness to execute a double-image strategy effectively, there is still a problem with this strategy. Here again, the problem arises from the fact that efforts at perceptual manipulation have side effects that cannot necessarily be controlled.

A key problem with the double-image strategy is that each image or message designed for one audience has a problematic side effect of sending the same message to another audience for whom it is not intended. Both audiences will often hear both statements.

To some extent this problem can be controlled by accounting for the

*This observation is not meant to imply that leaders should necessarily decide in advance what they will do in response to Soviet aggression. What I am pointing to is the fact that leaders harbor some confusion about what they mean when they say what they will do.

"other" statement. This can be done by implicitly projecting a reason for making the other statement. To the Soviets and to the hawkish constituency an American leader can, in effect, say, "I really do believe I could win a nuclear war; I just sometimes say I don't to please my allies and my dovish constituency." To the allies and the dovish constituency he can, in effect, say, "I don't really believe I can win a nuclear war; I just say I do sometimes to intimidate the Soviets and to keep the hawks happy." Such a multileveled statement has a kind of effect on the mind similar to the famous logic problem depicted below:

The statement on the other side of this line is false.	The statement on the other side of this line is false.

Perhaps it is because of this disorienting effect that policymakers can make such apparently contradictory statements without people fully noticing.

However, there are still messages being communicated that cannot be controlled. The Soviets and the hawkish constituency hear statements that war-winning policies are disingenuously designed to impress them and may then dismiss it as a mere bluff. Allies and dovish constituencies hear discussions of the need to assuage public opinion and they dismiss the discounting of war-winning policies as window dressing. There is no way to prevent all audiences involved from hearing both messages. Therefore, once again, it is possible that side effects of perceptual manipulations result in the net value of all such efforts being zero.

Furthermore this assessment does not take into account other potential costs to security that a war-winning declaratory policy incurs. To the extent that the Soviets are intimidated in the way that the perceptual strategy wishes them to be, this may well lead them to take counteractive steps. It may encourage the Soviets to build more countersilo and counter-command-and-control weapons to make it more difficult for the U.S. to execute a war-winning effort. Even if the Soviets do not believe it is possible for the United States to win, they may feel a need to disabuse American leaders of such notions by building more such weapons (a line of thought the Soviets I interviewed did in fact present, as we shall see in chapter 12). Such developments create a less stable strategic environment and are marginally harmful to American security interests, as American policymakers (including those who support a war-winning policy) will easily recognize. However, such concerns do not seem to lead these policymakers to reevaluate the war-winning policy.

CHAPTER 8

The Perceptual Value of
Hard-Target Kill Capability

AS DISTINGUISHED FROM the rationales based on military force considerations discussed in chapter 5, interview respondents frequently offered rationales for hard-target kill-capable weapons that emphasize their value in terms of the manipulation of perceptions. These perceptual rationales fall into two key types. One is that building hard-target kill-capable weapons refines American escalatory options and thereby enhances the credibility of American threats to use nuclear weapons. The second is that building hard-target-capable weapons enhances American destructive capability, which is necessary for accommodating certain Soviet delusions and idiosyncrasies. We will first explore these rationales separately; second, how they enter into conflict with each other; third, how they enter into conflict with other rationales; and finally, how some respondents attempted to resolve the apparent conflicts by cultivating a kind of double image.

Developing Limited War Options to Enhance Credibility

A theme that appeared in several contexts in the interviews and appears repeatedly throughout the defense literature is the concern that American threats to use nuclear weapons are not credible. As discussed above, this problem arises from the paradoxical character of nuclear deterrence, particularly in the NATO context—the fact that once deterrence fails, one would rather not execute the threat of escalatory nuclear response for fear of counter-retaliation. We have already seen how defense intellectuals have sought to enhance the credibility of the United States threat to retaliate by projecting the belief that the United States leadership believes it can win a nuclear war.

Closely related to this latter approach is the idea that American credibility would be enhanced by making it appear that a nuclear war could stay limited to military targets. To create such perceptions, the United States should build hard-target-capable weapons that would be appropriate for such a scenario. A strategic analyst explained,

> [We] want some hard-target kill capability so we can at least threaten—not totally incredibly—to engage in limited war-fighting . . . to the extent . . . that strengthens deterrence.

A former high-level Pentagon official elaborated on the underlying framework:

> I think it is true that if you really think you're going to cause a nuclear winter that would lead to death of all life on the globe that that means that deterrence is zero because nobody's ever going to do that. . . . [But by being able to] do something which isn't so obviously self-destructive . . . that makes [the threat] more credible.*

These same respondents, however, clarified that they did not take such limited war-fighting scenarios seriously. The formerly quoted analyst went on to explain that he felt this perspective was present on both sides.

> If you asked a different question—how are these calculations [of relative war-fighting capabilities] likely to be regarded in the kind of crisis in which there is even a small possibility of nuclear

---

*Glenn H. Snyder and Paul Diesing make a similar point, in *Conflict Among Nations,* that to "increase credibility," one can "reduce one's apparent net cost of war" by effectively saying, "We believe the war will be limited." (Princeton, N.J.: Princeton University Press, 1977, 199)

weapons being used—then I suspect the answer is that on both sides the political leadership will be extremely skeptical of these calculations in terms of (a) their own forces working as advertised, and (b) any of these more esoteric scenarios playing out.

A former member of the National Security Council also indicated that the value of countersilo capabilities was not based on a plausible war-fighting scenario.

R: If we have countersilo capability it seems to me [the Soviets] can plausibly come to the conclusion that we'd use it if the circumstance were right. Now they might be able to launch all out from under it . . . but at least it would make sense for us to attack. . . .

I: Is it that we have scenarios within which we might do that or that we want them simply to have the perception that we would have the capability and then that would have an intimidating effect?

R: I have trouble generating scenarios because you can't generate a scenario for nuclear war that is not implausible.

Some respondents did not articulate the relatively sophisticated concept of credibility enhancement but, nevertheless, presented an argument that was basically the same. For example, a member of the Senate Armed Services Committee explained the value of war-fighting plans and capabilities in terms of the "perception" they create in the Soviet mind that the United States believes that it can limit damage through limiting escalation. Noting that he consistently omitted any reference to the real war-fighting purposes of the weapons, I asked him directly,

To what extent are we trying to intimidate them . . . and to what extent do we really think we're going to limit damage [in a war]?

R: [smiling] I think the emphasis, or the realities, is more on the former than the latter.

While this kind of argument was most often presented in terms of the Soviets as the critical perceiving audience, in some cases allies were emphasized. Concern was expressed that an asymmetry in capabilities that support escalation control scenarios would lead to bandwagoning. A foreign policy aide to a prominent prodefense senator explained:

R: We've gone beyond this minimal deterrent because we're into this area now called escalation control.

I: Overall do you think [this doctrine is] based on realistic scenarios or that they're, again, [referring to an earlier comment of his] part of projecting a certain image of determination on our part?

R: I think it's image, posture. To prevent this coercion, if the West Germans feel or if the Japanese feel that the Soviet Union has such a predominant superiority over us, then they're going to— just to save their ass—tilt here and they're going to do this and that. So we've got to maintain a strong posture to maintain the status quo and all this.

A related rationale for hard-target kill capability is based on the idea that the Soviet Union has a unique means for measuring American resolve to escalate. This idea appeared in an unrecorded interview with a defense analyst. His rationale for hard-target kill capability was that it is necessary for countersilo purposes as an escalatory response to a conventional invasion of Europe. The United States would want to strike at something other than a countervalue target, not to achieve damage limitation but as a "gesture" that would have the desired amount of intensity to show United States resolve. When asked whether the United States has targeting options other than counter-value and countersilos, he said that the United States does but silos are uniquely impressive to the Soviets. But, again, this impressive quality arises from the nature of the gesture and not from any significant diminution of Soviet military capability that would be effected by the gesture.

He went on to say that it is also important to have a countersilo response to a Soviet countersilo attack. If the Soviets think that the United States could not respond in kind, they might think the United States would not respond. He agreed that even without hard-target kill capability, the United States would have many options for striking military targets—just not hardened ones. I then asked why the Soviets would think we might not respond. He answered that they "might" think this way and we must guard against that possibility. When asked

if he would see things this way if he were in Soviet shoes, he equivocated but then basically said no. When I probed into why he attributed
such reasoning to the Soviets, he did not offer any supportive evidence
but shrugged and said that "we might as well" guard against this
possibility and "there's no reason not to."

Asked whether there are any tradeoffs in our having hard-target kill
capability, he replied that there is always the risk of it leading the
Soviets to think that escalation to general war would be certain because
they would have to use or lose their missiles. He implied that he
thought the potential Soviet perception that hard-target-capable weapons would make escalation to general war more likely was more reasonable than the potential Soviet view that deploying hard-target-capable
weapons was a gesture of American resolve. Nevertheless he concluded
that having hard-target-capable weapons was esssential as a gesture of
American resolve.

Enhancing Destructiveness to Accommodate Soviet
Delusions and Idiosyncrasies

There were two rationales for hard-target kill capability based on the
need to structure American forces to accommodate spurious or idiosyncratic Soviet beliefs and attitudes about nuclear war.* The first rationale addressed the purported Soviet belief that they could attain escalation dominance in an intermediate-range or strategic nuclear war. The
second addressed idiosyncratic attitudes or spurious beliefs Soviet leaders may have about the consequences of a large-scale nuclear war.

ESCALATION DOMINANCE

The concern that the Soviet Union might incorrectly believe it has
the capability to achieve escalation dominance was a major rationale for
deploying hard-target capable weapons. Briefly stated, this argument is
that because the Soviets have an advantage on at least two rungs on
the ladder of escalation—intermediate- and strategic-range counter-

---

*Spurious beliefs and attitudes are those that respondents regard as patently false. Idiosyn-
cratic beliefs and attitudes are seen as arising from unique personal or national characteristics and,
while not necessarily spurious, are generally not the ones that respondents say they hold.

force (both involving hard-target kill capability)—they might believe that in a war they could escalate to the level where they could achieve an advantageous position and then force the United States to choose to escalate to the next higher level. Faced with the prospect of a painful counter-retaliation at the next higher level, the United States might refrain from escalating and accept humiliation. Filling in American capabilities at these rungs on the ladder of escalation would counteract such a Soviet belief. A current middle-level Pentagon official illustrated this kind of thinking in his rationale for current deployments:

> I would say that the principle thing we're trying to do is to influence the Soviet leadership—primarily the political leadership, but also the military leadership—into believing that no option for aggression looks attractive. If you are a Soviet planner, you believe that you have some option at some sort of intermediate level of violence of force, that the U. S. has no appropriate counter, then you may well believe that you can recommend that option to your leadership, and the leadership may believe that the risks are low enough, that the U. S. could not respond. That is, that having only responses of a major scale, which would entail the immediate initiation of Armageddon, that we couldn't respond. By building in flexibility to our forces and to our plans, we seek to convince the Soviet planner that for every option he comes up with we do have an appropriate counter.

This kind of thinking was used in support of deploying the MX and D-5 missile systems for responding to the potential for a strategic counterforce attack. The scenario most commonly cited was the window of vulnerability. According to this scenario, if the Soviets were to make an all-out counterforce strike, the United States—because it lacks invulnerable counterforce capabilities—would be forced into either surrendering or escalating to countervalue attacks. The middle-level Pentagon official explained:

> We were concerned that the Soviets might think that by hardening their silos and developing the first-strike capability they have against our Minuteman force, that they could come up with a large but nevertheless less-than-all-out attack against the U. S.

ICBM force and that, lacking weapons with sufficient yield and accuracy to go back against similar targets in the Soviet Union, we would be deterred from responding in any way. Clearly, rebuilding the capability to threaten their nuclear forces credibly gives us back a military response against this potential Soviet move.

A former member of the National Security Council made the same basic point in his analysis of Soviet thinking:

> I think you have to assume that because of MIRVing* that they would send out a first strike with a small portion of their forces. A part of the SS-18 force could destroy, theoretically, our whole Minuteman force. It would make sense only to them if they could then inhibit an American retaliatory strike by threatening a devastating countervalue strike—a ghoulish scheme . . . All the Americans have left is 15, 20 percent of a countervalue force, which you can neutralize by simply saying, you are going to be destroyed, wiped off the face of the earth.

This kind of thinking was also used in support of the Pershing IIs and GLCMs. Concern was expressed that because NATO did not have intermediate-range missiles, the Soviets might think they could use their intermediate-range SS-20s in support of a conventional advance into Europe. They might be tempted to use their SS-20s as part of a first strike against European nuclear weapons. They might think the United States would refrain from responding because the only available response would be to escalate to strategic weapons—something, again, the United States might prefer not to do for fear of the consequences of further retaliation. Whatever the actual outcome in the event of a war, the Soviets might in the present be so certain that they could get the United States to relinquish Europe that they would become overly confident and rash. Harold Brown wrote in 1980:

> With these new and more accurate weapons [SS-20s], the Soviets might make the mistaken judgment that they could threaten our allies without

*The term *MIRVing* refers to the addition of multiple independent re-entry vehicles (MIRVs) to ballistic missiles, so that a single ballistic missile, instead of delivering just one warhead, would be able to deliver several warheads, each independently targeted.

fear of retaliatory attacks on their territory. . . . To avoid any such error of perception, we are proceeding with the development of . . . the PERSHING II and the Ground-Launched Cruise Missile.[1]

It was rarely flatly stated that the Soviet belief that they could effectively win a limited intermediate or strategic counterforce war was a delusion or derived from idiosyncratic assumptions. Nevertheless this was clearly implied. First, it was frequently stated that it would be impossible to keep a nuclear war limited and, sometimes, that anybody who thought so was crazy. Second, it was sometimes recognized that in the event of a Soviet counterforce attack, the United States would in fact have response options of a counterforce nature even if it did not have hard-target-capable weapons, because many Soviet military targets are soft. Third, in the case of strategic counterforce it was also recognized that the United States already had survivable hard-target kill capability (before deploying the D-5) in the form of cruise missiles. (There were complaints that cruise missiles were not prompt, but no one explained why this would lead the Soviets to believe the United States would not counter with them in response to a strategic counterforce attack.) However, all such considerations were easily shrugged off with the statement that, nonetheless, the Soviets might perceive a usable advantage for themselves unless the United States has a survivable response that is both hard-target capable and prompt.

I sometimes asked if the concern was simply that the Soviets could, in theory, hold such beliefs or if there is also reason to believe they in fact do now. Some said that there is a possibility that the Soviets might think this way now and that, if not, they might get such ideas. In either case the United States must act to "deter" such thinking. Others were more certain that the Soviet Union does think this way now, that such escalation-dominance goals have been foremost in their minds for many years now, and that it has shaped their force deployments. When I asked for evidence of this, the responses were a little thin. They pointed to the fact that the Soviets have developed such extensive counterforce-capable weapons, that many of their weapons are in vulnerable silos (suggesting that they are meant for first-strike purposes), and that their strategic doctrine has eschewed countervalue targeting in favor of counterforce targeting. I pointed out that the United States also has vulnerable counterforce weapons, that it eschews countervalue targeting, and that the preponderance of ICBMs in the Soviet arsenal can largely be attributed to geography. The only response this produced was frustration with my inability to correctly perceive Soviet intentions. I also pointed out that Soviet doctrine explicitly rejects notions of limited war. This was dismissed as propaganda despite the fact that Soviet doctrinal rejection of countervalue targeting had previously been used as supportive evidence.*

The next question, then, is how building more hard-target kill capability will effectively counter the Soviet belief that it can achieve escalation dominance. The dominant argument was that building such weapons would make it clearer to the Soviets that any limited conflict they would start would inevitably escalate. Such thinking was applied to the INF weapons, as in the explanation of a former high-level Pentagon official that the purpose of such weapons was not to keep a war limited to Europe but "without using central strategic systems, to attack targets in Soviet territory." A former member of the National Security Council staff explained with a mechanical cadence that the INF missiles would be at the site of the European battle, thus ensuring that they would be struck at, thus ensuring that they would be fired against Soviet territory, thus ensuring that the Soviets would strike against the United States, and thus ensuring that the United States would use its central strategic forces. A current middle-level Pentagon official affirmed, "The United States has said repeatedly that we do not

---

*Although the overriding explanation for Soviet belief in their potential for achieving escalation dominance rested on the assumption that the Soviets' judgment was distorted, another image of Soviet thinking may have been operating. No one articulated it, but my sense was that some individuals who refrained from elaborating on Soviet thinking may have assumed that the Soviets themselves were carrying out a subtle perceptual manipulation. By projecting the false belief that they can achieve escalation dominance, the Soviets could intimidate the United States. Soviet disclaiming of such beliefs could even strengthen the desired perception because that is what they would want to do if they, in fact, did believe that they could achieve escalation dominance (because otherwise the United States would counter this option through new deployments). Possibly no one articulated such an idea either because it would sound too implausible or was too difficult to spell out. But there is an image of strategic behavior, which has been developed throughout the defense literature, suggesting that a player might, in fact, have such a convoluted strategy. The net effect might be that some policymakers and strategists would feel a need to guard against a particularly clever Soviet strategy while they cannot clearly articulate the strategy they are guarding against.

seek to confine a nuclear war to Europe." A Rand analyst described the INF weapons as "a sort of fuse to bring other larger American weapons in." And a member of the Senate Armed Services Committee staff explained that the purpose of the Pershing IIs and GLCMs is "to make sure we get hurt" so that we will then necessarily escalate.

The MX was also cited as a means for ensuring that the Soviets would perceive that a counterforce strike would lead to escalation. The ability of the MX to strike silos and command and control centers was seen as a means of enhancing the perception that the escalation process would go out of control. The probability that the Soviets would launch out from under incoming MX warheads was not seen as a problem but as part of the desired perceptual effect. It emphasizes to the Soviets that a counterforce exchange would necessarily escalate to a general war. A current middle-level Pentagon official explained:

> If you're a Soviet planner and you want to avoid general nuclear war, you don't want to face a situation in which you would launch a strike and then be faced with launching or losing your silo-based reserve within a matter of thirty minutes. What MX does is it forces the Soviets to realize that the silo-based reserve will no longer be there—that is to say that if you start with a counterforce strike, you will shortly be pushed into general nuclear war so you don't start with a counterforce strike in the first place. . . . We would deny them the option of withholding a significant portion of their ICBM force.

A strategic analyst went a bit further and explained that the MX is also important because it increases the certainty that the American president would react angrily. Because ICBMs can be fired more quickly than other systems, the president would not have time to think. If the president did have "time for sober thought," it might give him a "cooling-off period" and "in a situation like that [he] might say it's enough."*

*Colin Gray has made a similar point: "Flexibility, per se, carries few advantages. Indeed, if the flexibility is very substantial and if the enemy agrees tacitly to a fairly slow pace of competitive escalation, it provides noteworthy time for the self-deterrence process to operate." (in Robert Jervis, *The Illogic of American Nuclear Strategy* [Ithaca, N.Y.: Cornell University Press, 1984], 84)

The Perceptual Value of Hard-Target Kill Capability

A former Rand analyst formulated the theoretical perspective under-lying this general emphasis on the need to assure escalation:

> We're going to create a world with . . . each step of the escalatory ladder [such] that there is only one choice for the Soviet Union, and that's massive total attack or none. . . . You want a situation where, if it starts at the lowest level it's responded at the lowest level . . . because it deters them from attacking at that low level. It says there's no gain at a low level. So when you guys pencil it out, don't pencil out the onesie-twosies, don't pencil out the potential coercion at one hundred here [gesticulating as if he is moving up an imaginary escalation ladder]. Might as well go back to the big correlation of forces because there's never going to be even a thought because at each step whatever you would try to do to say [speaking as if a Soviet], "Hey, we don't want to go to the big thing, no. But there's this little one that maybe we could do that would give us an added . . . no, damn it! They have a capability that would respond to that. But how about moving up here? Same thing. So that's the only thing it'll get is just top-level stuff." And the reason they would look top-level is because they're matched all the way down.
>
> If they look down and there's a big gap, they might go, "Hmmm. If we threaten this move, his only credible response is up here. That means he's going to have to eat what's back up here because we've got them all the steps [in between]." . . . leading the Soviet to say, "You can either accept the stepping on your toe and like it or be coerced or you can bash me and I could bash you right back." . . .

In order to focus attention on the top line, you have to have an appropriate response at each and every step in between. If you don't have an appropriate response at each step intermediate to the totality, then you create not an interest at the top line but at the gap. That's where the attention is focused because now there is an alternative for which there is an advantage that could be gained, for which the only response on the part of the United States is one that is at a much higher level of escalation. That little

gap down there is going to draw your attention. If all gaps are
plugged, then you look at the totality. And we want them to look
at the totality so we plug each gap along the way.

A former middle-level Pentagon official put it more succinctly.

I: Do we want the Soviets to think that a nuclear war could be
     controlled?
R: . . . We want the Soviets to think that a nuclear war will be an
     unmitigated disaster . . . because that helps deterrence.

SOVIET BELIEFS AND ATTITUDES ABOUT LOSSES

Another set of arguments for hard-target kill capability stressed that
such weapons were necessary to counter spurious Soviet beliefs and
idiosyncratic attitudes about their potential losses in the event of a
nuclear war. The central concern was that their beliefs and attitudes
about the costs to them of a nuclear war might lead them to not be
deterred from aggression. Hard-target kill capability was seen as a
means of strengthening the perception that they would indeed suffer
unacceptable losses.

A key argument was that the Soviets have the mistaken belief that
their civil defense efforts will greatly reduce their population losses. A
high-level arms control negotiator explained:

I think they would say, and they do say, that their civil defense
programs and the one percent of their gross national product
which they put into civil defense and the several hundred thousand people they have in their civil defense program would protect
them so much that they could absorb anything that we had to
launch at them and "only suffer twelve to sixteen million casualties," which they suffered in World War II and therefore is
tolerable. They would not want to suffer those, but if necessary
they would sacrifice these to protect Mother Russia. I don't believe that their civil defense figures have any validity to them.*
That's, again, not what we think—it's what they think.

*I do not know what figures he was referring to nor why he had earlier intoned the 12- to
16-million figure as if he was quoting some source.

Closely related was the argument that the Soviets do recognize that they would suffer major population losses, but that they have the idiosyncratic attitude that this would be acceptable. Therefore, as long as they can protect their leadership, they might not be deterred and may still believe they can win an all-out nuclear war. For example, when a senator was asked whether the Soviets think they can win a nuclear war, he answered:

> I don't think that in the normal sense we think about winning . . . But you've got a different mentality, which I can't describe. We would consider it unacceptable—surviving—if we had 80 percent of the country devastated and 60 percent of the population killed, and we preserved our leadership and said, "We will rebuild from here." That would not be winning in our terms. But in their terms, I think they see that as a winnable situation; they lost twenty million people in World War II.

Some respondents elaborated on why the Soviets have such willingness to accept these losses. Usually it was attributed to unique features of the Russian character.

> I: What is it about them that makes them willing to put their population at risk to such a great extent?
> R: Well, in addition to the whole Russian traditional heritage, which is very different from our own in looking at the individual, it's a totalitarian system. And those systems aren't well known to put the lives and safety and creature comforts and security of their people, per se, at the highest level of priority.

In some cases these explanations were given with a tone that conveyed a curious mixture of admiration and disdain, as in the following reply:

> They have a history of storming; that is, like the great collectivization drives, like putting the missiles in, like the purges, of trying to overcome structural difficulties. There's a very interesting history [of doing things] by storm . . . really macho. And when you plan your move . . . you don't wait for invisible market forces like some

damned pansy. So if they felt their system was threatened, they then might launch a strike in order to conserve it.

Deploying hard-target kill capability was seen as a way of countering these spurious beliefs and idiosyncratic attitudes. In some cases the assumption seemed to be that despite the Soviets' misconception that in a major war they would suffer minor loses to population, they would correctly perceive that they would lose their protected weapons, comand-and-control capabilities, and leadership, and thus would be deterred. In other cases the assumption seemed to be that despite their unusual willingness to suffer major losses to their population, the possibility of losing their protected assets would give them pause.

Closely related to this latter argument was the assumption that the Soviets place an idiosyncratically high level of value on their military weapons. A high-level Pentagon official spoke of "the value placed so heavily upon military capabilities" in "the Soviet scheme of things," using as evidence the fact that "they have invested so vigorously in [military capabilities]." Paul Nitze, in a 1976 *Foreign Affairs* article, expressed concern that the Soviets might even initiate a large-scale nuclear war with the goal of improving their advantage in the relative throw-weights of the nuclear arsenals. He argued that "such a counter-force strategy appears to fit with Soviet ways of thinking and planning."[2] Harold Brown, in his FY 1982 Report to Congress, wrote, "Because the Soviets may define victory in part in terms of the overall post-war military balance, we will give special attention . . . [to] targeting of the full range of military capabilities."[3]

This emphasis on targeting Soviet weaponry was frequently justified in terms of the need to "threaten what the Soviets most value." By stressing that the issue was what the *Soviets* most value, respondents did not feel a need to explain how the target in question was intrinsically valuable or would be valuable to a rational actor. There was also usually little felt need to give evidence for these valuations. Hard-target kill capability was seen as a hedge against the possibility that the Soviets might make such valuations.

In a way, this argument is similar to the one given for a response to the possibility that the Soviets might believe they can achieve escalation dominance. In both cases the concern is that the Soviets might believe there is some way to meaningfully limit the damage of a nuclear war. Hard-target kill capability is, then, meant to sternly neutralize such Soviet fatuity.

Conflicting Objectives

So far, we have examined two general rationales for hard-target kill capability, both of which involve the strategic manipulation of perceptions. The stated objectives of these rationales not only are quite different but even enter into conflict. One rationale seeks through improved hard-target kill capability to create the perception that, because of the increased flexibility granted by hard-target-capable weapons, a nuclear war is more likely to be kept limited. This is desirable because it enhances the credibility of American threats. The other rationale sees improved hard-target kill capability as a means of creating the perception that a nuclear war is more likely to go out of control and be generally annihilating. This is desirable because it counters potential Soviet beliefs and attitudes about the possibility of surviving or winning a nuclear war. By being more afraid of nuclear war, the Soviets will then be more deterred from taking potentially provocative actions. These rationales enter into conflict because each incremental increase in the Soviet perception of the probability of limitation will, theoretically, incrementally increase the credibility of American threats to use nuclear weapons but will decrease the Soviet fear of nuclear war. Each incremental increase in the Soviet perception that a nuclear war will be annihilating will incrementally increase Soviet fears of nuclear war but will decrease the credibility of American threats to use nuclear weapons. An asset on one side of the ledger is a deficit on the other.

One could argue that it is not necessary to resolve this conflict because both arguments point to the same conclusion—deploying the hard-target weapons. But it is not so simple. If one accepts the objectives of either argument, the other argument becomes a reason *not* to deploy. The net effect is that the arguments cancel each other out. A logical solution is to choose one rationale and reject the other. But in fact this was not generally done. Many respondents used both rationales to support deploying hard-target kill-capable weapons. This was even done with enthusiasm, as if the cumulative effect of the two rationales should strengthen the argument. There was a marked resistance to seeing any tension at all between the objectives of the two rationales. Several respondents simply asserted, "We're trying to do both."

Besides the general discussion of objectives, there were several specific areas in which the same conflict emerged. One had to do with deploying the INF weapons in Europe. A recurrent rationale was that without an improved nuclear capability based in Europe, the credibility of the American threat to use nuclear weapons in response to a conventional invasion would be too weak. The weapons need to be based in Europe to create the perception that a nuclear war in Europe might not escalate to the intercontinental level and thus the United States would be less self-deterred from using them. On the other hand, some of the same people argued that the INF weapons were important as a means of strengthening the perception that a war in Europe *would* necessarily escalate to the intercontinental level. Pershing IIs and GLCMs were presented as a kind of hostage to strengthen the perception that American strategic forces would be drawn in or as a means of provoking the Soviet Union to strike the United States by striking Soviet territory—thus, again, assuring an American strategic response. The conflict between the goal of enhancing credibility by attempting to create the perception that a nuclear war could be limited to Europe and the goal of attempting to create the perception that a nuclear war would inevitably be intercontinental was rarely recognized.

This tension also surfaced in relation to the question of whether the United States should target Soviet missile silos. A common argument was that it is important to be able to strike Soviet silos because, as a limited response, it would be a more credible threat than striking populations. Two other arguments depicted countersilo capability as a means of convincing the Soviets that any nuclear war would ultimately become all out. One stressed that the Soviets value their missiles so highly—more, even, than their population—that striking their missiles would essentially be full escalation. Another was that by our striking at silos, the Soviet Union would be forced to use or lose their missiles, thus ensuring escalation. Increasing the Soviets' perception of the certainty of general escalation would strengthen deterrence. However, it was not always clearly seen that this objective conflicted with the goal of strengthening American credibility by enhancing the perception that an American response might be limited.

More Rationales, More Conflicts

Respondents frequently used other rationales for hard-target kill capability in addition to those described. These involved addressing the perceptions of audiences other than the Soviet leadership and bringing in the military rationales described in chapter 4. These various rationales conflicted with each other in so many different ways that it was hard to keep track. Here again, the same individuals frequently offered several rationales despite the conflicts.

The key audience stressed, in addition to the Soviets, was the European allies. A common theme was that hard-target-capable Pershing IIs and GLCMs are important because they provide the ability to strike at the Soviet homeland, thereby ensuring that any European conflict would escalate to the intercontinental level. As a former Pentagon official explained, the primary purpose of the INF weapons is to "ensure in [the Europeans'] mind that the [strategic] U. S. nuclear forces would be used if they were attacked." The Europeans could then feel confident that they would not be abandoned in the event of a limited Soviet attack against them, and, more important, they could feel more certain that both superpowers would be deterred from making risky moves on the Continent on the assumption that a war could stay limited to Europe.

Obviously, there is a tension between the desire to communicate to the Soviets that the United States believes a European nuclear war would not necessarily escalate and to assure the Europeans that the United States does not plan to use Europe as a battlefield. This contradiction was thrown into the foreground particularly during the INF debate, when American leaders were saying that the INF weapons were being deployed to balance out local asymmetries thus increasing the possibility of escalation control and simultaneously saying that they were being deployed as a kind of hostage to ensure escalation. When leaders made statements unambiguously on one side of this duality—

such as Reagan's comment that he could imagine a nuclear war limited to Europe—it created major political repercussions.*

As discussed in chapter 4, the two military rationales for hard-target kill capability conflicted with each other. The goal of limiting damage to the United States in the event of a war by acquiring the capability to comprehensively destroy missile silos, command and control centers, and leadership bunkers conflicted with the goal of signaling the intention to keep a war limited. Nevertheless, respondents sometimes used both rationales.

Making the phenomenon even more complex, respondents sometimes mixed military and perceptual rationales, which also conflicted with each other (see figure 8.1). The most common was to mix the military rationale that called for limited options as a means of increasing the probability of limiting war with the rationale that called for promoting the Soviet perception that a nuclear war would go out of control. Several respondents felt that they could resolve the apparent conflict between these two rationales by saying that before a war the goal would be to enhance deterrence by creating the perception that a war would escalate; however, once a war started, the goal would be to keep it limited. As one former Pentagon official said, "You would have different goals at different points in time." This argument makes some sense as a general policy. But as an argument for deploying hard-target kill capability, it presents problems. Either the United States does or does not deploy hard-target kill capability, and the Soviets will perceive this as either increasing or decreasing the probability that a nuclear war will stay limited. (If it does both equally, there is no net gain in either direction and the effort is pointless.) If deploying hard-target-capable weapons succeeds in strengthening the Soviet perception that a nuclear war will necessarily escalate, it may satisfactorily enhance deterrence. But once war starts there is no way to abruptly change the meaning of the deployment so that the Soviets perceive the deployment as signaling the possibility of keeping a war limited.

---

*Ronald Reagan, on October 16, 1981, when asked about a limited exchange of nuclear weapons in Europe and whether the exchange would inevitably grow into direct war between the U. S. and the USSR, replied, "I could see where you could have the exchange of tactical weapons against troops in the field without bringing either one of the major powers to pushing the button." (Robert Scheer, *With Enough Shovels: Reagan, Bush, and Nuclear War* [New York: Random House, 1982], 131)

FIGURE 8.1.

Rationales for Hard-Target Kill Capability (HTK)

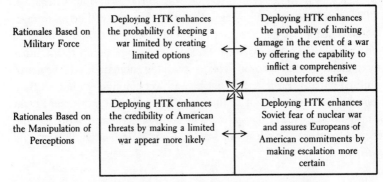

Rationales Based on Military Force	Deploying HTK enhances the probability of keeping a war limited by creating limited options	Deploying HTK enhances the probability of limiting damage in the event of a war by offering the capability to inflict a comprehensive counterforce strike
Rationales Based on the Manipulation of Perceptions	Deploying HTK enhances the credibility of American threats by making a limited war appear more likely	Deploying HTK enhances Soviet fear of nuclear war and assures Europeans of American commitments by making escalation more certain

NOTE: Two-way arrows indicate four different conflicts between the various rationales.

The military rationale that seeks to limit damage through counterforce targeting also conflicts with the perceptual rationale that seeks to enhance the credibility of threats by promoting the idea that a nuclear war can be limited. Deploying hard-target kill capability could significantly limit damage only if it was done in such large numbers that Soviet silos and command and control centers were threatened on a very large scale. Obviously, the Soviets know that they could launch out from under any limited counterforce attack. Consequently, only an all-out surprise attack could conceivably limit the number of warheads arriving on American soil. Therefore, employing a damage-limiting, hard-target kill option is at least as likely to strengthen the Soviet perception that American actions will be large scale as it is to convince the Soviets American actions will be limited.

Apparent Confusion

Given that most respondents did not limit themselves to one rationale for hard-target kill capability and given the various ways in which rationales conflict, it is not surprising that many respondents at times appeared somewhat confused and inconsistent.

When a former middle-level Pentagon official, quoted above, who had worked on PD-59 was asked, "Do we want the Soviets to think that a nuclear war could be controlled?" his initial answer was negative. ("We want the Soviets to think that a nuclear war will be an unmitigated disaster . . . because that helps deterrence.") I then referred to an unpublished paper by Notre Trulock in which he points to a number of indications that the Soviets are thinking increasingly in terms of limited nuclear war. He said that he was "very familiar with it." I then asked, "Is the movement in that direction a positive movement from our point of view?" Despite his previously expressed wish for the Soviets to think a nuclear war would be an "unmitigated disaster," he answered:

> I think so . . . but it's a little different kind of talk than what we talk about in escalation control. For example, they might limit use by sector, by country, by type of weapon.
>
> I: But to the extent that they move in that direction, is that a positive—
>
> R: I think so.

This inconsistency also appeared in discussing the Soviet idea of limiting exchanges to the conventional level. Initially he viewed this emerging idea favorably.

> I think . . . the most marked trend of Soviet strategy is to back off from the automatic early use of nuclear weapons and try to handle theater situations with conventional weapons. And I think that's a trend to the good.

But just moments later he indicated that such trends in both the nuclear and non-nuclear realm were actually ominous in terms of deterrence. He commented that the development of the conventional option was even "more worrisome" than the limited nuclear option because it "might make them less deterred from starting a war because they believe they can keep it [limited]."

An interview with a high-level arms control negotiator followed a similar pattern. Initially, he seemed to wish that the Soviets would take on some of the ideas of limiting escalation and was concerned that the Soviets had a doctrine that opposed the idea of control. When I pointed to Soviet trends toward the idea of limiting escalation, he seemed to view them as being consistent with American interests but discouraged premature optimism.

    I: Recently [the Soviets] have made some movements toward talking about the possibility of limitations [on escalation]. Is that a positive development from our point of view?

    R: It is, but it can't be taken too seriously because it could be a propaganda ploy . . . to get us to believe they're as reasonable as we are or as restrained as we are. . . . I think the Soviets are pretty fundamentalist in their approach. . . . Their military writings are replete with the idea that these weapons should be used and will all be used rather early in the game.

Later in the interview, however, he seemed to be concerned that the Soviets might think there is a way to gain some control over the escalation process. This might make them feel freer to take risks. Therefore, an objective of American policy, he argued, is to make an impression on the Soviets that would enhance their perception that a war would probably escalate.

    We want them to think that . . . they stand to lose so much more by starting something which they don't know how to control and [that] it might get out of control. . . . I think that has by and large worked. They're cautious. They don't take very grave risks, or any risks at all with nuclear weapons.

With one respondent, who had held a high-level position doing war planning at NATO headquarters, I pursued these questions at length. From the beginning he stressed that the purpose of hard-target-capable weapons in Europe was primarily perceptual—to send signals. The first signal he emphasized stressed the potential for escalation to strategic weapons. "There must be the perception of using weapons in a way that signals further use—strategic use." He then went on to say that the Pershing IIs and GLCMs are useful for destroying hardened targets. When asked, "Why can't you use strategic forces for that?" he responded by invoking a ladder-of-escalation framework, asking rhetorically:

> Do you want to have as your only option to destroy hardened targets in the Soviet Union using strategic weapons, which means that you are now engaged in nuclear conflict at the strategic level, in which case you have no alternative but for more massive use of strategic weapons? . . . In a general sense, there's always an interest in showing restraint . . . such that the Soviet leadership doesn't feel that its only recourse is for massive use of nuclear weapons.
>
> I: So the hope is that the Soviets would show some corresponding restraint?
>
> R: That's correct.

We then discussed what targets hard-target-capable weapons would be used against. He said that, in general, command and control centers would not be a good target, "You want to maintain an ability for effective command and control on both sides." He did, however, say that there might be some lower-level command and control centers one might want to strike at.

On the whole, he felt that countersilo targeting would also be inappropriate, though at times he wavered. First he said that he could not "conceive of limited attacks" involving attacks on missile silos. Then he qualified that statement by saying that one could make a limited attack on a "subset of strategic weapons with INF weapons." But shortly thereafter he seemed to shift to saying that attacking strategic weapons would necessarily be a major escalatory move.

> R: To the extent that you mount an attack, albeit against a more limited set of strategic assets, I would put it in the context of what you are now attacking is primary military weapons.
>
> I: So that's not a tit-for-tat kind of thing. If they use the SS-20s against Europe and we strike at their strategic weapons, that's not exactly a response in kind.
>
> R: It's not exactly a response in kind, no. [laughs]
>
> I: So it's an escalatory response?
>
> R: I think most people would cite that as an escalatory response

. . . now you are attacking the homeland directly. That suggests very strongly what the next step in escalation will be, and that is a coupling to the West's strategic weapons.

By bringing in the concept of coupling, it seemed to me that he was shifting away from his previously stated goal of trying to project a willingness to show restraint in a European war. When I pointed to the potential conflict with that previously stated goal, he first denied it and then resurrected it in a more politically neutral form.

I: But there's some tension there between that [coupling] and the goal of keeping the war limited to Europe.

R: We have an objective of keeping the war limited to Europe? You're sounding very parochial. [laughs]

I: I thought that's what you said earlier.

R: No, I didn't say that.

I: Well, to keep it limited to a certain level on the ladder of escalation.

R: Again, I think the more desirable objective is to bring about a cessation of the war.

I: At the lowest level?

R: At the lowest level of conflict, right, you got it. You're reading well.

But then, when I brought back the concern for coupling through the perception of the possibility of escalation, he embraced it.

I: And yet, if the Soviets have the perception that the United States is putting these efforts into making sure the war is limited to Europe, then theoretically that reduces the intimidating effect of deterrence that is derived from perception of coupling—that is, that it will go all out of control if anything gets started in Europe.

R: I'm not sure you would want to create a perception that *everything* is out of control . . . [but] there is a certain element of that . . . it's part of the strategy because you want to convey to the other side there's a possibility of escalation.

He then tried to put his two rationales together by asserting that both signals can be sent.

> It should be in the attacker's interest to have this idea of restraint and the possibility for escalation. . . . Our signal, hopefully, is very clear; our restraint is clear, our ability to escalate further is clear. And you can't muddy the waters.

When I pointed out how it is hard to send both signals with countersilo weapons, he first denied having said that the United States should strike at silos (though he had).

> I: It seems you're putting a lot of effort into making sure that the signal comes through that you want to keep it limited to this level, but at the same time, the way you're doing it—by striking at silos—is a very provocative gesture that would almost—
>
> R: But I didn't say I was striking at silos.

When I then asked him what the purpose of hard-target kill capability is, he implied that countersilo capability was actually a secondary concern; that the primary concern was having an assured retaliatory capability. But when questioned, he abandoned this argument.

> I: Then why do you need hard-target capable weapons?
>
> R: . . . [countersilo targeting] is only one of a series of objectives in terms of hard-target kill capability.
>
> I: What are the other ones?
>
> R: Well . . . first of all, it seems to me there should be a fundamental thesis, certainly, that our basic policy is one of having an assured retaliatory capability.
>
> I: Is that a question here?
>
> R: · No.

He then seemed to shift, now embracing the importance of destroying silos as part of a straightforward damage-limiting strategy.

> R: All I'm suggesting is that in having an ability to attack and destroy his hardened ICBM silos, you have an ability to destroy

the launchers. There's even value in destroying those launchers if the missile has been launched. . . . All you want to again be able to do is to say to the other side, "We can destroy that military capability."

I: Do you mind me asking why? I don't know that it's self-evident. You have to say what your goals are.

R: I grant you it depends on what your goals are. One goal is a real military goal, it's the fact that you would destroy his ability to ever use that launcher again. Another is that you're running on the assumption that inevitably such systems would be used in a major, all-out attack. . . . So, therefore, there's limited value in destroying that capability.

But when I restated this thinking, he abruptly discounted it.

I: So you're trying to draw down [that is, reduce the number of] their forces in the event that the whole thing escalates?

R: Well, the idea of drawing down I have some trouble with because, it seems to me, if you, in fact, engage in a major attack against his ICBM silos, the notion of drawing down forces is a little bit [makes a dismissing gesture]—

He then reverted to his argument that hard-target-capable weapons can signal the intention both to keep a conflict limited by their ability to strike at military targets and to escalate to strategic use if necessary. The fact that the United States would have the ability to destroy silos and command and control centers, he said, would not be a problem because the United States could strike at less vital military targets. As we were running out of time, I formulated the problem with some emphasis:

But given that before the conflict you're trying to communicate to the Soviets what your intentions would be in the circumstance— because you'll have the capability to destroy the missile silos and the capability to destroy significant command and control centers, then the Soviets are going to tend to interpret your whole force posture as being an escalatory force posture. So it almost doesn't matter what you *would,* in fact, hit. What matters is what

you *can* hit, it's perceptions. What impression do you want to
make on the other guy as to what you would do?

At this point, he seemed to fully grasp the problem. There was a very
long pause as he stared straight at me. Finally he said, with apparent
discomfort, "I understand the point." Although he had expressed ideas
about the importance of perceptions at the very beginning of the
discussion, he seemed to be assimilating it now in a new way. He said
reflectively, "We are dealing primarily here with questions of deployment policy, which is a very important area, which is embedded in the
idea of perceptions." He then made some mild efforts to resurrect his
previous arguments, but by the end of the interview he seemed to
implicitly confirm that he had not seen the incompatibility of his
positions. I asked him if, in all his years at NATO headquarters, anybody had ever pointed out this problem to him, or if he had ever heard
anybody else discussing it. He answered negatively.

The Double Image

In a very small number of cases, respondents did recognize the conflict
between these objectives and did have a way of reconciling them. This
generally involved trying to create a double image in the minds of the
Soviets. One image suggests that Americans believe a nuclear war can
be controlled and war thus continues to be a viable instrument of
policy. Building hard-target-capable weapons, declaratory policy, and
publicly discussed war plans support this image. On the other hand, an
effort is made to create an image in the Soviets' mind suggesting that,
in fact, a nuclear war would go out of control. Building hard-target-
capable weapons supports this image as do the statements by American
policymakers regarding the improbability that nuclear war can stay
limited. In short, the Soviets are supposed to perceive that *Americans*
are emboldened by the belief that a nuclear war *can* be controlled, and
at the same time, they are supposed to be deterred by the perception
that *in fact* a nuclear war *cannot* be controlled.

A former high-level Pentagon official, who was involved in developing the escalation-control-oriented PD-59, explained,

> I believe it to be true that if they think it's all going to go out of control, they won't start the process. And that's the conclusion we'd want them to come to.
>
> I: Oh, is it? That it's going to get all out of control?
>
> R: That's a conclusion we want them to reach. If they reach that conclusion, the game is over and we've won—that is, we have deterred Soviet actions. . . .
>
> I: It's a little confusing because in the countervailing PD-59 vein the whole idea is to put emphasis on the possibility that it will be controlled, but at the same time you're saying that we want the Soviets to think it won't be controlled.
>
> R: If the Soviets think that it won't be controlled, then they will judge that it's not in their interest to strike. . . . The difficulty is that going out of control, from their point of view, means we're going out of control from our point of view, and launching the whole SIOP at the Russians is a wonderful deterrent if the Russians believe it will be launched. It's not effective in its credibility, is the problem. Greater threats are more effective but less credible. Smaller threats are more credible but less effective. The idea is to do both. . . . We want the Soviets not to attack. There are two ways to convince them . . . there are two things we want them to worry about. One is, I think, inevitably, a major factor is that it'll all go out of control. . . . The trouble with that is, as a general deterrent it lacks credibility. . . . [Therefore, second,] we increase the threat of effective retaliation by saying we have options other than launching the whole SIOP at them.

When I started to raise a point that implied that the United States might consider whether, in fact, a war could be controlled, he cut me off, saying, "No. We are agnostic on the subject of whether it can be controlled."

A general involved in arms control ultimately arrived at a similar conclusion. Initially he said that in the event of war our goal would be "to limit that at the lowest possible level . . . [so] that this brings us back to the bargaining table and restores stability in a crisis situation rather than allow it to escalate." However, when asked what impression we want to make on the Soviets, he changed his tune.

> I: What do we want them to think we would do?
> R: We want them to think that . . . it might get out of control.

He then began to explain, though, that it is important not to be too precise about what you intend to do.

> R: You tell somebody specifically what you're going to do in a situation . . . in the first place, it's not credible, and in the second place, it may lead him to believing that he's got freedom to move. . . .
> I: So you see it as valuable to create some ambiguity?
> R: Absolutely.
> I: About what we would do under the circumstances?
> R: Exactly.

He explained that war-fighting plans are not really plans as such but are designed "only" for their psychological impact. "You only talk about what might happen if it fails, to be sure that you assure deterrence in the first place."

This emphasis on the value of ambiguity was echoed by a middle-level Pentagon official. Initially he made the statement that in the event of a European war "we would seek to halt the aggression at the lowest level of violence possible." However, when asked, "What do we want the Soviets to think?" he gave a more complex answer.

> We want the Soviet leadership to understand that active aggression against NATO could ultimately lead to the destruction of the political, military, and economic assets which the Soviet leadership values most. We want them to understand that active aggression against NATO carries with it the risk of having nuclear weapons used on a massive scale against the Soviet homeland. What NATO would do in response to this kind of attack or that kind of attack is deliberately left unclear. . . . To be too clear about

what we would do, to reduce the ambiguity somewhat, might allow the Soviets to calculate—however incorrectly—that certain risks were acceptable. And so there is a deliberate element of ambiguity as to what we would do.

To make sure my understanding of the overall pattern was accurate, in some cases I formulated what I am calling the "double image." In general, respondents concurred with the description. In an interview with a former middle-level Pentagon official who had been involved with developing PD-59 (a different official from the one quoted above), I made the following comment:

> It seems to me that [in PD-59] you were trying to project a fairly complex image, and I want to see if this makes sense to you. We want to project that [because there is the possibility of keeping escalation under control] we're not inhibited, we're not self-deterred, we will go ahead, there's credibility in our threats. On the other hand, we want to project to the Soviets that it'll probably escalate to the top, because that will deter them. So there are two images.

He nodded comfortably and said, "Yeah, I think that's a fair assessment." Interestingly, he then went on to say that the Soviets are also projecting such a double image.

> I think to some extent the Russians are doing the same to us. There is at least more discussion by the Russians about limited use of nuclear weapons, and yet in their public statements to us they continue to stress that nuclear war can't be controlled.

In addition to the concern for Soviet perceptions, this double-image thinking was also applied to European perceptions. The previously quoted former middle-level Pentagon official continued the discussion about the double image.

> There are really several audiences involved, not just the Russians . . . you have the ally angle to it too. . . . Most of the allies

. . . don't want to believe in escalation control because that implies limiting the war to Europe. And so to them we project: We're prepared to escalate all the way to the top.

The Problem of Side Effects

It is not difficult to understand how a policymaker or strategist can feel satisfied with the double-image approach to the question of escalation control. It may be tricky to simultaneously suggest to the Soviets both that the United States thinks that it can control escalation and that, in fact, escalation cannot be controlled; and to assure the Europeans that the United States believes that a war will not be controlled—but it does make sense. It also makes sense conceptually that one would want to pursue a variety of political and deterrence-related objectives before a war which may include escalatory signals but once the war begins to try to limit it as much possible.

However, when one is faced with the need to make a specific decision about whether or not to build hard-target weapons, such concepts turn out to be quite inadequate. Each rationale tends to be canceled out by another rationale which respondents also embraced. The double-image approach attempts to compensate for this problem by trying to separate the effects of different efforts. In this way, the United States can try to project to the Soviets that it *believes* one thing while simultaneously telling the Soviets that something else will *happen* and also convince the Europeans that it believes something else again. The problem, as in the other double-image strategies discussed above, is that the deployment of hard-target kill capability creates side effects possibly as strong as the desired effects.

The effort to increase the perception that the United States believes it is possible to limit a war has the potentially undesirable side effect of strengthening the Soviet belief that a war may, in fact, be controlled, which may then incrementally weaken deterrence. The effort to increase the perception that a nuclear war will necessarily escalate weakens the perception that the United States believes it will stay controlled and therefore incrementally diminishes the credibility of American threats.

The Perceptual Value of Hard-Target Kill Capability

There is also the problem of all audiences hearing all messages. Messages designed for Soviet consumption, to the effect that the United States is confident it can limit a war and is therefore not deterred, are heard by Europeans, who become less assured that the United States will not try to limit a war to Europe. Messages designed for European consumption, to the effect that the United States means to enhance coupling, are also heard by the Soviets and weaken the perceived American confidence in limitations.

In short, I found no convincing reason to believe that the effects desired from the deployment of hard-target kill capability, even in its most sophisticated form, did not also lead to opposite side effects of a similar magnitude.

Furthermore there are additional costs to American security interests that are not taken into account by such perceptual rationales. Developing weapons with hard-target kill capability encourages the Soviets to keep their missiles on a higher level of alert so that they will be able to respond quickly enough to launch out from under incoming warheads. It is widely believed, among strategic thinkers, that such a situation decreases stability and increases the chance that a crisis or a miscalculation (perhaps based on faulty data) will lead to a nuclear conflagration. This argument is rarely contested in strategic circles: some simply accept such costs as acceptable in the pursuit of other values.

Once again we are led to consider the possibility that the desire to build weapons capable of destroying Soviet hardened targets is significantly shaped by values unrelated to security concerns.

CHAPTER 9

Eliminating Population Vulnerability Through Strategic Defenses

EVER SINCE President Reagan's now-famous speech on March 23, 1983, there has been a steady stream of statements suggesting that the Strategic Defense Initiative is a means of undoing the condition of nuclear vulnerability and thereby moving away from a strategy based on deterrence. In his original speech Reagan pictured a world in which "security did not rest on the threat of instant U. S. retaliation to deter a Soviet attack." SDI was described as a "means of rendering these nuclear weapons impotent and obsolete." Over the next few years this theme was repeated and amplified. In April 1985, Reagan described SDI as "a way out of our nuclear dilemma." In his 1986 State of the Union address, he claimed that "a security shield can . . . free mankind from the prison of nuclear terror." And addressing a high school class in Glassboro, New Jersey, he made a call to "leave behind . . . the defense policy of Mutual Assured Destruction."[1]

Others in the Reagan administration echoed such statements. Shortly after the March 1983 speech, Defense Secretary Weinberger elaborated the president's vision on NBC's "Meet the Press":

> The President's whole motive here is to . . . *ensure that no missiles could get through,* and thereby release the whole strategic arms problem from

this idea . . . [of] threats of retaliation . . . *[t]here would be no longer any danger from—from nuclear missiles. . . . What we want to try to get is a system which will develop a defense that is thoroughly reliable and total. . . . And I don't see any reason why that can't be done* [emphasis in original].

In May 1984 Weinberger said, "We've proposed once and for all to remove any temptation to return to a policy of mutually assured destruction." The following year, before the House Armed Services Committee, he claimed that SDI "is going to remove the shadow and the terror of these most destructive weapons." In July 1986 he assailed more limited objectives for SDI that could "possibly lead us to mistake something less than total defense as sufficient for our requirements." General James Abrahamson, director of the SDI program, rejected MAD and said that SDI is "really a search for a strategy of what some people call mutual assured survival." George Keyworth, science advisor to the president, denounced limited objectives for the SDI program short of doing away with MAD.

> Protecting weapons represents no change in present policy. It simply strengthens—*entrenches*—a de facto doctrine of Mutual Assured Destruction. Protecting people, on the other hand, holds out the promise of dramatic change. This clear purpose of the President has been repeated time and time again by Cap Weinberger, Bud McFarlane, and myself.[2]

At the same time, members of the Reagan administration have expressed strong reservations about such objectives. In 1982, before the president's speech, numerous administration officials, including Secretary Weinberger, rejected a proposal very similar to the current SDI program as "unrealistic and unworkable."[3] Even after the president's speech, numerous statements have been made that cast the SDI program in a light quite different from Reagan's vision. A recurring theme is that SDI will not change the condition of mutual deterrence. Rather, SDI is a means for enhancing deterrence. A 1985 Defense Department report to Congress says, "With defenses, the U. S. seeks not to replace deterrence, but to enhance it." A White House publication on SDI says, "Providing a better, more stable basis for enhanced deterrence is the central purpose of the SDI program." And General Abrahamson said unambiguously, "In pursuing strategic defenses it has never been our goal to eventually give up our policy of deterrence."[4]

Consistent with this view is the attitude that it is not really possible to fulfill the vision of a totally effective defense. Gerold Yonas, chief scientist at the Strategic Defense Initiative Organization (SDIO) in the Pentagon, stated unequivocally, "There's no such thing as a perfect defense."[5] Kenneth Adelman, director of the Arms Control and Disarmament Agency, described the idea of "a leakproof defense shield" as "farfetched."[6] Even SDI zealot retired Lieutenant General Daniel Graham conceded that a strategic defense system would not be leakproof.[7]

What is occurring here is not simply a conflict of opinion between individuals about whether the goal of the program is a perfect defense. Some individuals themselves have appeared to be quite inconsistent. General Abrahamson testified to the Senate Armed Services Committee on April 24, 1984, "I think what the President has outlined for us is . . . a goal that says let's strive for an absolutely effective defense." However, just a few weeks later he stated, "Nowhere have we stated that the goal of the SDI is to come up with a 'leakproof' defense." A few months later he reiterated, "A perfect astrodome defense is not a realistic thing."[8]

Inconsistent statements have been made by administration figures on other points as well. One is whether SDI would also involve air defenses against air-breathing systems (that is, bombers and cruise missiles)—something that would be essential for a total defense. Weinberger, when interviewed on "Meet the Press," seemed to assert that such defenses are part of the SDI program.

MARVIN KALB, NBC NEWS: That [ballistic missile defense] would take care of incoming nuclear missiles, but what would it do for cruise missiles . . . ?

SECRETARY OF DEFENSE WEINBERGER: Well, the defensive systems the President is talking about are—are not designed to be partial. What we want to try to get is a system which will develop a defense that is—

KALB: Total?

WEINBERGER: —thoroughly reliable and total, yes. And I—

KALB: Against all incoming missiles of any kind?

WEINBERGER: Yes. And I don't see any reason why that can't be done.

However, Richard DeLauer, then undersecretary of defense, said, "The Strategic Defense Initiative is a technology program against ballistic missiles, not against air-breathing threat."[9]

There has also been inconsistency as to whether SDI ultimately has cooperative objectives or if it is a way for the United States to pursue a unilaterally advantageous position even to the point of gaining a first-strike capability. President Reagan has asserted categorically that "we seek neither military superiority nor political advantage." He has, on several occasions, said that "we welcome the day when the Soviet Union can shoot down any incoming missile, so long as the United States can shoot down any incoming missile, too." Weinberger, in the "Meet the Press" interview, dismissed Soviet concerns about the United States trying to acquire a first-strike capability.

MARVIN KALB, NBC NEWS: Mr. Secretary, but do you understand that the Soviet Union could think, in its own planning, that the United States and this administration particularly, is seeking a first-strike capability?

WEINBERGER: No, I don't see any way in which they could think that. . . . [T]here is no basis for that thought.[10]

At the same time there have been numerous statements that suggest the United States is indeed seeking such an advantageous position. Weinberger testified to the Senate Armed Services Committee that SDI is a means of re-creating the condition in which the United States was the only nation able to pose a nuclear threat (essentially a first-strike capability). "If we can get a system which is effective and which we know can render their weapons impotent, we would be back in a situation we were in, for example, when we were the only nation with the nuclear weapon." George Keyworth embraced SDI as a means of pursuing superiority: "I see this shift [from offensive to defensive weapons] as a decided advantage to the West. . . . [The Soviets] have to play catch up when it comes to advanced technology. . . . In that way, by the expedient of always staying several steps ahead, *we can thwart even the most aggressive attempts by adversaries to keep up* [emphasis in original]." Elsewhere he also said, "We must start to play our trump—technological leverage." General Abrahamson called for the United States to "have a much more effective defense than they have." Richard Ruffine, a senior Pentagon analyst, was perhaps the most bold, declaring, ". . . [If] it went all out with the technology in hand—we could eat them up."[11]

Finally, an ambiguity exists about whether administration officials genuinely believe that it is possible for both sides to cooperatively seek a condition of mutual assured survival or if strategic defense will inevitably lead to unconstrained efforts to undermine the defenses of the other side. President Reagan, with characteristic optimism, has said, "I think [SDI] could be the greatest inducement to arms reduction," that SDI "will improve the opportunity for arms reduction because missiles, no longer the ultimate weapon they are today, will be more negotiable," and that "by making missiles less effective . . . the arms spiral will be a downward spiral, hopefully to the elimination of them."[12]

Other administration spokesmen, though, appear to assume that SDI will have quite a different effect, as in Caspar Weinberger's testimony to the Senate Armed Services Committee.

> SENATOR EDWARD KENNEDY (D-MA): What makes you believe the Soviet Union's response is not going to be just increasing their offensive capability, increasing their production of warheads and missiles?
>
> SECRETARY OF DEFENSE WEINBERGER: I think they are doing that. They have been doing it right along.
>
> KENNEDY: Do you expect that will be their response if this program is implemented?
>
> WEINBERGER: . . . I think they will make every effort to negate it if they can. . . .
>
> KENNEDY: You mean they will increase their offensive capability?
>
> WEINBERGER: I think they will try to overwhelm or otherwise defeat a strategic defense.[13]

In another Senate Armed Services Committee hearing, General Abrahamson commented that such a response would be generically prudent. Senator William Cohen first quoted from the Future Security Strategy Study (the Hoffman Report):

SENATOR WILLIAM COHEN (R-MI): . . . [The report] says: "Their current program emphases suggest that they would be more likely to respond with a continuing buildup in their long-range offensive forces."

The question is: If that is our perception now, is it wise to spend these billions to get that level only to say they are going to continue with their offensive system?

LIEUTENANT GENERAL ABRAHAMSON: I understand the point that is made there. It certainly is what a prudent military planner would look to as a first step.[14]

Furthermore, there are indications that the United States would not restrain itself from seeking to undermine Soviet defenses. Weinberger states, "Even a probable [Soviet] territorial defense would require us to increase the number of our offensive forces and their ability to penetrate Soviet defenses." Indeed, the United States already has a program for improving American capabilities for penetrating defenses. Thomas Cooper, assistant secretary of the Air Force, described this program: "The Advanced Strategic Missile Systems (ASMS) program is . . . focused on providing options to counter [Soviet] defenses."[15] In addition, I am not aware of any American efforts to seek, through arms control, mutual constraints on countermeasures against defenses—something that would seem essential for the goal of eliminating the condition of mutual assured destruction.

Interview Findings

As mentioned in chapter 1, the issue of strategic defenses was not part of the original design of the study. Later in the study, as SDI became increasingly prominent in public debate, I began to focus on it more directly. Also, in earlier interviews, a number of respondents spontaneously spoke about it. This led me to investigate further whether respondents genuinely believed that strategic defenses could ultimately eradicate the condition of vulnerability or whether the policy of pursuing such a goal was designed for certain perceptual effects.

ALTERING STRATEGIC REALITY

Only a very small number of respondents explicitly embraced the idea that strategic defense would be so effective that it would cancel out the effects of population vulnerability on strategic reality.

One prominent defense industry figure said that SDI made "the concept of winning" plausible again. However, he complained that "the way it is going, it's off for the next century." A congressional defense analyst explained how SDI could resurrect the traditional concept of war.

> It seems to me that while the idea of any strategic defense that can prevent any damage from nuclear weapons to the United States's strategic forces is preposterous because no defense is leakproof, . . . it is reasonable to think about a system of strategic defense that could reduce the level of damage in a strategic exchange to a level that would not destroy the United States as a functioning society. It would inflict horrible amounts of damage. . . . I come back to a good definition being what was the level of population and industrial damage proportionate to what the Soviet Union sustained in World War II? Maybe that's a good index. . . . I think [SDI] would be useful to us in that if there was a war with the Soviet Union, say, and if you had a functioning strategic defense of this kind, it might turn into a protracted conflict. And if it's a protracted conflict, then it's conceivably winnable; it's conceivably winnable with us surviving as a functioning society.
>
> I: So the net effect is to kind of cancel out nuclear weapons?
> R: Yeah.
> I: And you see that as positive for us?
> R: I think so, yeah.

Some respondents were ambiguous about whether they actually believed it was possible to defend populations. A former Pentagon official described himself as "agnostic." A Rand analyst seemed to have trouble determining exactly what he thought as he described other people's beliefs. While he began by downplaying the idea of population defense, he seemed to gradually take on the idea as he was describing it:

I think the primary motivation for SDI is close to what the president expressed. He was maybe a little nutty, some would say, a little visionary, but a lot of people—many, many people, *most* people [his voice rising]—would say, this is a hell of a situation, where we have no defenses! [gesticulating] What kind of a situation is that?! Now, yes I understand about mutual assured destruction and all that stuff, but NO defenses?! [getting very animated] You must be kidding! That's just not something that any—

Stopping in midsentence, he paused for a moment. Then, changing his tone, he began to say that in fact sophisticated people do not take the idea of defenses seriously.

—person is going to regard as reasonable, unless he's been spending an awful lot of time on stategic doctrine and has become inculcated. . . . Most of the people who work on this have very different objectives for realistic strategic defense than the president. . . . Only in a much more theoretical sense do they have much faith in real survival. . . . It's something that only a fraction of the supporters of defense believe in.

When I asked him directly what he believed, he seemed surprisingly comfortable with his uncertainty.

I: Where would you place yourself [on this issue]?
R: Well, we're going to be doing some studies in depth this year, and I suspect I'm going to be changing my mind back and forth as we go through the analyses.

Some respondents also noted an apparent ambiguity in the administration position. A member of the Scowcroft Commission observed:

I think it's interesting that from the beginning there's been a certain duality about this, because although there was the phrase "trying to make nuclear weapons impotent and obsolete" in the president's March of '83 speech, certainly some spokesmen in the administration talk very much still in terms of perfect defenses and what-have-you. Others don't and, indeed, the March '83 speech had as its key part of the operative sentence in what was being recommended the phrase (I think this is right) "an attempt to define a long-term R and D program to begin"—five qualifiers in the one phrase! So I think from the beginning there's been a certain duality about this, as there was in the initial U. S. work on ballistic missile defense in the 1960s. And you could possibly see some similar tendencies as SDI work gets folded into the more traditional deterrence notions.

Setting aside the few examples of minor equivocation quoted above, however, the overwhelming weight of opinion in the interviews unambiguously rejected the idea that populations could, in fact, be defended in a way that would alter the fundamental reality of mutual vulnerability. Even representatives of the Reagan administration who are generally viewed as hardliners and supporters of SDI, when interviewed, dismissed such a possibility. For example, a high-level ACDA official said that scientists had convinced him, "there's no such thing as a perfect umbrella which is a shield." A high-level Pentagon official stated flatly that the SDI program was aimed at protecting missiles and that the hope of protecting populations was purely abstract, speculative, and something he did not take very seriously. A high-level arms control negotiator said, "Is it possible to give [the] population, with any foreseeable technology, a hundred percent protection? Nobody foresees that today—I don't know of anybody who foresees that." Naturally, it is possible that there are some administration figures who do believe in such a possibility, but no one I spoke with cited any individuals other than Weinberger and Reagan.

There were also indications that the dominant sentiment in Congress was not that SDI would fundamentally change strategic reality as much as that it was useful as a point of leverage with the Soviets. A staff member of the Senate Armed Services Committee said,

> . . . I think our members voted as strongly as they did for SDI a couple weeks ago because of their perception that this was a very important program for the future arms control. They saw it, I think, as being a primary reason why the Soviets came back to the bargaining table. . . . Whether they had really bought into the president's vision or anybody else's vision of what this might

ultimately be is not altogether clear. . . . Whether their perception of it is something that will ultimately eliminate nuclear weapons from the face of the earth, I'm not sure if any of them have bought into that.

Among the strongest advocates of SDI I observed an evolution over the two-and-a-half-year period of the interviews. In the earlier period respondents shrugged off questions about the feasibility of population defense by referring to the skepticism originally held toward the Wright brothers. Later, though, it became more common to hear that SDI would "defend" populations by enhancing deterrence through lessening the potential of a Soviet strike. This argument is quite different from the president's original vision, but it was still phrased in the absolute terms reminiscent of some of his earlier calls for abandoning deterrence as the basis for defense. This may have been prompted by a political need to obscure discontinuities with previously stated objectives.

For example, an official in the Pentagon's Strategic Defense Initiative Organization (SDIO) first said that the goal of SDI was to "deprive [ballistic missiles] of any military utility." On closer examination it became clear that it was not implied that *all* ballistic missiles would be stopped but enough to generate uncertainty. "[When] there are great levels of uncertainty about which missiles would reach what targets . . . then there's no ballistic missile striking capability." When I brought up the notion that the goal of SDI might be to move away from deterrence, this was corrected, "No—it remains deterrence." But then deterrence was quickly defined so as to include the concept of defense: "Deterrence is the prevention of attack. There's nothing to say that deterrence has to be based on the threat of retaliation." However, it soon became clear that there was no expectation that retaliation would really ever be abandoned. I inquired whether, in a world in which the goals of SDI had been fulfilled, we would be free to do away with our offensive weapons.

R: Oh, no—of course not.
I: Well, then, what would be the purpose of those weapons?
R: You're sure that's a serious question?
I: Retaliation, I assume—right?

R: Well, of course!

I: So you're saying that you don't necessarily foresee completely removing the retaliatory function of our offensive weapons as part of our defense, but you'd like to change the ratio [of defense to offense]?

R: That's right. And it's a long-term process, obviously.

This is certainly a cogent position, although it is somewhat different from the original objectives that the SDIO was established to pursue.

PERCEPTUAL RATIONALES

In some cases it appeared that the interest in strategic defense was derived from an effort to manipulate perceptions. The goal of SDI was not to create a real population defense and thereby reconventionalize the world. Rather, it was to play a strong card for America in the competition for political perceptions dominated by conventional thinking.

The perceptual orientation of some respondents was not always immediately apparent. In some cases, initially it appeared that respondents were embracing the idea that SDI could give the United States a genuine strategic advantage over the Soviet Union. For example, a prominent strategic analyst asserted that through SDI the United States could "recapture" the "golden age" of absolute American superiority, which he identified as the 1950s, when the United States was not significantly vulnerable to the Soviet Union. However, on closer questioning, he either shifted or clarified that he only meant to create the political perception of such decisive superiority, stating bluntly, "The prospect of being able to defend the Americas, building an astrodome over it, that's a technological fantasy." Because he had earlier used perceptual rationales to argue for the need to appear technologically more advanced, I asked,

How much do you see SDI development as rooted in the need to be perceived as moving forward into the future, and how much do you see it as based in actual belief that it is technologically possible to achieve a meaningful strategic defense?

R: Ninety-five percent the former. Because [pause] it's not, in fact, possible to build a leakproof defense. . . . What we ought to have is SDI, to make the Soviet ballistic missile force look rusty and old-fashioned; to reaffirm the fact that the United States has regained strategic nuclear superiority.

A Rand analyst echoed this view, saying that SDI, by demonstrating American technological superiority, created the perception that "America is on the rise again" and that the Soviet Union "is going downhill." He saw these perceptions as derived from the misperception that SDI would grant the United States a significant military advantage.

A State Department official who has been part of the negotiating team in the Geneva negotiations described the interest in SDI as largely derived from a desire to match the Soviets in the realm of political perceptions. He said that the Soviet strategic defense program produced

> . . . [a] political-perception reaction that we need to have something similar . . . that says they are building system X, therefore we should build system X-prime, which can do the same thing, whether we need it in a military sense or not. . . . [If the U.S. has] a gap in this particular capability—whatever it is—people find that's a disadvantageous position to be in.
> I: Politically?
> R: Yeah.

Another Rand analyst also pointed to the attitude that SDI was a means of competing with the Soviets in the realm of perceptions as distinguished from the president's goal of acquiring a population defense.

> Some people, I think, are less interested in strategic defense from the president's point of view than they are from the competitive point of view. They feel we have lost the offensive arms race—we just don't have the will to pursue it—and they feel that the only recourse left to us is therefore to open a race in high-technology defense, which we could win. Implicit in that is, again, this belief

that the strategic equivalence is important to perceptions, and if enough people believe it, then it is true.

Consistent with this line of thinking was a statement in an editorial in the *New York Times*. It dismissed the possibility of a leakproof shield, pointed to its probable cost ineffectiveness, and observed that, in this light, no coherent rationale had been formulated. Nevertheless it concluded that the SDI program "makes sense" largely because "[it] maintains pressure on the Soviet Union in a field of American advantage."[16]

While some respondents focused on generalized political perceptions, others specifically emphasized Soviet perceptions. This was often based on a greater-fool type of argument. For example, a former member of the Joint Chiefs of Staff first recognized that SDI would not fundamentally alter the nature of the Soviet-American strategic relationship even if one side was significantly ahead. Nevertheless he strongly supported building SDI because "it makes the Soviets nervous." Another respondent referred to a phrase similar to one used by Ronald Reagan and then Assistant Secretary of State Richard Burt: "If SDI won't work, why are the Soviets so worried about it?" This was said with a smile that indicated that he was not borrowing on Soviet credibility to support the feasibility of strategic defense; rather, he was saying that the question of feasibility was largely irrelevant given that the Soviets seem to be intimidated.

Even Edward Teller made a similar argument when speaking to a group of journalists:

> I was asked in 1969 to explain the ABM program to the media at a conference in Montana. . . . A hundred yards from the hotel, I picked up a stick—not a big stick, just a branch. . . . One of the conference staff asked me what the stick was for . . . I said the stick was for protection against grizzly bears. "Don't you know, Dr. Teller," the staff member said, "that a stick is not good enough against grizzly bears?" "Yes, I know that, but I hope the grizzly bears don't!"

In case his point was not already clear, Teller added, "that is my answer" to those who say SDI would not be effective.[17]

Other respondents emphasized that SDI is necessary as a response to the Soviets' belief that they can win a nuclear war. A former member of the National Security Council said:

> If you believe, as I do, that they believe a nuclear war can be won and then take steps in that direction, then clearly you must accept countersteps, of which SDI is one. . . . The result will be that the Russians will have to look upon their strategic forces as we do— essentially as a deterrent and nothing else.

When I probed into what he thought about the military realities involved, it became clear that he regarded them as completely beside the point. I asked whether he thought the Soviet Union could, in fact, win a nuclear war.

> R: It's irrelevant whether I think a nuclear war can be won or not.
> . . . The question is whether I'm right in interpreting what they say or not . . .
> I: Is it something you haven't investigated?
> R: I think it is irrelevant—I have never given it any thought.

Likewise he said the Soviets had to assume that U. S. behavior would be conditioned by the assumption that SDI would be effective even if the Soviets themselves did not think so.

> Take their point of view of SDI. Suppose we were sitting in Moscow, and you came to me and you say, what do you think? Is SDI possible or not? I'll say it's immaterial. Reagan believes it is. And Reagan is going ahead with it—that's what matters.

Overall, though, I did not get the impression that respondents strongly believed this greater-fool argument. When I pointed out that the Soviets have consistently asserted that SDI will not effectively protect populations, it did not seem to trouble them. One respondent answered by asking why the Soviets, then, seem so set against it. But this can easily be explained by the logic given at the end of the previous paragraph—they might be concerned that American leaders will think it will work (which is, in fact, what they told me, as we will see in chapter 12). Mostly, though, respondents seemed to shrug off the question. Even if the logic of the argument did not hold up relative to a specific audience, there seemed to be a vague feeling that somewhere there was an audience that responded to the SDI program in a way that was valuable for American interests. As we will see in the next chapter, some respondents eventually said that that key audience was actually the American people.

CHAPTER 10

Satisfying Psychological Needs

THE RATIONALES explored so far have had as their ostensible goal the promotion of American security. Rationales based on military force have sought to enhance American capabilities to effectively wage war and thereby enhance deterrence of a rational adversary. Those based on the strategic manipulation of perceptions have sought to counteract potential bandwagoning effects, to signal resolve, to enhance the credibility of threats, or to increase an adversary's fear of nuclear war. In all cases the focus of concern has been extrinsic threats to American security.

A number of rationales, however, were based not on security interests but on the gratification of psychological needs. Rather than addressing objective considerations related to security, they were concerned with achieving certain subjective psychological states. Most often such rationales appeared in a spontaneous fashion, but sometimes they emerged after the logical problems with security-related rationales became apparent. For example, in an interview with a Rand analyst, I asked why he felt a need to maintain equality of nuclear forces relative to the Soviet Union. Each argument he raised led to another question which pointed at its weaknesses. With a refreshing intellectual candor, he freely recognized the problems in his arguments and then either relinquished or distanced himself from them but nonetheless went on to another. Finally, after probably thirty minutes of this, it seemed that all of his security-related rationales had effectively fallen apart, but he did not indicate any change in his attitude that the United States should maintain equality. I came back to the original question: "So why do you feel a need to maintain equality with the Soviet Union?" He was silent for a while, looking a bit befuddled by the problems in his arguments but nonetheless apparently still feeling compelled by the desire for equality. Finally he said, with a slight embarrassment, "I don't know. I just feel better that way" and then, with more finality, "I just do."*

Such an answer can be regarded as a defensive ploy. By abandoning all "reasons" for his positions, he made it impossible to probe any further. However, I do not interpret his remark this way. It seemed that he was genuinely reporting the emotional gratification derived from maintaining American status relative to the Soviet Union independent of its security relevance.

A closer analysis of the rationales based on psychological needs revealed several recurring themes. Some respondents emphasized that competitive defense policies were valid because they gratified the desire for prestige and status in the eyes of others. The pursuit of dominant military and political positions in some cases was seen as enhancing national morale. Others explained that certain policies suppress the awareness of the condition of vulnerability and thereby alleviate domestic fears. There was also a somewhat obscure argument that competitive policies should be pursued because they fulfill the fundamentally competitive nature of being.

In a minority of cases, respondents did clearly differentiate these arguments from those based on security interests. When the distinction was not clearly made, it was pointless to ask respondents directly whether they made such a differentiation. The context of questioning, obviously, invited individuals to try to bolster their arguments by trying to show some relation. Concerns for status and prestige could easily be tied to a concern for bandwagoning. Concerns for American morale could be tied to perceived resolve. Suppressing awareness of vulnerabil-

---

*When describing emotional gratifications derived from certain defense policies, respondents sometimes spoke in terms of their own feelings and at other times they spoke in terms of the needs of the general public. I regard these two forms of description as functionally equivalent. Although respondents may be talking partly about their personal feelings, I think that when they describe their feelings about policy issues they are primarily describing desires they feel when they identify with the needs of the collective.

ity could strengthen determination. Fulfilling the competitive nature of being could be further justified with the argument that "if we don't, they will." But this does not mean that arguments were not also seen as sufficient by themselves. By examining the context within which these arguments were presented, I have concluded that they are not simply derivative of security concerns. Respondents did not always feel a need to justify them in terms of extrinsic security. In many cases they seemed to assume that it was self-evidently worthwhile for the United States to pursue prestige, bolster domestic morale, assuage fear, or fulfill the competitive character of being.

Prestige and Status

An argument sometimes used to support maintaining the strategic balance was that the United States would suffer a loss of prestige and status relative to the Soviet Union if it failed to uphold its end of the competition. The strategic balance, grossly measured, was seen as a symbol of America's stature as a superpower, and maintaining this stature was seen as intrinsically worthwhile. To do so, the United States must at least equal the Soviet Union in its nuclear arsenal and, even better, strive to surpass it.

Although many aspects of this argument have a ring to them very similar to the perceptual rationales for maintaining the balance (examined in chapter 6), there is a fundamental difference. In the latter case, the concern for the perceptions of third parties is based on the potential effect of these perceptions on extrinsic security concerns. However, the concern for prestige and status discussed in this section is related to intrinsic emotional gratifications.

Perhaps the clearest description of this line of argument appeared in an article by Colin Gray titled "The Urge to Compete: Rationales for Arms Racing," in which he describes the concern for prestige and clearly differentiates it from perceptual rationales based on a misperceiving audience. First describing the latter, he writes:

the analyst must explore the diplomatic and domestic bureaucratic meanings widely believed—though not by arms-control experts—to be attached to different states of strategic balance. . . . Militarily meaningless weapons are significant politically if political leaders believe them to be important.

Then, "in contrast" to this proposition, he formulates another rationale for arms racing that says:

A state may engage in an arms race in order to preserve or enhance the measure of dignity or prestige it deems appropriate (or essential). . . . The armed forces do not serve the state only as instruments of defense, deterrence, or national development; they also serve (in the eyes of others) to identify the state's estimate of its relative standing in the world . . . armaments yield satisfactions worth purchasing for the good of national morale.

He goes on to interpret this concern as playing a key role in the Jackson Amendment, which calls for the United States to maintain numerical equality with the Soviet Union. However, he notes, with some humor, that this was not openly stated:

These relative judgments were actually of little (if any) significance, because the United States had and would maintain "sufficient" weapons to devastate the Soviet Union. The prestige proposition was a fairly strong undercurrent in Senator Jackson's exposition of his views, but he and his supporters did not . . . [openly] contend that the United States should be first, or at least *primus inter pares* simply because it feels good to win—and Americans are a very competitive people.

Gray counsels those who desire "for the United States to be *first*" to "clothe" such desires in the "garments" of the more familiar perceptual arguments, based on a misperceiving audience, because it is "familiar and acceptable." He notes:

Many analysts who are devotees of the theory of assured destruction would admit that appearances are reality and must be taken seriously—if adversaries are likely to believe that gross asymmetries in military postures have military or diplomatic meaning.[1]

The thrust of *his* argument, though, was that the prestige significance was intrinsically worthwhile.

Although no one interviewed for this study was as precise as Gray in differentiating the status argument from the standard perceptual argument, many respondents did present rationales for defense policies based on concerns for prestige. A former high-level Pentagon official, who himself had been a significant critic of SALT I, described the SALT debates as follows:

> Numbers became very important, oddly enough, and the symbolism became very important. Indeed, a great deal of the fight over the SALT I agreement—and even more clearly, subsequently, over the SALT II agreement—had to do with these numerical issues more than the fighting capabilities of the two sides. The critics of SALT I said it was an unequal treaty. . . . They weren't really sure it was all that important [militarily], but they knew that when the United States signed an unequal treaty it suffered a lowering of prestige.

A strategic analyst who played a role in formulating the concept of the window of vulnerability gradually clarified that in developing the concept he was not really concerned with the condition of deterrence. He also made it clear that building the MX missile or Trident submarine was not really meant to improve America's strategic position. Rather, the concern was about prestige.

I: So [what is] the difference between having the Trident and the MX or not having the Trident and MX? In a crisis situation, do you think that margin where we would have counterforce capabilities after an all-out counterforce strike on their part, versus a situation where we wouldn't have a substantial amount of counterforce capability for second-strike purposes, do you think that would alter their decision?

R: No.

I: Do you think deterrence would be unstable in one situation and stable in the other?

R: No. I don't think—unless a madman gets in there, in command to do it—because a sane guy looks at what the results would be, and it isn't there.

I: Either way?

R: Either way, right.

I: So it sounds like what you're saying is that deterrence is still—

when you talk about the window of vulnerability, you're not really saying that deterrence is threatened.

R: No. Let's put it this way, in more understandable terms. All roads in the strategic equation lead to MAD. All the other ones— the first ones in all these other parts—are games, are window dressings, and they are window dressings for upmanship.

I: Why? To what end?

R: Prestige, self-assurance.

An arms control negotiator differentiated two kinds of responses American leaders have to new Soviet deployments: one, a concern for the genuine military implications; two, an irrational urge to match the Soviet deployment.

So it leads to two reactions: one is the direct, sensible military counter-reaction—how do we counter this new system, what do we build to fight against it? And the other reaction being a more political-perception reaction that we need to have something similar. The first is more rational than the second . . . but the second one is just as real.

By diagnosing this second reaction as less than rational, he was—or so it seemed—attributing it to psychological needs, not to security-related concerns for the political consequences derived from, for example, bandwagoning. Although he implicitly expressed some chagrin about these nonrational factors playing a role in American defense politics and arms control positions, he did not reject them and described himself as a full participant in the effort to act on such concerns.

James Schlesinger, in his FY 1976 Report to Congress, differentiated his concern for the status significance of equality from military considerations and from the political and military consequences that might be derived from a misperception of the balance. He asserted, with philosophical regret, that maintaining the strategic balance had become necessary to maintain the symbolism of being a superpower. "Equality is also important for symbolic purposes, in large part because the strategic offensive forces for us have come to be seen by many—however regrettably—as important to the status and stature of a major power." He then went on to attribute to the Soviet Union a preoccupation with parity along these lines. "Clearly the Soviet Union places a very high value on achieving parity, at the very least, with the United States."[2]

In the interviews, respondents also asserted that there was a general consensus about the prestige significance of the balance and attributed to the Soviet Union the goal of achieving the status of a superpower by building nuclear weapons beyond its military requirements. For example, in an interview with a former member of the Joint Chiefs of Staff, I asked:

I: Are they building up their weapons because they're not sure we believe they have a survivable retaliatory capability? Do they think that we might have some ideas that we could get away with a first strike?

R: . . . I think they are wise enough to know that there's no threat that we would initiate an attack and just deliberately destroy them. I don't think they worry about that too much. . . . There's a prestige item associated with this, where the Soviets want to be considered imagewise as being on an equal with the United States.

A Rand analyst explained:

[The Soviets decided] they would spend big bucks to get into the big leagues. They would also do arms control to become seen an equal of the United States—and that was very high, grand strategy. . . . They made that as a conscious, positive decision, as the best mechanism to be seen as a superpower.

Then, on a more general basis, he commented:

I think the higher the level of people, the more they think of them as instruments of the political competition. So there is a notion— whether it's correct or not—that national vigors are somehow measured by strength of strategic forces.

Third parties were also seen as attentive to the prestige significance of the nuclear balance. In a few cases, the Europeans were described as a bit uncertain about whether the balance was primarily of symbolic or military importance. The French were once cited as being more sophisticated—that is, more aware of the symbolic relevance—than the Germans. In two cases the Chinese were cited as being especially sensitive to the intrinsic symbolism of prestige. A former Pentagon official commented:

> It's not so much the military attributes. It's the prestige that they see associated with one or the other of the two superpowers. So it's less numerical in the Chinese case. But they are sensitive—even more sensitive than the Europeans—to these perceptions of competing prestige.

Given that the audiences in question are not concerned with real military capabilities, this implies that the concern is not that these audiences will bandwagon. Rather, it appears that some respondents regard it as worthwhile to pursue prestige in the eyes of other nations, independent of security considerations.

Although the dominant focus of status considerations was the relative military capabilities of the two sides, there were indications that the ability of each side to achieve perceived dominance in arms control negotiations also had prestige significance. After the Reykjavik Summit, some individuals expressed satisfaction that Reagan had not "given in" to Soviet proposals.* This satisfaction had elements that seemed distinguishable from the attitude of these individuals toward the specific proposals considered. Such considerations also entered into the INF debate. Kenneth Adelman advocated resisting Soviet proposals (largely the same as earlier American proposals) because going along with them would give the Soviets "credit." Speaking to a group of students at Georgetown University, he said, "So I'm sitting next to Schultz and I say I *don't* agree to negotiate because [the Soviets] want

---

*This zero-sum, gamelike orientation is frequently enhanced by the press in virtually any Soviet-American confrontation. For example, after the Danilof affair there were numerous assessments as to "who won." Reporters will also press political leaders to assess their performance in these terms, and leaders will, not surprisingly, often comply. For example, after the Danilof affair, the *New York Times* reported, "When President Reagan was asked today by reporters whether he had given in by agreeing to a Soviet proposal . . . Mr. Reagan said, 'No one on our side has blinked and I didn't blink.'" ("U.S. Continues Political Discussion with Moscow," *New York Times*, September 16, 1986)

to get credit for bringing it up to show on the world stage how peace-loving they are." A student inquired, "Is it just the credit that's important?" To which Adelman replied, "Yes!"[3]

Maintaining American Morale

Rationales emphasizing the significance of status and prestige, in most cases, were oriented to the perceptions that other nations might have of the United States. Other rationales, however, emphasized the value of certain policies for positively influencing how Americans feel about themselves. Competitive policies were seen as a means of maintaining or improving the collective psychological health.

Such arguments were used to rationalize the concern for marginal asymmetries. A Rand analyst explained:

> A country can have, in its own psyche, a notion that it is slowly going downhill, or it can have in its psyche a notion that the best is yet to come, and by God, we can solve any problem and do anything. And these things tend to be correlated with—irrationally, per-haps—but they do tend to be correlated with: "How well are you doing in the superpower [arms] competition?"

A senior CSIS analyst said:

> The older I get the less confident I am that you can change sort of instinctive reactions very much. . . . Self-confidence seem[s] to come from sources that are not on the whole totally rational anyway. And I think the concept of a dynamic military capability is one that really is very impressive—especially to Americans who are very change oriented and very modernization oriented. And I do think the fact that we've modernized things—big weapons, visible weapons—very little between '67 and '80 really upset a lot of people in this country.

A middle-level State Department official explained how the symbolism of strategic gains the Soviets made in the 1970s led to an enhanced sense of vulnerability and a crisis of faith in the United States. The feeling was

> that whatever the Russians have that's excessive we're not going to do anything about it—that their forces and our inability to respond, or unwillingness to respond, makes us vulnerable. And I think that a lot of it was psychological and not based wholly on the numbers. I think in part "the window" was an expression of this sense of uncertainty about where we were going in a larger sense.

The arms buildup that followed was then meant to counteract this feeling:

> The strategic force modernization program probably was an expression of saying, "Well, we're willing once again to spend what we think is necessary to create a viable deterrent." So that was one manifestation of the era of feeling good about yourself. And Congress also got severely scared, but not by the Soviet nuclear threat.

He clarified that the building was not aimed at solving strategic problems but rather for morale.

> I don't think the weapons themselves were in the end specifically designed to shut up the window; that was one of the rationales given to it. In the end, though, if you want to discuss what buying weapons is about, it's to make yourself feel that you're doing your part for the national defense. And in Congress's way, this is, "Yeah, we agree there's a problem—they took our embassy in Tehran and there are troops in Afghanistan; we lost the civil war in Angola, or our proxies lost. So, yeah—we'll spend more money on defense." And they don't think through the use of the weapons—nobody does. . . . We don't only build to impress [them]—in part you build to impress yourself. . . . That's the way countries tell themselves they're doing a good job.

But he clarified that it was essential not to make it explicit that the weapons were being built for reasons other than security interests.

[But] you don't say to yourself, "We're building this so . . . we'll feel better."

Arguments based on domestic morale were also used to support policies of seeking advantageous termination in the event of war. A Rand analyst said:

The word *prevail* is a reaction to the more passive terms or the more defeatist terms in previous years . . . *not lose* wasn't strong enough. I don't think these words mean necessarily what they seem to mean. I think they have to do with attitude. It has to do with vigor. [changing voice] "We're gonna be in this competition—blasted!—no matter what the circumstances . . . we should come out on top!" . . . If you don't analyze weapons and forces from a viewpoint of how to do the best you can at winning a war . . . morale is poor, . . . above all, we've got to avoid defeatism.

A former high-level Pentagon official, who had been involved in formulating such concepts, said that the ideas of achieving an advantageous termination are

primarily for the American audience—[changing voice] "Yeah, we're tough . . . we're prepared to carry through American policies," and that's not serious looking at the military possibilities. That's cheerleading, . . . and there's a big difference between the two. . . . It's quite schizophrenic . . . the statements that sound that way just come from bravado, because of defiance and bravado.

A State Department official explained the emergence of the policy of seeking to prevail in a nuclear war, differentiating between perceptual concerns vis-à-vis the Soviets and those related to the allies and to domestic morale.

R: It was for perceptual reasons—not simply though to impress adversaries—[but] to impress ourselves, our allies. It was kind of a big announcement, a proclamation, a sort of "We are here!"
I: Say more—what was the purpose of saying that?
R: I think it was sort of a more positive declaration about "Amer-

ica's back" and there's a sense that it was an instinctive or instinctual attempt to be positive . . . to get away from total nuclear defeatism.

At times this kind of thinking took on a slightly mystical quality, as if affirming that the possibility of winning would in some way help, or "sustain," the American way. An ACDA official explained:

> Nuclear war is not a winnable proposition. . . . That having been said, . . . we have to think about the follow-on exchanges. We have to think about the preservation of the human and social experiments that have been the heart of this country from its beginning . . . so if the language of prevailing is the vehicle for sustaining this body of thought, I'll sign right up.

Some respondents emphasized the value of war-winning policies in terms of the emotional gratification of the American public. A State Department official explained:

> American leaders have to say that they will prevail—it's the responsibility of their office. They cannot say, "Well, we're building these things, but I can't guarantee that we'll win." You can't do that to your population. People don't go to war for the sake, in the end, of preserving the status quo. War brings up all sorts of terrible emotions.

However, he added that people do not always like to recognize such feelings, saying, "Grenada was fun . . . but that part you can't admit to yourself."

Sometimes war-winning policies were described as gratifying vengeful feelings. A Pentagon analyst said, a bit defensively, with shoulders shrugged and palms turned upward, "Revenge is not a particularly laudable motivation . . . [but] it would be nice to make them pay retribution," then adding more sternly, "We will indeed wreak revenge."

Members of the military who were questioned explained that it is simply emotionally unfeasible for the military to think in any terms other than winning. As one officer said, "That's what the military is for!" This was said with a curious mixture of embarrassment for the military (he had already made clear he did not believe winning was possible) and irritation with me for asking questions with such self-evident answers.

Alleviating Fear

The third major rationale based on psychological needs emphasized the value of certain policies in terms of their ability to assuage the fears of the American public. This kind of rationale was generally accompanied by a clear recognition that the policies did not, in fact, reduce actual security threats, but because they made Americans *feel* more secure, they were worthwhile.

Such considerations entered into rationales for hard-target capability. It was argued that building weapons consistent with the idea that a nuclear war can be controlled would help alleviate public anxiety about the probable consequences of a nuclear war. A State Department official who had roundly dismissed the possibility of controlling escalation nonetheless supported it for "internal psychological reasons."

> I don't think any society wants to admit that [nuclear war] is going to be the end of everything. You have to, just for various internal psychological reasons, continue to believe that you can get out of this thing okay. . . . I think you need the [escalation control] policy for political reasons, for the sake of the public.

James Schlesinger, when originally proposing more limited options in NATO strategy, called for designing "rational missions credible to our adversaries and *ourselves* [emphasis added]."[4]

There were also indications that such factors entered into the movement for the SDI. A former high-level Pentagon official analyzed Reagan's decision to pursue SDI as follows.

> The origins of the SDI, that was pure perception, pure vision of the president—even the Department of Defense didn't want to have anything to do with it. This is a president who is well attuned to

the American viscera. Somewhere in the American viscera we don't want to believe that some son-of-a-bitch on the other side can destroy us, and he's offering us that wonderful defense-in-the-sky. It has nothing to do with military planning; anybody who takes a serious look at this knows that the Reagan vision is unattainable. And the Department of Defense, which falls in line behind its commander-in-chief, has resurrected an advanced form of the Safeguard, which is to say we protect our missile fields. And that's a little different than protecting our people and population. That was taken solely as a result of the instincts of Ronald Reagan—I think you have to treat SDI not in terms of rational military planning; it's just this gut reaction that comes from the deepest, deepest recesses of the American viscera that Reagan is attuned with.

He seemed to feel that a narcissistic resistance to vulnerability is particularly prominent in the United States.

Deep down, Americans feel that America should be invulnerable. No other country in the world feels that way. The Japanese may have felt that way till 1945; the Russians feel that they ought to be able to defend themselves unilaterally—that, despite the damage that Hitler did or Napoleon did, "We prevailed. We prevailed on our own." But that's different from thinking that you should be invulnerable. The Europeans are quite different; they have lived for five centuries of the balance of power, and sometimes your opponent is a little bit ahead. You gotta survive through those periods. And sometimes you're a little bit ahead, and when you're a little bit ahead, don't forget your opponent's gonna be a little bit ahead later. You're going to be vulnerable against something even if you're not today. So it's only the Americans who have this psychology.

Another respondent, who holds an advisory position to President Reagan, spoke of the value of having the public believe that the United States is simply moving in the direction of invulnerability. He explained that when people make their economic plans according to a longer "time-horizon," they "always do better." He expressed concern that

Americans, because of their sense of vulnerability, were not planning according to a long enough time-horizon, and that this was harmful to the American economy. The SDI program might encourage Americans to do their planning within a longer time-horizon by making them feel more confident about the future. My impression was not that he presumed that this was a rationally considered process, or that Americans would necessarily fully believe that population defense is possible; rather, SDI would create a feeling of greater invulnerability which would unconsciously lead to longer-term planning.

There are also good reasons to believe that some of the perceptual rationales for maintaining a balance were actually trying to address domestic emotional anxieties. Some argued that maintaining the balance was important for reassuring the American public. In one of the original formulations of the perceptual argument, Schlesinger stressed the importance of maintaining "a range and magnitude of capabilities such that everyone—friend, foe and *domestic audiences* alike—will perceive that we are the equal of our strongest competitors [emphasis added]." He warned that if the U.S. leadership failed to do so, "our own citizens may doubt our capacity to guard the nation's interest."[5] One respondent worried that if the Soviet Union gained a larger arsenal, Americans might get an "inferiority complex" and feel that "we shouldn't do anything to upset the Soviets." Another worried that if there were a "general perception of U.S. weakness," this might create a situation in which the president "feels weak." Maintaining a balance was seen as a means of neutralizing all of these potential feelings even though the respondents recognized such a response as irrational.

It is possible to rationalize this concern for domestic perceptions in terms of security interests; a domestic population that feels more secure will more likely support a strong foreign policy and dissuade a potentially adventurous adversary. However, my impression was that it was also seen as worthy in itself for the American public to feel safer. Policymakers see it as their responsibility to address these domestic psychological needs even if it involves maintaining illusions such as the idea that maintaining a balance makes one significantly more secure.

Fulfilling the Competitive Nature of Being

An intriguing rationale for competitive defense policies was based on the assumption that competitive behavior is intrinsic to human identity, nation-states, and even being itself. A tautological argument was made that because such competitive behavior is natural and inherent, it must be pursued without reservation (that is, people or nations should be competitive because they are competitive).

This argument is in substantial contrast to those based on considerations of military force or perceptions. Both of these latter rationales were based on the assumption that states follow competitive policies to achieve certain instrumental objectives, such as power, security, or economic advantages. In the pursuit of such objectives, states rationally consider the objective conditions, such as the distribution of power, that indicate their probability of achieving success. As we have seen, these arguments are often hard-put to explain how nations can rationally pursue such objectives in a militarily competitive fashion given the objective condition of mutual vulnerability.

The tautological rationale, however, avoids many of these problems altogether. It asserts that nation-states pursue competitive policies largely irrespective of the objective conditions. Driven by the innate, intrinsically motivated human urge to compete, nations will behave competitively and will go to war or engage in an arms race even if that behavior is irrational. The most curious element of this rationale, though, is its prescription that given this state of nature, the United States should pursue competitive policies with even greater aplomb. This prescription rarely held out much hope for an improved outcome. In fact, it was often accompanied by pessimistic predictions. Nevertheless, it was argued that humans should fulfill their competitive nature unreservedly because to do otherwise would be an unnatural distortion.

A former Pentagon official presented such an argument in some detail. He made it clear from the beginning that he was quite pessimistic about the potential for rational control over the propensity for war.

The chances are there will be a [Soviet-American] war one of these days. So that'll be the end. So I'm very gloomy, really despondent, okay? I'd like to hope that there's some way out of this dilemma, but I don't see it. Now, why don't I see it? Now I go below the surface.

He then began to elaborate a rather complex theory based primarily on psychoanalytic concepts. Briefly stated, he argued that humans—especially males—are genetically coded to be competitive. The original context for this competition is the Oedipal conflict between the son and the father. To deal with this competitive energy, when sons come of age, fathers direct this energy to the periphery of the society in the form of war. This then evolves into interstate conflict. In summary, he said, "[Nations] want to fight . . . [because of] these genetic factors and Oedipal factors and everything else like that." He felt that because of the irrational character of this urge, deterrence is not a reliable foundation for defense.

R: I don't believe in deterrence, and the Soviets don't believe in deterrence.

I: Why don't you believe in deterrence?

R: Wars are just going to go on.

I: Because deterrence is based on rationality, and war is not rationally motivated?

R: Yeah, so I think that sooner or later someone is going to start one.

A presidential advisor was equally pessimistic about the potential for inhibiting the tendency to war.

My whole theory of history is based on patterns. If a thing happens again and again and again, and it reflects a facet of human nature, it'll happen again. The most important pattern about war can be stated in two words: it's recurrence.

He also did not feel that the rational concern about nuclear annihilation would necessarily prevent another major war. Conventional wars have also been irrational in terms of real gains. He asserted, "For people to act rationally goes against all history."

A State Department official used a kind of hydraulic model to describe the intrinsic urge to war. He explained that emotional energy builds up in periods of political tension, an energy that ultimately seeks release through war independent of rational considerations.

> Tensions begin to build up with you and [leaders] start making decisions to release the tension . . . at a certain point everyone just decides, "Fuck, let's go to war!" It's just easier . . . I mean, you're not worried about, well, should we, shouldn't we do it. It's not a rational decision.

Several respondents argued that arms races were also inevitable and not derived from rational military planning. A noted hawkish academic was pressed to give a rationale for the deployments he supported. After some futile efforts, I took an aggressive approach,

> I still haven't heard the answer to the question about what the purpose of the weapon is . . .
> R: . . . as always, I am rejecting your question because this is a product of historical evolution.
> I: But there's still the question of what is their purpose? And I assume that you mean that their purpose is deterrence.
> R: But you see I'm objecting to this—the way you're putting this— because you're trying to say somebody sat down and said, "What is the purpose here?"
> I: But why are we building weapons here? We certainly must have a reason for building them.
> R: A reason, yes. And the reason is that others have them. They build them because we have them. And that is a product of historic forces . . . that's an historic reaction.

Others projected the driving force of the arms race onto technology itself, depicting it as moving ahead irrespective of human intentions. When I raised policy questions that suggested that we might consider not pursuing certain options, several respondents said, in nearly reverential tones, "You can't stop technology!"

Some respondents described an intrinsic urge to compete, in subjective terms. For example, a defense analyst supported SDI on the basis that the United States should exploit its technological advantage. However, he had some difficulty explaining the military utility of this advantage. Recognizing this, he finally said, in a thoughtful tone, "I guess, too, I suppose—and this comes back to some of the psychological aspects . . . I am viscerally unwilling to give away any advantage over an adversary." When I asked him why, he explained his wishes in terms of the intrinsic nature of states: "It comes back to what is the nature of international politics? What is the nature of relations between nations?"

This kind of thinking also led to attitudes about the arms race. The predominant attitude was a philosophical acceptance of the arms race and an insistence that it should not be judged negatively. The State Department official quoted above, in a discussion of the potential for an arms race in strategic defenses, said:

> Weapons always bolster counterweapon research. And the guy who invented the bow forced someone to invent the shield. And you can just take it from that simplistic example on. And for every measure there's always a countermeasure. And that's just the nature of weapons development . . . and that's what drives it and I think there's nothing wrong with it.
>
> I: So you see it as something reflexive?
> R: Yeah, to a certain extent it is. But there's nothing wrong with it.

A current high-level Pentagon official betrayed a bit more ambivalence but nonetheless embraced the same position.

> I: When you step back and look at [the arms race] as a whole—when you view the entire process in the last several decades that has led from just a handful of weapons to the arsenals that we both have on each side and the ongoing competition—when you look at that whole process, what's your feeling about it? Is that an unfortunate process?
> R: No.

Then, shifting his tone a bit, he said,

> Well, it's all a shame that we couldn't have frozen every nation into a kind of technological impasse in weapons development.

And, finally, with more resolve:

> But the reality of the situation in this is our aspirations, or whatever, don't gear to the technological process or to the adversarial quality of the relationship we have with the Soviet Union which primarily drives all of this.

To explore this attitude further, several respondents were asked whether they felt that the United States had made a mistake by not pursuing a ban on MIRVing in the late 1960s to early 1970s. At that time, the United States was well ahead in this technology. However, in the middle-to-late 1970s, as the Soviets caught up, the counterforce advantage of the larger Soviet ICBM force greatly troubled many defense planners. Because this advantage would not have materialized to such a great extent were it not for the development of MIRVing, the question of whether it was a mistake not to pursue a MIRV ban has been discussed in the defense literature. Even Henry Kissinger, as early as 1974, expressed some regret that the United States did not make such an effort. In a December 1974 press conference he said, "I would say in retrospect that I wish I had thought through the implications of a MIRVed world more thoughtfully in 1969 and 1970 than I did."[6]

However, of the seven respondents questioned, only one expressed any reservations about the United States decision to not pursue such a ban. Some expressed doubts that the Soviets would have accepted it, but this did not explain United States efforts to refrain from trying early enough in the process of development to make an offer attractive to the Soviets. A few (some had been directly involved in the decision) said there was concern at the time that the United States needed a hedge against a Soviet breakout from the ABM Treaty. Retrospectively, though, none of them felt that this was really a very strong reason. The predominant tone was that it was simply inconceivable that the development of MIRVing would not occur.

Perhaps most interesting were the responses received when I tried to point out the connection between the emergence of MIRVing and the vulnerability of American land-based ICBMs. To my surprise, most respondents said they did not see the connection. I found myself awkwardly explaining to sophisticated nuclear strategists that given that each Soviet warhead had a kill-probability of not more than 0.5, the Soviets could only threaten the United States ICBM force, within the SALT constraints, by MIRVing their missiles. Once the connection was made, no one contested it, but nonetheless no one had an explanation as to why it had not been a mistake for the United States to not pursue a MIRV ban. In one case, I pressed several times for an answer to this question until the respondent snapped at me, "I don't have to answer your question! You're not the district attorney, you know." Overall, I had the distinct impression that no one really held a strong belief that it was in the United States's interest for both sides to proceed with MIRVing. To most respondents this was largely beside the point; much more fundamental was the belief that this kind of arms race behavior was simply inevitable.

Not surprisingly, the belief in the inevitability of competition led to the active rejection of any efforts to constrain competitive behavior through international agreements. Here again, a tautological argument was used to the effect that such efforts were contrary to human nature and even aberrant. A congressional defense analyst elaborated such a view.

> I: So you're saying that there is a competition here, and notions of arms control and setting up these regimes to constrain the use of force and move the competition out of the military realm, you're just very dubious about all the effort?
>
> R: Yes. It seems to me antithetical to the fundamental nature of man.
>
> I: And do you have an attitude about that? Do you see that as sort of fortunate, inevitable?
>
> R: I don't consider it fortunate or unfortunate. I don't object to it in that I don't dislike the human race, and it seems to be a real integral part of the human race.
>
> I: If you could change it, would you want to try to change it?
>
> R: To me it's almost like saying it would be like going from being bisexual to having three sexes—I mean, it's such an integral part of our nature, as I say, that I can't see it changing.

A presidential advisor rejected any notion of mutual restraint. "My whole view of international morality—and this has always been true . . . [is that] it is the most duplicitous—it's one dirty trick after another." He went on to make such strong statements about the impossibility of achieving any kind of trust in human relations per se that I asked if he had ever lent money to a friend. Undaunted, he said "Yes," and then, with admirable consistency, pointing his finger at me for emphasis, "but I never expected to get paid back." Another presidential advisor expressed similar sentiments, saying in a philosophical tone, "We live in a world in which you can't trust."

Efforts for arms control were roundly dismissed. A strategic analyst scoffed, "[Arms control] is one of those funny American ideas. It just doesn't make it, you know, it just doesn't work." A former Pentagon official expressed this view by referring to David Lillienthal's change of attitude after his major involvement in nuclear disarmament.

R: Lillienthal, who couldn't have been more antinuclear right after World War II—just rabidly so—swung around. He was one of the prime architects of United States disarmament policy. And by 1963 he had swung around, and he'd turned against the disarmament process—it was hopeless, and the reason being that it just ignored human nature; it ignored countries; it ignored history; and everything else—just a great speech . . .

I: So do you essentially agree with the idea that disarmament is, in a sense, against human nature?

R: Well, sure it is. It would never work, for whatever the reasons may be. Human beings are human beings, and nations are nations, and underneath they've never really had any really serious intent of going by disarmament rules.

A presidential advisor asserted:

It's ridiculous to rely on a treaty. It would be ridiculous if they weren't Soviets. . . . Most nations have broken their treaties (although the Soviet Union was probably the champion for a short time, but only by a narrow margin—England would qualify just as well). The United States, with the few treaties it has had to break, has done remarkably well in breaking them—including George Washington, Thomas Jefferson, Alexander Hamilton, and you could go on. . . . Everybody breaks treaties.

Another presidential advisor asserted that establishing arms control limits simply redirects competitive energy to a slightly different arena of arms competition. Once this has been exhausted the limits will ultimately be abrogated. Citing historical patterns, he said:

> You've got caps on certain kinds of things, and then the changes began to occur around those things. We capped one thing, and even taking the most neutralist view of this, the most abstract historical view, . . . these things are meaningless. Take the Washington Arms Treaty in the 1920s, for example. Great triumph, you know—the British, the Japanese, and the Americans, the French, even the Italians got together and established systems—some kind of parity in battleships, tactical ships. So what happens? Then everybody starts making cruisers and submarines. You hold to that until the cap bursts and then go back to building the battleships again.

A political analyst carried this idea further, saying that arms control treaties even exacerbate the competition.

> It may well be that looking back we will see that each agreement is followed by larger defense systems. Partly because the military said, "Oh, my God, we're limited here, and therefore we have to do it elsewhere." Partly because it sets up a different structure of competition.

When I asked respondents for the prescriptive implications of their general perspective on competitiveness, the overriding theme was that competitive policies should continue to be pursued and in most cases that competitiveness should even be intensified. In some cases this was articulated in terms of certain desired outcomes, one of which was the maintenance of a certain stability to be derived from both sides actively and effectively pursuing competitive policies. A State Department official went so far as to say that it was positive that the Soviet Union finally had a dynamic leader who could more effectively uphold its end of the equilibrium.

Others supported the arms race and opposed arms control based on the psychoanalytic concepts of symbolic substitution and sublimation. A former Pentagon official said:

> Arms control is a false activity in itself. That is to say it is an attempt to cope with what is, in fact, a beneficial symptom of the malevolent, of the malignant conflict, the arms competition. It is an outlet for this compoundment. One of the ways that we have avoided a war has been because the energies of war have gone into other things, such as low-intensity warfare—but also the strategic arms competition. It's a substitute. And when you perversely enough go in there, and you preclude that, then . . . arms control is self-defeating in a most literal sense. If arms control were completely successful in itself, it would have created a far more dangerous world.

Colin Gray, in his article "The Urge to Compete," makes a similar point:

> An arms race may serve . . . to satisfy a potentially aggressive state with a[n] . . . arms race victory (the arms race as a cheaper substitute for war). . . . Of a number of unpleasant alternatives, a rearmament program could be the least harmful both for national security and international order.[7]

Overall, though, my impression was that the dominant motive for sustaining competitive behavior was not tied to an instrumental end. Respondents who asserted the intrinsically competitive nature of humans and states, when asked the reason for sustaining competitive behavior, would often simply reassert that it was natural. In some cases they recognized the danger of the competition but still embraced it. This would not necessarily even be derived from a concept of maintaining deterrence, because sometimes this was rejected on the basis that deterrence was not strong enough to override the irrational human urge to war. For example, the former Pentagon official who had based his theory of the inevitability of war on psychoanalytic concepts was asked for his prescriptions.

> I: Given the situation, what needs to happen in regard to nuclear arms? You seem to believe there's a real danger here . . .

R: So what needs to happen to avoid war, the impossible, the unthinkable, and so on? I've got this deep feeling—way down deep—that we're incapable of avoiding it, that we really don't want to. And all the signs that I see pretty well back that up. But as to what I would do, I would emulate the Soviets, and I would build up a military machine (this sounds awful, just atrocious to those people)* capable of actually fighting nuclear war, the object being to win—well, let's put it this way: at a minimum, not lose it . . . so that we can present to them a general posture that "we're every bit as good as you are in all departments."

Referring to his earlier statement that he did not believe in deterrence, I said, "I don't quite get how that solves the problem." He seemed a little confused about what he was trying to say but was nonetheless quite intense, almost passionate. "I don't believe in deterrence. . . . Wars are just going to go on."

In some cases these views about inherent conflict extended beyond the human dimension. The nature of being itself was seen as based on a dialectical conflict. As each part pursues its competitive course, the equilibrium of the whole is maintained. To go against the competitive nature of being was seen as not only unwise but even dangerous. For example, a congressman explained that a dynamic arms race has an inherent equilibrium, "As long as you keep things in balance, just like the balance in the atom, you don't have an explosion."

This did not necessarily mean that maintaining stability was always the goal of the competitive behavior. As discussed above, some respondents recognized that such behavior could very likely lead to war, but they nonetheless favored the competitive behavior. At the deepest level it seemed that the most fundamental motive was almost mystical in nature: the desire to align oneself and fulfill not only one's own deepest nature but the deepest nature of being itself.

---

*It was not clear from the context whom he was referring to by "those people." Presumably he meant people of a more dovish persuasion. However, given how abruptly it appeared in his sentence, it can also be interpreted that he was referring to a part of himself that had some reservations about what he was saying.

CHAPTER 11

The Two Streams in Soviet Military Thinking

THERE ARE unique difficulties for a Westerner attempting to discern the impact of nuclear weapons on Soviet thinking. Beside the differences in culture and language, one is faced with a government shrouded by a remarkable level of secrecy and with a tradition of presenting a unified front to the world.

However, despite the high level of control exerted, Soviet thinking about the significance of nuclear weapons is far from unified. As in the United States, two clearly distinguishable streams of defense thinking conflict in visible ways: an adaptive stream that firmly recognizes not only the existence of a condition of mutual vulnerability derived from nuclear weapons but that this condition radically alters the utility of military force, and a more traditional stream that questions the reality of mutual vulnerability or plays down its significance and asserts that pre-nuclear concepts about the role of military force are still valid.

This former stream had its fledgling beginnings in the middle 1950s. Georgi Malenkov, then chairman of the Council of Ministers, asserted that a general nuclear war would mean "the destruction of world civilization."[1] This declaration was, at that time, not well received and apparently played a role in Malenkov's fall from power. Nevertheless, in 1956 Party General Secretary Khrushchev, at the Twentieth Party Congress, recognized that nuclear weapons now made a general war with the West no longer "fatalistically inevitable."[2] By 1960 Khrushchev went further and described the condition of mutual vulnerability between nuclear armed states, saying that even "the state which suffers [an all-out] attack . . . will always have the possibility to give the proper rebuff to the aggressor."[3] And with even more emphasis he asserted, "Nuclear war is stupid, stupid, stupid! If you reach for the button, you reach for suicide."[4]

Eventually even military writers began to make such statements.* In 1965 Major General Nikolai A. Talensky, former editor of the journal *Military Thought,* wrote in *International Affairs:* "In our days there is no more dangerous illusion than the idea that thermonuclear war can still serve as an instrument of politics, that it is possible to achieve political aims by using nuclear weapons and still survive."[5] In 1973 Lieutenant General P. A. Zhilin, chief of the Institute of Military History of the Ministry of Defense, wrote, "The contemporary revolution in means of conducting war . . . has led to a situation where both combatants can not only destroy each other, but can also considerably undermine the conditions for the existence of mankind."[6] In 1976 he made the same basic argument in an article in *Red Star.*[7] Marshal Nikolai Ogarkov, as chief of staff, in a major book described the transition from the thinking of the 1950s and 1960s, when nuclear weapons were regarded as simply a means of increasing firepower, to the thinking of the 1970s and 1980s, which involved "a fundamental review of the role of [nuclear] weapons, breaking with previous views of their place and significance in war, . . . and even questioning the possibility of waging war with nuclear weapons at all."[8] A 1983 article made a direct reference to the concept of mutual assured destruction. "Given

---

*Readers may well wonder whether the statements made by military writers reflect genuine military thinking or are propaganda designed for public consumption. The quotes presented in the following pages were taken from a variety of sources. Statements made in the newspapers *Pravda* and *New Times* are clearly meant for public consumption. Statements made in the journal *International Affairs* are directed to a more specialized, elite readership. Books on military strategy and the articles in *Red Star (Krasnaya Zvezda)* and the *Soviet Military Encyclopedia* (published by the military) are aimed primarily at the military but with the assumption that other audiences will be taking note as well. The journal *Military Thought (Voyenna Mysl)* is very much an in-house military publication, and the Soviets have at times tried to restrict Western access to it. In terms of the issues being explored in this chapter, there is, at most, only a difference of emphasis between the statements made in these various publications. For example, there is a tendency to put greater emphasis on the impossibility of winning a nuclear war in statements for the public. But such statements can be found in military journals as well. It is intriguing to think that high levels of the Soviet military have ideas that are highly discrepant from the views presented publicly. While it is not possible to disprove such a hypothesis, there is little evidence to support it.

the present development and spread of nuclear arms in the world, a defender will *always* retain that quantity of nuclear means which are capable of retaliating against the aggressor by inflicting '*unacceptable damage*'—as former U. S. Defense Secretary R. McNamara once put it [emphasis in original]."[9]

Meanwhile, party leaders also affirmed the fundamental changes engendered by nuclear weapons. Then General Secretary Konstantin Chernenko countered the classic notion of Clausewitz (embraced by Lenin) that war is a continuation of politics by violent means, saying: "no political aims can be achieved by means of [nuclear war]. Any attempt to use nuclear weapons would inevitably lead to a disaster that could endanger the very existence of life on Earth."[10]

On the other hand, a palpable orientation in Soviet thinking has discounted the significance of nuclear weapons, questioned the notion of mutual vulnerability, and continued to approach military issues in pre-nuclear, conventionalized terms. Forces in the military opposed to a new orientation not only played a role in Malenkov's deposition but contributed to Khrushchev's removal, partly in response to his concepts of minimum deterrence and his resulting interest in reducing the size of the military.

Several military writers directly opposed the notion that nuclear weapons have fundamentally altered the nature of warfare. Major General A. Milovidov, a prominent military theorist, criticized those who emphasized the condition of mutual vulnerability, complaining that they "absolutized the quantitative analysis and arithmetical calculations of the destructive power of nuclear weapons" and did not take into account the qualitative factors that would work unilaterally in the Soviets' favor—that is, the Soviets' moral superiority.[11] Rear Admiral V. V. Shelyag dismissed "arguments about the death of civilization and about there being no victors in a nuclear war" as a "one-sided approach" derived from "over-simplified mathematical calculations."[12] A recurring theme has been that war, even nuclear war, continues to be an instrument of policy. In the influential book *Marxist-Leninist Doctrine on War and the Army* (first published in 1957 with numerous revised editions, most recently in 1984), this principle has been reaffirmed for the nuclear age: "It must be said quite categorically that nuclear-missile war fully retains the general social essence of war within its genetic foundation: it is a *continuation of politics,* by other, violent means."[13] Another military writer in *Red Star* sniffed, "no weapon can change the political essence of war."[14]

Consistent with this perspective is the tendency to apply conventionalized concepts. In a 1968 article in *Military Thought,* then Minister of Defense Vasily D. Sokolovsky and General M. I. Cherednichenko wrote that "the resolution of many strategic problems is still essentially based on the habit of leaning on the combat experience of past years."[15] Sergei Gorshkov, admiral of the fleet of the Soviet Union, said in 1979 that "Soviet military doctrine is based . . . on the experience of past wars."[16] At times there has been a reference to "fundamental changes" but still a tendency to employ pre-nuclear models. For example, Army General and candidate member of the Central Committee Ivan Gerasimov, in a 1979 article addressed to junior officers, speaks of "fundamental changes in the nature of a battle." He then goes on to refer to this World War II experience as applicable to battles involving nuclear weapons: "From my own experience at the front I can say. . . ."[17]

Closely related is the Soviet tendency to use images suggesting that the USSR is not truly vulnerable and that nuclear weapons directly defend it from nuclear attacks. Khrushchev said in 1961 that "the Soviet people can be confident and calm—the Soviet army's present armament makes our country completely impregnable." Major General Vasily Zemskov, in a 1969 *Military Thought* article, wrote of the Soviet capability for "repulsing a nuclear attack." Colonel Konstantin Vorob-'yev, a well-published military academy professor, in a 1980 book, has written that the Soviet Union can "repel" a "simultaneous strike on all the armed forces . . . and even on industrial and administrative centers in the deep rear."[18] A common image is of a "shield" supplied by nuclear weapons, as in a statement by Commander of the Strategic Missile Forces and Deputy Defense Minister Yuri Maximov: "The Strategic Missile Forces are called the nuclear-missile shield of our Motherland [because of] their high degree of readiness to repulse at any moment an aggressor's attack."[19]

Perhaps, though, the most significant indications of the perseverance of conventional thinking are defense policies similar to those explored in previous chapters. The concern for maintaining the balance, the goal of winning a nuclear war, and the pursuit of hard-target kill capability all suggest that pre-nuclear concepts still shape Soviet policies. There are indications, however, that at least some Soviets recognize the invalidity of these policies given the nature of nuclear weapons. Making it more complex, in some cases the same individual publicly both embraces a policy and recognizes principles that invalidate it.*

Maintaining the Balance

A consistent theme in Soviet defense policy statements is that the USSR must maintain, at a minimum, a level of forces equal to the United States. The Soviet concept of balance was recently defined by Deputy Defense Minister Yuri Maximov, who said, "The strategic balance means a rough parity of strategic arms, both in terms of numbers and combat might."[20] Then Defense Minister Dimitri Ustinov stressed that the Soviet missiles should be "in no way . . . inferior."[21]

Maintaining the balance, as distinguished from having a secure retaliatory capability, has been seen as having a major influence on American behavior. General Secretary Yuri Andropov asserted that equality had undermined "the possibility of blackmailing us with a nuclear threat" and is therefore "a reliable guarantee of peace."[22] Ustinov claimed that "military strategic equality . . . hinders the United States' aggressive intention in the world arena and limits its expansionist actions."[23] Major General Zemskov warned that with a change in the "nuclear balance of power" in favor of the West, "the danger of a nuclear war will increase manyfold."[24]

Consistent with this thinking is an interest in having military superiority over the imperialists. A 1972 article in *Communist of the Armed Forces* said: "The military-technological policy of the Communist Party of the Soviet Union is directed toward creating and maintaining the military superiority of the Socialist countries."[25] The entry on "military-technical superiority" in the *Soviet Military Encyclopedia* says that "Soviet military doctrine . . . gives a program of actions for

*By excluding the pursuit of strategic defense from the policies explored, I do not mean to say that the Soviets do not have such a research and development program. I was simply not in a position to investigate Soviet attitudes about their strategic defense program, since at the time of these interviews Soviets were still denying its existence.

ensuring military technical superiority over the armed forces of probable enemies."[26]

In contrast to this chorus of voices expressing concern for the balance, there is a consistent line of thinking that downplays the significance of marginal asymmetries and denounces the pursuit of superiority as pointless. V. Kuznetsov, in a 1977 *New Times* article, said:

> One more aircraft. One more submarine. One more missile. . . . What can that alter in a situation where both sides already possess weapons capable of killing everything on earth many times over. . . . The addition of new batches of weapons or the raising of their destructive power . . . is hardly capable of yielding substantial military, still less political, advantages.[27]

Major General Rair Georgiyevich Simonyan echoed similar ideas:

> neither the addition of fresh consignments of armaments nor the increase of their destructive force can produce any substantial military advantage.[28]

Marshal Ogarkov, in *Red Star*, labeled the further buildup of nuclear weapons as "senseless,"[29] while Leonid Brezhnev denounced the striving for military superiority, saying that it "becomes pointless in the presence of today's huge arsenals."[30] Gennadi Gerasimov elaborated this point:

> Superiority has become a concept that has no bearing on war. No superiority can save an aggressor from retribution. . . . It is not true that he who has more nuclear weapons has greater chances.[31]

While it would be easy to assume that these two orientations toward the significance of the balance represent the attitudes of different groups of people, a closer analysis reveals that, in some cases, they represent different mindsets within individual people. Henry Trofimenko, a political analyst at the Moscow Institute for the Study of the U.S.A. and Canada, in an article titled "Changing Attitudes Toward Deterrence," makes comments about the military significance of the balance that appear quite inconsistent. First he recognizes that the condition of mutual vulnerability is highly robust and largely immune to changes in the relative capabilities.

Even if the United States managed to break away from the Soviet Union in some parameter of strategic power, this lead could not restore the military invulnerability of the United States. In any situation the United States remains open to a devastating counterstrike.

But then he goes on to say that "parity" or "approximate equality"—not a secure retaliatory capability—"assures the security of the Soviet Union and its allies." Furthermore, he expresses concern that the United States might achieve marginal qualitative advantages even within the framework of a general balance:

> the Pentagon is striving to introduce certain material and conceptual amendments into the situation of mutual deterrence—without visibly disturbing the balance—which would make U. S. deterrence of the Soviet Union "more efficient" than Soviet deterrence of the United States.

He worries that these might give the United States both political and military advantages. But then, some pages later, he once again becomes more sanguine, recognizing the robust character of the balance:

> It seems clear that neither the United States nor the Soviet Union are likely to make qualitative improvements in existing systems sufficient to change the condition of approximate parity.

Two pages later he says that deploying MARVs (maneuverable re-entry vehicles) "would destabilize the present bilateral strategic balance." However, he does not give a military explanation of how they would upset the balance. He also asserts that such American attempts to gain superiority "compel" the Soviet Union "to adopt a similar approach."[32]

Seeking Advantageous Termination

The notion of winning a nuclear war has played a prominent role in Soviet defense policy. In the 1962 book *Military Strategy*, Marshal Vasily Sokolovsky formulated some of the seminal Soviet concepts of nuclear war. From an intensely ideological perspective, he asserted that nuclear war, while not inevitable, was a significant possibility due to the inherent contradictions between capitalism and socialism. Such a war "will be first of all a *nuclear rocket war* . . . [which] will impart to the war an unprecedented destructive and devastating nature."[33] Nevertheless the aims of the war will be to gain "complete victory over the enemy" by "completely defeating the enemy's armed forces and capturing his territory."[34] For many years afterward, such thinking was very common in military writings, as, for example, in this statement by Lieutenant General Vasily G. Reznichenko, a major authority on military tactics, in a 1973 issue of the journal *Military Thought,* "To achieve total victory, however, it is necessary to implement the results of these nuclear strikes, to complete the defeat of the enemy, to occupy his territory and to deprive him of the capability of offering resistance in any form."[35]

Such thinking appears to be heavily laden with pre-nuclear concepts of war. Arguing on the basis of age-old principles of conventional war has been a common practice. For example, Reznichenko wrote, "Many centuries of the history of warfare convincingly attest to the fact that a decisive offensive alone enables one to gain total victory over the enemy."[36]

Of course, the most intriguing question is how such ambitious objectives can be pursued when there is also such a high level of vulnerability. Some authors recognize the devastating potential of nuclear war and then blithely assert that victory is nonetheless possible, with no explanation for the potential discrepancy between these statements. Khrushchev's minister of defense, Marshal Rodion Malinovsky, recognized that "a future world war . . . will take on an unprecedentedly destructive character. It will lead to the death of hundreds of millions of people, and whole countries will be turned into lifeless deserts covered with ashes." But then he said, "we nevertheless come to the conclusion that final victory over the aggressor can be achieved."[37]

The problem of vulnerability of troops to nuclear strikes (in most scenarios critical to efforts to achieve victory) is given prominence in Soviet military writings. Numerous strategists have struggled with a paradoxical feature of combat when nuclear weapons are involved. A principle in Soviet strategy involves massing troops at critical points on the battlefront to break through enemy lines. Such an approach is seen as essential for victory. However, concentrated masses of troops become prime targets for nuclear strikes. One solution offered to this problem is for the troops to move *quickly* in and out of formation. An article in *Military Thought* reads:

> a certain contradiction arises here. The fact is that under conditions of the constant threat of enemy use of nuclear weapons, the concentration and disposition of a large number of troops in limited regions is highly unsafe. In such a situation, assault groupings . . . can be allowed to form only for the shortest period of time in order to deliver a strong blow at the necessary moment, to defeat the enemy, and develop the attack on dispersed formations in planned directions.[38]

It is hard to understand how such quick troop movements can solve this problem. The time required to mass troops and to execute a mission is many hours, if not days, while nuclear weapons can be delivered in a matter of minutes. Even if NATO responses were slowed by reconnaissance problems in some specific instances, the Soviets could hardly be confident that they could launch a massive attack without at least many of the major troop formations being quickly identified.

The tortuous difficulty in solving this problem is palpable in Soviet writings. Major General Aleksandr A. Strokov, in a 1971 textbook for use in Soviet military academies, seems to go around in circles.

> The principle of concentration of forces in the decisive directions has not lost its significance. However, the delivery of a nuclear rocket strike can bring to naught the superiority in forces in any chosen direction. The danger of a nuclear strike demands dispersion of troops. . . . At the same time the dispersal of troops has not changed the principle of massing forces at the most important place.

Finally he asserts that "troops will have to . . . carry out measures of defense from means of mass destruction,"[39] but he gives no explanation as to how this can be done.

Lieutenant General Reznichenko, in a 1973 article in *Military Thought,* recognizes that

> nuclear weapons have produced radical changes. . . . [This] presents tactics with a number of important problems, such as combating the numerous enemy offensive tactical nuclear weapons and elaboration of effective methods of troop operations within the effective range of these weapons.

But rather than presenting the solution to such problems, he simply asserts, "It is possible to solve all these problems . . . on the basis of thorough theoretical elaboration and practical verification of elaborated recommendations." A few years later he struggles with the problem in another article. He recognizes that massing troops "does not provide protection against nuclear attacks" but that using "dispersed formations . . . does not assure success." He candidly concedes that "the solution to this contradiction" is "no easy matter."[40]

At times the efforts to resolve the problem of vulnerability while pursuing victory take on a bizarre character. The arguments become so unrealistic that one is forced to wonder whether they are serious or if they are simply a form of cheerleading.

One theme is the categorical assertion that it is simply inevitable for the Soviet Union to win a war against the imperialists because this would be consistent with the deep-seated forces of socioeconomic evolution. Marshal Sokolovsky, in the book *Military Strategy,* asserted, "This war will naturally end in victory for the progressive Communist social-economic system over the reactionary capitalist social-economic system, which is historically doomed to destruction." Then Chief of the General Staff Marshal Ogarkov, in his article "Military Strategy" in the *Soviet Military Encyclopedia,* echoed similar claims, adding that the moral superiority of the Socialist efforts will afford them special advantages:

> The Soviet Union and fraternal socialist states in this event will have, in comparison with imperialist states, definite advantages, . . . and the advanced character of its social and state structure. This creates for them the objective possibilities for achieving victory.[41]

Another theme is that maintaining a high level of troop morale will somehow play a decisive role in overcoming the enemy despite the problem of vulnerability. Minister of Defense Andrey A. Grechko, in his book *The Armed Forces of the Soviet State,* asserts, "The morale factor will play a particularly large role in the event of nuclear strikes," and then confidently claims that "moral-political and psychological conditioning helps a soldier overcome *all* obstacles and adversities on the way to a goal" [emphasis added].[42] Sokolovsky asserts that, rather than being relatively less important because of the long-range capabilities of nuclear weapons, "the importance of the morale and the combat esprit of the troops increases to a greater degree than in any war in the past."[43] Another military writer recognizes that massive nuclear strikes will put the Soviets "in an extraordinarily difficult position," but goes on to say, "Nevertheless, troops possessing an adamant will for victory and inspired by the lofty aims of a just war, can and must wage active offensive operations . . . and strive to rout the enemy completely.[44]

At times it is implied that Soviet troops will somehow be miraculously immune to nuclear strikes even though it is emphasized that enemy troops will be highly vulnerable. Numerous writers extol the benefits of using nuclear weapons against enemy troops. Major General Strokov, in an important military textbook, proclaims, "The road for offensive movements of troops will be paved by nuclear weapons," and that "they must quickly use the results of the nuclear strikes, annihilating enemy troops in their path." He continues, "The massive use of the nuclear weapon will permit tank and motorized rifle units to conduct the offensive at higher tempos." The only explanation given for why Soviet troops will not be subject to similar nuclear attacks is a comment that troops advancing against the enemy should "destroy . . . his nuclear means."[45] But it is hard to understand how advancing troops, even when equipped with long-range artillery and tactical nuclear weapons, could comprehensively pre-empt NATO use of nuclear weapons. A substantial portion of NATO's nuclear arsenal is in basing modes essentially invulnerable to such attacks.

Another military writer, in a famous collection of military articles published in 1973, first describes in mathematical detail the devastating effects of nuclear weapons and then says, "For this reason, the troops in an offensive can be given missions to defeat superior enemy forces," and "to create breaches in its battle formation," all "under the conditions of using nuclear weapons."[46] Here again, there is virtually no consideration of the possibility that NATO will use nuclear weapons in an equally effective fashion. Perhaps there is an assumption that NATO would refrain from using nuclear weapons against advancing Soviet troops to preserve NATO territory. But there would be little incentive for NATO to do so, as the areas Soviet troops would be moving through would already have been devastated by Soviet nuclear weapons as part of their original advance.

Furthermore, in the same book it is claimed that Soviet troops will not only defend Soviet borders as well as internal targets in the midst of nuclear attacks but will also take actions that, somehow, will undo the effects of the nuclear attack.

> The creation by nuclear blows of enormous zones of destruction and radioactive contamination require a large number of troops for the defense and protection of national borders, rear targets and communications, and for the *liquidation of the consequences of the atomic blows* [emphasis added].[47]

Marshal Grechko adds that with proper moral preparation, the general population can join in this effort to "quickly eliminate the aftereffects of enemy nuclear strikes . . . and to ensure conditions for normal operation of the country's national economic installations."[48]

At times it is asserted directly that high morale can be so strong that pre-nuclear war principles can still hold. Grechko writes:

> the principle of attaining victory over an enemy in men and equipment at the decisive moment and at the decisive place will not bear the desired result if qualitative indications relative to the troops are disregarded. Among the most important of these is the morale of the personnel.

He expresses confidence that indeed this high level of morale will give Soviet armed forces yet another victory continuous with those of the past.

> There is no doubt that if imperialist reaction should impose a new war on us, the Soviet Armed Forces would display high moral stability in defense of the socialist Motherland and write vivid new pages in the annals of our glorious victories.[49]

In contrast to the war-winning orientation in Soviet military thinking is an equally palpable orientation that recognizes the condition of mutual vulnerability and the impossibility of victory. As mentioned, in the 1950s, then Premier Malenkov suggested that the newly developed power of military weapons had undermined the logic of war. Khrushchev, while less definitive, made similar statements about the irrationality of nuclear war. The 1961 Party Program declared, "War may not and must not serve as a method of resolving international disputes."[50]

During the early 1960s this line of thinking was developed by a number of theoreticians. The historian N. M. Nikolsky of the Ministry of Foreign Affairs argued that military power had reached its limits in nuclear weapons and had "dialectically 'negated itself.' " Such an outcome, he claimed, was predicted by Lenin. Major General Bochkarev, deputy commandant of the General Staff Academy, in 1963 said that the superpowers had acquired "enormous stockpiles of nuclear weapons . . . many more than required for the complete annihilation of the entire population of the earth. Thermonuclear war . . . will create a real threat to the very existence of mankind." In this context, war had become a morally unacceptable instrument of policy.[51] Lieutenant General P. A. Zhilin of the Defense Ministry's Institute of Military History, wrote in 1977:

> The contemporary revolution in means of conducting war . . . has led to a situation where both combatants can not only destroy each other but can also considerably undermine the conditions for the existence of mankind.[52]

Fedor Burlatsky, a prominent writer of the State and Law Institute, wrote in 1974:

> [General nuclear war] has become unthinkable as a result of the threat of mutual annihilation or of the infliction of unacceptable damage. . . . [Nuclear weapons have] made the victory of either side in a world conflict doubtful (or impossible) . . . inasmuch as the victors will be in no better position than the vanquished.[53]

This line of thinking gained particular eminence as it was increasingly embraced by General Secretary Brezhnev. In a 1977 speech in Tula, as part of his denunciation of nuclear superiority, he declared the impossibility of winning a nuclear war. There was some slight ambiguity in that he specifically said that the imperialists could not hope to achieve victory, leaving open the possibility that the Socialists still might achieve it. However, at the Twenty-sixth Party Congress in February 1981, he dispelled any uncertainty, declaring categorically that "to expect victory in nuclear war is dangerous insanity."[54]

There have been numerous efforts to explain this apparent inconsistency in Soviet military thinking. Some have given a chronological explanation, stressing that there has been a clear linear evolution away from victory-oriented thinking. Indeed, after the 1977 Tula speech, there was a precipitous decline in war-winning rhetoric. However, this explanation is not entirely satisfactory. There is no "alternative" set of military objectives that Westerners have had the opportunity to hear Soviet military writers describe. More important, there has been no clear change in Soviet force posture that suggests such a change in strategic thinking. Finally, statements about the pursuit of victory have persevered to some extent in Soviet writings.

Most notable was the entry on "military strategy" by Marshal Ogarkov, then chief of the General Staff, that appeared in the edition of the *Soviet Military Encyclopedia* published in late 1979. Citing Sokolovsky's *Military Strategy*, Ogarkov repeated the basic maxims that

> a future world war . . . [will] be waged without compromise. For the most decisive political and strategic goals. . . . [T]he Soviet Union . . . will have definite advantages, conditioned by the just goals of the war and the advanced character of its social and state structure. This creates for them objective possibilities for achieving victory. . . . [T]he achievement of victory in war as a whole, is possible. . . . [D]efense on any scale must be active, must create conditions for going over to the offensive (counteroffensive) for the purpose of the complete destruction of the enemy.

Perhaps in recognition of the potentially perceived contradiction with Brezhnev's statements, he quotes a 1970 statement by Brezhnev that "combat readiness . . . is the key to victory in war." Other writers also continued to make references to victory. In 1980 Colonel Konstantin Vorob'yev spoke of seeking "complete victory over the enemy" in a war with the West involving nuclear weapons.[55]

Such ideas have even persevered since the Twenty-sixth Party Congress, after which Brezhnev unambiguously denounced the notion of victory. In a 1982 book, Ogarkov begins by praising the Twenty-sixth Party Congress and says that "the character . . . of today's nuclear war imposes heightened demands." Nevertheless he goes on to assert that "the basic principle . . . has remained and continues to remain unchanged: to learn that which is necessary in war, to learn to defeat a powerful, technically equipped adversary in any and all conditions of modern war," and calls for "retain[ing] the will to achieve victory over the enemy in any and all conditions."[56] In a 1983 issue of the *Communist of the Armed Forces*, A. Dmitriev states, "The high goal of military art is to obtain victory."[57]

Another explanation is that there is a split between military and civilian thinkers—the latter recognizing that nuclear war cannot be won and the former continuing to hold traditional perspectives. Indeed there is a significant asymmetry along these lines. However, there have been numerous military writers who have recognized the impossibility of victory and civilians who have called for it.

This leads to the seemingly obvious conclusion that different individuals must have different opinions on the question—but even this explanation is inadequate. Many individuals express contradictory viewpoints. As noted above, Ogarkov has repeatedly called for pursuing victory while also clearly recognizing the condition of mutual vulnerability. Further, he has theorized that nuclear weapons have led war to negate itself as an instrument of policy.

Another prominent military writer, Colonel E. Rybkin, has made seemingly inconsistent statements repeatedly over several decades. In 1959 he denounced the theory of war's "self-elimination" due to nuclear weapons and called for a renewed will to victory. Five years later he recognized that nuclear weapons had fundamentally altered the nature of war because a nuclear defense "cannot be created."[58] In 1973 he wrote about "the role of spiritual forces in achieving victory," saying, "Victory in modern war will be on the side . . . [with] the ability to keep the will for victory under conditions of the most severe tribulations." In the *same* book, however, he seems to thoroughly discount the possibility of victory because of the devastating effects of nuclear war, saying, "even if a modern aggressor estimates that he will be able to save a certain portion of the population and national wealth, the price of aggression becomes too great and does not justify those goals for which it is undertaken."[59] In the same year, he wrote that "a total nuclear war is not acceptable as a means of achieving a political goal."[60]

Developing Hard-Target Kill Capability

Soviet spokesmen have also shown remarkable inconsistencies on the subject of Soviet hard-target kill capability. At times, some have even denied that the Soviet Union is pursuing such a capability. Henry Trofimenko has written, "The United States emphasizes the increase in the counterforce potential of its strategic forces . . . this approach is groundlessly attributed to the Soviet Union."[61] This is difficult to reconcile with the tremendous investments the Soviets have made in developing weapons with high levels of accuracy. Trofimenko offers no suggestion of an alternative purpose for developing such accuracy. Furthermore, Soviet military writings explicitly downplay countervalue targeting and describe counterforce targets as central in their planning. Major General Aleksandr Strokov, in a major military textbook, writes, "In nuclear rocket war, the greatest significance has been acquired by the actions of the Strategic Rocket Forces . . . in frustrating the enemy's nuclear strikes." A list of key strategic targets includes "communication centers, the basic means of waging war (nuclear weapons, rockets) and also centers of . . . military control." General Nikolai A. Lomov has written of the need to "defeat the enemy's basic nuclear weapons."[62] And Colonel M. Shirokov, in an article in *Military Thought,* says the objectives of nuclear strikes are not to destroy civilian targets "but to deliver strikes which will destroy strategic combat means."[63]

On the critical question of whether the United States would simply launch out from under such countersilo and counter-command-and-control strikes, Soviets are generally silent. However, for some years Soviets have stated that they will launch on warning. Marshal N. I. Krylov wrote in 1967, "an aggressor is no longer able suddenly to destroy the missiles before their launch. . . . They will have time during the flight of the missiles of the aggressor to leave their launchers and inflict a retaliatory strike against the enemy."[64] More recently, Henry Trofimenko has written that "a capacity to make a counterforce—disarming—strike . . . makes immediate response by the other side imperative."[65] In a recent *Pravda* article about a launch control center, it was reported that "each officer here knows the time in which a Pershing-2 or Minuteman-3 would reach his very specific silo, the so-called flight time." It was implied that detection capabilities had become so refined that specific Soviet missiles could be launched out from under specific incoming missiles. An officer at the launch control center said that "during that [flight] time we have to carry out our military task. And if it is necessary, we will fulfill it."[66]

During the INF debates in the early 1980s, a theme in Soviet arguments against the Pershing IIs was that their short flight time would be destabilizing, implying that the Soviets could be forced to use, rather than lose, their nuclear forces and, when command and control centers are threatened, to launch weapons under their control. Assuming that the Soviets presume that the United States has similar capabilities for detection and quick launching, it is not entirely clear why the Soviets pursue such an extensive capability to destroy hard targets.

There is also ambiguity about whether the Soviets believe it is possible to use hard-target-capable weapons to inflict a disarming first strike. An often-repeated concern is that the United States is attempting to acquire such a first-strike capability through its hard-target weapons. For example, the *Soviet Military Encyclopedia* says that the United States seeks to acquire capabilities "having sufficient efficiency not only to launch a first, i.e., preventive, strike with nuclear weapons, but also to make a second, i.e., retaliatory, strike impossible."[67] The urgency of tone suggests some genuine danger is involved.

At the same time, there has been strong confidence that the Soviet Union is immune to such a disarming attack. Sometimes this is expressed in bold terms which say that Soviet ICBMs are simply invulnerable, as in an interview with Deputy Defense Minister Yuri Maximov. *"What are the chief requirements put to modern ICBMs?* High reliability and invulnerability. . . . At present our ICBMs have . . . all-round invulnerability. *How is the invulnerability of our ICBMs maintained?* By a set of organizational and technical measures intended to ensure their high combat readiness and their protection on earth and in flight."[68] This reference to "combat readiness" as a means of sustaining the invulnerability of ICBMs probably implies a readiness to launch out from under a countersilo attack. How ICBMs are to be protected "in flight" is harder to understand. More common is the statement that any effort at a disarming strike will fail in that retaliation will be assured.

Such statements are cogent arguments. Assuming they are believed, it is not clear, then, why the Soviets worry about American aspirations to develop a hard-target kill capability. Even more perplexing is why the Soviets feel a need to develop a hard-target-capable arsenal at least as powerful as that of the United States. It is not a satisfactory explanation to say that the Soviet Union is seeking to offset American developments. If the Soviets are concerned that American counterforce weapons put their ICBMs at risk, it does not follow that they should improve the accuracy of their ICBMs. Hard-target-capable weapons are no less vulnerable to an American attack than other weapons—if anything they are more vulnerable because (at least until recently) they require fixed basing modes.

Naturally a particular significant question is whether Soviet defense planners, like American planners, see hard-target kill capability as being essential to fill in rungs on the ladder of escalation as part of an effort to improve the chances of keeping a nuclear war limited. Here again there is remarkable ambiguity.

The loudest message that prominent Soviet military spokesmen have made sharply dismisses the possibility of keeping a nuclear war limited. Defense Minister Ustinov said in a 1981 *Pravda* article:

> Can one seriously talk of any limited nuclear war whatsoever? For it is clear to everybody that the aggressor's action would inevitably and instantly invite a devastating retaliation from the side attacked. None but utterly irresponsible individuals can claim that nuclear war can be fought under some rules established in advance whereby nuclear missiles will have to go off under a "gentlemen's agreement": only over specific targets without hitting the population in the process.[69]

Also in 1981, Brezhnev asserted, "if a nuclear war breaks out, be it in Europe or elsewhere, it would inevitably and inescapably assume a worldwide character."[70] Marshal Ogarkov, in a 1984 article in *Red Star,* was even more definitive, saying, "any so-called limited use of nuclear means will lead inevitably to the immediate use of the entire nuclear arsenal of the sides."[71]

Soviet spokesmen have also rejected the notion of a ladder of escalation differentiated according to the geographic origin of the attacking missiles. Georgi Arbatov asks rhetorically, "Why should we care where a missile aimed at our territory takes off from, be it Montana or North Dakota, West Germany or Holland?"[72]

Despite such rejections, there is, nevertheless, concern that if the United States has flexible capabilities along the ladder of escalation, the United States, in fact, could have a significant advantage. An article on "escalation" in the *Soviet Military Encyclopedia* says that American "flexible response" capabilities serve the "American drive for world domination."[73] Henry Trofimenko elaborates this point, saying that even within the strictures of arms control treaties, the United States might gain such superior flexibility that it could achieve an advantageous outcome in the event of a military conflict.

> [American deployments may] be interpreted as a way to favor the United States (without violating the letter of the arms limitation treaties) with certain partial advantages that would not guarantee the success of the first strike but would still allow for greater flexibility in the use of strategic offensive arms, thus making it possible to impose on the other side "rules of exchange" (in case of conflict), unilaterally beneficial for the United States.

He goes on to say that in fact, "if actual engagement of the main forces should occur, the Soviet Union would undoubtedly act in accord with its own military doctrine, aimed at eliminating the opponent's marginal benefits and defeating the aggressor."[74] But despite such bravado, Trofimenko does not shrug off these futile efforts. His tone continues to be worrisome and implicitly supports Soviet efforts to match such American developments.

Even though the Soviets reject the notion of the ladder of escalation, they still feel a need to match American deployments in much the same way as if they took the "ladder" idea very seriously. Georgi Arbatov explained that the SS-20s are "our response to the forward-based systems the United States has in Western Europe. . . . The Soviet MRBMs are called upon to perform the role of our deterrent against all these [forward-based] weapons." Likewise, he says, intercontinental counterforce capabilities require a corresponding response:

> The latest technological advances in armaments make it possible to produce weapons systems with an increased counterforce capability. . . . The MX missile and the new warheads like the MK-12A are examples. All this in itself is sufficient to increase the worries of the other side [presumably he means the Soviets], which, it can be assumed, will consider these programs threatening, detrimental to . . . strategic stability, and will therefore take appropriate measures in response.[75]

Furthermore, despite vociferous claims to the contrary, a closer reading of Soviet military writings reveals that there is a substantial amount of thought about the possibility of fighting a limited nuclear war—thinking that, possibly, has led to an interest in hard-target kill capable weapons. General Nikolai A. Lomov wrote in 1968 that "the armed forces must master the methods of waging operations in existing organization with limited use of nuclear weapons."[76] Marshal Sokolovsky and Major General Cherednichenko wrote in 1968 of the possibility of wars involving "the limited use of nuclear means in one or several theaters."[77] In 1972 Colonel A. A. Shirman criticized the "nuclear fatalism" based on the "idea of unlimited employment," saying, "The very nature of [nuclear] weapon[s] presupposes particularly rigid control by political means over its development and utilization."[78] More recently, in 1982, General M. M. Kiryan described Western plans for graduated escalation from conventional weapons "to the use of nuclear weapons, at first tactical, and then later possibly to more powerful weapons." In response to such plans, he explained, the Soviet Union has created "a well-proportioned military . . . permitting the accomplishment of missions of any scale, in varying conditions."[79] Colonel General N. A. Merimsky, in 1984, stated more directly, "The presence of nuclear weapons in the armies of the probable enemy does not exclude the conduct of combat operations with the limited use of nuclear weapons."[80]

Developments under Gorbachev

Naturally, the question arises whether there has been a significant change relevant to the problem of adaptation to nuclear reality under General Secretary Mikhail Gorbachev. It does seem clear that the adaptive stream in Soviet thinking has become incrementally stronger with what the Soviets call "New Thinking." Gorbachev has stated, "Now it is perfectly obvious that the old notions of war as a means of achieving political aims are completely outdated."[81] In his speech to the Twenty-seventh Party Congress, recognizing the dangers of nuclear war, he stressed that "security can only be mutual" and reiterated that "it is no longer possible" to win a nuclear war. Perhaps most interesting, he introduced the concept of "reasonable adequacy" in force sizing. Though he did not really define the term, it appears that he was implying something along the lines of minimal deterrence.[82] In arms control negotiations, the Soviets under Gorbachev have shown more flexibility than their predecessors and seem relatively less occupied with precise measures of parity. This was particularly apparent in their willingness to accept asymmetrical reductions in the recent INF treaty.

On the other hand, there are also indications that some pre-nuclear-style thinking perseveres, particularly in the military. This was evident in a speech on Warsaw Pact military doctrine given by Defense Minister Marshal D. T. Yazov, reported in *Pravda* on July 27, 1987. I have given particular attention to this speech because one of my Soviet respondents mailed it to me as evidence of the changes occurring under Gorbachev. Indeed, in the speech, Yazov did talk about the need for a "new philosophy of security" given "the realities of the nuclear age," and how "a nuclear war cannot be used as a means of achieving political aims." He also spoke of "the principle of defense sufficiency," which he related to the need "in any circumstances" to inflict "unacceptable damage."[83]

However, a number of traditional military concepts were still evident. Rather than incorporating the principle of sufficiency, Yazov asserted that "the decisive factor in preventing war at present remains military-strategic parity," which he defined as "the approximately equal correlation of the two alliances' military forces."[84] Deputy Defense Minister Yuri Maximov has expressed similar thinking, defining "the strategic balance" as "a rough parity of strategic arms both in terms of numbers and combat might"[85] and proclaiming that the Warsaw Pact will not "tolerate anyone's military superiority over themselves."[86]

On the question of war-fighting strategy, there was some vagueness. Yazov stressed the "defensive nature" of the pact's military doctrine. But then, rather obliquely, he said, "The defensive military doctrine of the Warsaw Pact . . . by no means signifies that our actions will be of a passive nature."[87] Furthermore, there have been no major changes in the Soviet force posture to suggest a radical departure from their traditionally offensive orientation.

This is not to say that under Gorbachev significant changes are not occurring. Indeed, I believe that the adaptive stream has gained some strength; nevertheless, the traditional stream continues to exist. The Soviet Union, like the United States, seems to still have internal conflicts and resulting inconsistencies as part of its struggle to cope with nuclear reality.

CHAPTER 12

Interviews with Soviets

G AINING INTERVIEWS with Soviets proved to be quite difficult. My primary approach was through the Soviet Academy of Sciences. Initially, high-level officials expressed a strong willingness to cooperate. However, a long period passed before this willingness finally resulted in a formal invitation. From that point they were most gracious, though I still had trouble gaining access to the range of people I understood would be available for interviews. I also made contact with interview subjects through the Soviet Embassy in Washington and the USSR San Francisco Consulate, and contacted Soviet scholars visiting the United States.

A list of the affiliations of the individuals interviewed can be found in table 12.1. Clearly, the sample is fairly thin and oriented more to those who study the United States than to those who specialize in specific areas of Soviet policy. Only a few had more than a general knowledge of Soviet military strategy, and even they were reluctant to say much about it. By no means should this sample be regarded as symmetrical with the American sample.

In nearly every case the respondents spoke fluent English. With those who did not, I spoke through an interpreter.

In many cases, the Soviets were fairly uncomfortable with the interview process, insisting they were not accustomed to it. Sometimes the interview took the form more of a discussion in which they also asked questions. Only a small number of respondents consented to the tape recording, and some seemed uncomfortable when my note taking became too vigorous. Some expressed concern that attributions not be

TABLE 12.1

Soviets Interviewed

Institute for the Study of the USA and Canada	15
Diplomats (active and former, including 1 former arms control negotiator)	5
Institute of World Economy and International Relations (IMEMO)	4
Retired military officers (1 involved in nuclear strategy, 1 retired General)	2
Institute of Economics of the World Socialist System	2
Institute of International Relations	1
Journalists	2
Institute of U.S.-USSR Relations	1
Soviet Committee for Security and Cooperation in Europe	1
Other members, Academy of Sciences	3
Total respondents interviewed	30[a]

[a]The totals from the above categories are more than 30 because a few individuals fell into more than one category.

made based on their institutional affiliation (which is why such references have been omitted in the presentation of the material). A few seemed to regard official published statements as an adequate explanation for government policy. Nevertheless, despite these apparent discomforts, quite a few respondents made a number of interesting and, at times, surprisingly candid statements.

An obvious concern is that the Soviet respondents' statements may have little or no significance because the only Soviets given permission to be interviewed were those specifically trained to deal with foreigners. Their goals, then, would be simply to promote certain Soviet interests; therefore, it is impossible to discern what these individuals really think. I have several comments about this concern. First, my goal was not to try to elicit dissident points of view; I *wanted* them to explain the official Soviet viewpoint as cogently as possible. Second, their task was not so simple as it might seem. They were being asked to account for apparent inconsistencies in stated policies. During the interviews, I learned how to counter their stock phrases in a way that forced more creative responses. Their replies under these conditions were far from homogeneous. Finally, it seemed to me that there was a significant degree of candor in the responses. Many respondents made at least some comments that were implicitly, and sometimes explicitly, critical of certain government policies. It was not uncommon for them to be openly critical of the military. Nonetheless, in every case the dominant tone was one of support for the general outlines of government policy and pervasive optimism that, from their point of view, things were improving (something that may also be attributed to the changes anticipated with Gorbachev). In short, the level of candor seemed fairly parallel to what I found in members of the present administration in Washington. They felt free to make oblique criticisms on specific points, but in general they came across as team players.

Overall, the Soviets' rationales for their policies were quite similar to American rationales, falling roughly into three categories: those based on conventionalized military thinking, those based on the strategic manipulation of perceptions, and those based on identity needs.

Rationales Based on Conventionalized Military Thinking

MAINTAINING THE BALANCE

The majority of respondents clearly embraced the notion that it is essential to maintain a balance of nuclear forces or parity relative to the United States. This was sometimes presented as so self-evident that there was some resistance to explaining it any further. However, as I probed further it appeared that there were really two different reasons for this resistance.

In a small number of cases, there seemed to be some genuine confusion about the military significance of the balance. A few respondents expressed a concern that if the United States continued to build up its offensive arsenal and the Soviet Union did not match such efforts, the United States might gain a disarming first-strike capability. When I tried to introduce the notion of a minimal deterrent, it was not clearly differentiated from the concept of parity.

I: I'd like to understand a little bit better about the Soviet perspective on the purpose of arms beyond minimal deterrence. The Soviets have put a lot of emphasis on parity. . . . If you have a secure retaliatory capability, why do you need to maintain parity?

R: As far as I can see, when the Soviet Union talks about parity, they're mainly talking about maintaining a balance. . . . So I do think that the basic Soviet concept is their understanding of a minimal deterrent.

When pressed, he dissociated himself from this line of thinking, claiming a lack of knowledge, but continued to defend the concern for a general balance as militarily necessary.

I: But there is a significant difference between the concept of balance and the concept of minimal deterrence.

R: Well, I don't really know. . . . [But] I think it's extremely difficult to talk about minimal deterrence when the other side develops new weapons. . . . So how do you maintain what you would call minimal deterrence without developing some kind of new capacity every time a new weapon comes up? . . . Had the United States not developed these weapons, the Soviets would not have developed them either. They have found themselves forced to do so.

Considerably more common, though, was a highly nuanced response to my request that they explain why parity was necessary as long as the Soviet Union has a secure second-strike capability. Some respondents communicated through body language that they did not take very seriously their previous statements on the importance of the balance. Ostensibly they simply avoided answering questions by saying, "I am not a military expert" or "You will have to discuss these things with a military expert." At the same time, they sent other signals. Some shrugged their shoulders and rocked their heads as if to say, "Oh, come on, please don't try to embarrass me by pushing this point." Others rolled their eyes as if to say, "Oh, that old question again." Still others gave me a fixed gaze as if to say, "You're not going to get me to talk about anything I don't want to." In every case the clear implicit message was that they were fully aware that the military rationale for maintaining the balance did not really make logical sense. They also seemed to feel that I should know that they understood this, and they thought me a bit thick-headed for being so impolite as to force the issue.

I have since discovered that I may have been violating an age-old

Russian tradition called *vranyo*. Vranyo can be defined as a very gentle, nonmalicious, and sociable form of lying, distinguishable from *lozh*, which is a harsher, self-interested form of lying. David Shipler writes that a Russian friend characterized *vranyo* as follows: "You know I'm lying, and I know that you know, and you know that I know that you know, but I go ahead with a straight face and you nod seriously and take notes."[1] Ronald Hingley, in his book *The Russian Mind*, says that a cardinal social rule is never to challenge someone who is engaging in vranyo.[2]

Another pattern was for respondents to shift between asserting the importance of a balance and implicitly recognizing its unimportance by attributing the concern to elements in Soviet society that have trouble grasping nuclear reality. For example, one respondent started by explaining the concern for parity as an "inertia in Soviet thinking" leading to a tendency to think "in conventional terms in which quantity is still very important," thus leading to deployments at high levels of "overkill." But as he began to blame the United States for setting this trend and being the "pacemaker," he gradually began to take on this point of view. Speaking in first-person plural, he said in a serious tone, "To be on the safe side we must duplicate trends and capabilities." But then, distancing himself again with a faint smile, he said, "We don't believe in saying there's too much of a good thing. From our point of view, too much is wonderful."

He shifted in this subtle manner on other points as well. Saying, "We underestimated our own capabilities twenty years ago. We didn't perceive MAD until later," he seemed to imply that the Soviet Union had actually acquired an assured destruction capability before it achieved parity. But when I tried to make this implication explicit, he changed his tone: "For me it is difficult to make the distinction between assured destruction and parity." But just moments later, he said, "From my point of view [parity] is not important, but functionally, for arms control, it is important." He then explained that assured destruction and parity are at "two levels of conceptualization," though he did not define these levels.

He continued to make numerous statements which, while not directly contradictory, had distinctly different implications. He described a fear that the United States might achieve a technological breakthrough which would give it a breakout option. At first he seemed to embrace this idea as a valid rationale for Soviet deployments, but when questioned whether increasing the number of ICBMs was the appropriate response to a potential breakthrough, he attributed such ideas to Soviets who think in outdated terms, saying, "If I was an old man from World War II . . . I would be worried." But shortly thereafter he seemed to resurrect this kind of thinking, stressing that the Soviet Union must build large quantities of ICBMs to compensate for the American SLBM advantage derived from its larger number of submarine ports.

As in this last example, a common pattern was to explain the concern for the balance in terms of people in Soviet society who do not really understand nuclear reality. One respondent drew direct parallels with the problem of accommodating public opinion in a democracy, explaining that in public meetings Soviet citizens question officials about foreign policy issues. When they perceive the Soviet Union as lagging behind the United States in military power, citizens complain and challenge the officials. Having been the official at such meetings, he confided that it was very difficult to deal with such challenges. While not the only reason for the official policy of upholding parity, he explained, it is a significant factor—and one he seemed to regard as valid.

The part of Soviet society most commonly cited as being preoccupied with a conventional concern for parity was the military. Some military people, it was explained, would be satisfied with a minimal retaliatory capability. A stronger element, though, wanted something more "luxurious" with "alternative target coverage," "broader ranges," and high levels of "redundancy" so as to "match" American capabilities. One respondent said that the Soviet military "tries too hard" and even may be "harder to convince" of the nonutility of large arsenals than the American military.

A common theme was to view this difficulty in grasping the irrelevance of marginal advantages as a generic human problem. Describing the ludicrous desire for ever greater quantity, one respondent told an anecdote about a character who claimed that if he was czar he would be even wealthier than the present czar because he would supplement his income by digging ditches. Citing some psychological research, he said that "crowds act by the lowest common denominator." This tendency was attributed to Soviets no less than Americans.

SEEKING ADVANTAGEOUS TERMINATION

When asked what Soviet objectives would be in the event that deterrence fails, virtually none of the respondents spoke in terms of seeking advantageous termination. One respondent said that in the event of a Central European war, Soviet troops would attempt to move past the Elbe River. But this action would be quite limited and would be meant simply to prevent NATO from damaging Warsaw Pact territory when firing against Soviet troops. Ultimately, he saw a restoration of the status quo ante as part of a negotiated solution. One former military officer said that it was not possible to win a nuclear war but that it might be possible to win a conventional war, though it was very unlikely that a conventional war would stay limited. The dominant theme of the answers was that any superpower war would almost certainly be all out and both sides would be effectively annihilated. Soviet civil defense efforts were dismissed as simply the result of "bureaucratic inertia" or efforts to "calm down the population." Overall, respondents projected a high level of certainty that it was not Soviet policy to seek advantageous termination.

I then raised the point that concepts of winning a nuclear war had appeared in Soviet military writings. In my first interviews this was frequently dismissed as simply not true. When I presented translated quotes, these were sometimes discounted as mistranslated or taken out of context. As a result I photocopied the entire entry on "military strategy" in the 1979 *Soviet Military Encyclopedia* along with several other military articles written in the Russian language (some as recent as 1982), with the passages on achieving victory marked in fluorescent yellow. This, finally, did elicit some explanations.

A common theme was that a transition had occurred during the 1970s (a perspective supported by numerous Western Sovietologists as well). One respondent explained that there had been a debate between the journals *Military Thought,* which supported the concept of victory, and *Questions of Philosophy,* which opposed it. A recurring comment was that with Brezhnev's 1977 speech at Tula, it became firm Party policy that a nuclear war cannot be won. However, one respondent concurred with the Western assumption that there was significance in the fact that at Tula Brezhnev said only that Western imperialists could not win a nuclear war, leaving open the question of whether the Soviet Union might be able to. But, he pointed out, in the 1980 Party Congress, Brezhnev made it clear that neither side can win. At most, respondents said, later writings on victory simply reflected a lag that had no political consequence and was probably already firmly under control.

In nearly every case, respondents pointed out that writings about the possibility of victory had essentially disappeared in the 1980s. They seemed to feel that this should firmly settle the matter. I forced the issue a bit by saying that although there had been a clear change in declaratory policy, there was little evidence of change in force posture. Soviet forces are still deployed in a manner consistent with the traditional Soviet emphasis on an offensive orientation. Furthermore, no published military writings describe alternative strategies in the event of a war.

This frequently led to an implied concession that some traditional victory-oriented thinking does still occur. One respondent said, "In the Soviet military, as well as in other militaries, there are different views as to the whole issue of nuclear arms." A few others talked about different types of Soviet people. One respondent theorized in a general way that some people, in the event of a war, would like to "punish," wreak "revenge," or seek "political gain," while others are more sane and would simply try to "manage" the conflict and restore the status quo ante. Another respondent described two constituencies in Soviet society with different attitudes. He said that, although it has not always been the case, the constituency that does not believe in the possibility of winning is now definitely in the dominant position. Making a direct analogy to electoral processes in the United States, he said that this did not appear to be the case there. He described himself as a private citizen working to make sure that the more reasonable constituency in his country remains in a dominant position.

Once the advantage-seeking line of thinking was finally identified, respondents were asked to explain it as well as they could. Here again, though, they did not seem to take the idea seriously as a military concept and spoke instead in terms of perceptual strategies and psychological needs (discussed below).

HARD-TARGET KILL CAPABILITY

Respondents used military arguments most spontaneously in support of Soviet hard-target kill capability. When the question of why it is important for the Soviet Union to develop hard-target kill capability was raised, in many cases it elicited a perplexed look as if to say, "Why not?" It seemed to be regarded as self-evident that the Soviet Union would continuously try to improve its capabilities to destroy American military assets. One respondent said, "We just want improvements."

When I brought up the possibility that the Americans might launch out from under, respondents did not contest this. They seemed to regard it as an abtruse fine point with absolutely no potential to change their attitude that the effort to destroy American missiles was appropriate.

Several respondents tried to explain Soviet deployments as a necessary response to United States deployments. Three people said the SS-20s were a response to the Pershing IIs and GLCMs. Surprisingly, some respondents were a bit taken aback when I pointed out that some of the SS-20s were deployed some years before even the NATO INF deployment decision. Somewhat embarrassed, one individual corrected himself by saying that the SS-20s were meant to counter American forward-based systems. Another said that it was a pre-emptive move based on reading American plans for INF deployments.

When asked how the SS-20s were a militarily useful response to NATO deployments, a few respondents answered by stressing that NATO INF weapons have short warning times and an ability to strike at command and control center targets. When I asked how the SS-20s would be useful to offset this capability, they were, again, a bit surprised by the question and had no ready answers in terms of military capabilities. One respondent said that the SS-20s were meant to "threaten Europe," thus leading Europeans to put pressure on the United States not to deploy the Pershing IIs and GLCMs. However, this point had not been well thought out because he seemed a little thrown when I pointed out that the SS-20s apparently have had the opposite effect.

Some respondents implied that hard-target kill capability might limit damage, but, here again, on closer scrutiny they tended to discount the argument. They emphasized that there would be no efforts at mutual restraint in the event of war; the Soviet Union would "destroy all targets." When asked what the goals of such an effort would be, they simply said that a nuclear war will go out of control and both sides will be annihilated. It was not clear why, then, it would be important to go after counterforce targets. One respondent identified this inconsistency, saying, "There is a desire for damage control. At the same time there is a recognition that there is no rational way to do it." Asked if this split was derived from different constituencies with different attitudes or if it lies within specific individuals, he said that it exists within individuals. He then explained, quite lucidly, how individuals maintain the split with defense mechanisms. He said, "They simply don't think things through to the end, to all the consequences. There is a nonrational, nonscientific view that maybe something will remain." When asked whether the assumption of survivability affects war-planning, he replied that there are two "different levels." At one level there is "just a hope" that a war can be survived; at the other level, the level of planning, "this question isn't asked." At this level the military simply develops its plans according to traditional objectives of destroying military targets.

Perceptual Rationales

MAINTAINING THE BALANCE

The most common rationales for maintaining the balance were based on the need to manipulate perceptions. A recurrent one was based on a greater-fool argument that the Soviet Union must accommodate American misperceptions of the significance of the balance. One respondent began by affirming that numbers do not matter so much as they did before nuclear weapons. Nevertheless he said, "Dominant American leaders" believe that "more nuclear weapons make them more powerful." He felt that the Soviets tried to get across a new perspective but that this was only partially successful. Therefore, to prevent American leaders from believing that continued nuclear deployments offer a militarily usable advantage, it is important to match any American efforts to acquire superiority. When I asked how he knew American leaders had this belief, he said that it was evident in their deployments. Asked to explain how Americans acquired such an incorrect belief, he attributed it to Americans' "fascination" with technical things and their inability to see the "potential for failure" as illustrated by the Challenger accident.

Another respondent said that superiority would lead the United

States to "seek tests" to "diminish" and "ultimately get rid of the threat of socialism" and would even consider "preventive war." Arguing from the historical record, yet another respondent said that as the Soviet Union achieved parity, there was a dramatic decrease in American use of force. He cited specific numbers of incidents that correlated with this change. He also saw a recent increase in the number of incidents which he seemed to relate to the Reagan buildup. Similarly, another respondent worried that if the Soviet Union allows the United States to gain superiority, "they won't respect us" and will "deal with us like Grenada and Nicaragua."

Several respondents explained that maintaining parity was essential to address members of the American leadership who mistakenly believe that it is possible to meaningfully win a nuclear war.

I: Why is there this need to have equality in every area, if you have the capacity for retaliation?

R: Well, you know we have the capacity for retaliation, and the means of delivery are approximately equal. If this equality is destroyed, then one side will be in a weaker position. And then, you know, evidently there are people in the West who, say, who are ready to accept a lot of losses, who believe themselves to be victors in the possible war. . . . But what sort of victory would it be?

I: What do you think about these people? Psychologically what do you think is going on there? Do you think they're crazy? . . . Do you think they are serious when they say that they would consider a war, or are they just trying to bluff?

R: Evidently some of them are bluffing . . . but I wouldn't be surprised if maybe some of them seriously believe that they might gain something if they start a war.

I: So they think they personally would survive the war and would benefit from it?

R: Probably.

I: And do you think there is a rational basis for such a belief, or do you think that these people are in some way deranged?

R: I think they are at least on the border of being crazy.

Another respondent was more blunt, saying that parity is necessary to "deter" those "crazy" Americans who believe that even with 50 to 150 million casualties a nuclear war could produce "a worthwhile out-come."

Not all perceptual rationales were based on a greater-fool argument. Some respondents said vaguely that the balance had a very important "symbolic" function. In some cases it seemed that Soviets, like Americans, held the attitude that the state of the balance signals certain intentions. These signals occur within a framework that had genuine military significance in a pre-nuclear context. In a nuclear context, however, they have persevered as pure symbols. Ogarkov also seemed to express such a perspective, saying that "superiority has always been and continues to be a symbol of aggressive aspirations."[3]

Using a complex psycho-logic, it was argued that maintaining the balance would not only neutralize such symbolic gestures but would facilitate American adaptation to the condition of mutual vulnerability.

Another respondent explained that the United States believes superiority puts it in a position to use "coercion" to "fulfill its goals." His point was not that the United States misunderstands the military significance of nuclear weapons but that it believes asymmetries have "political meaning," which gives the United States the right to "do what it likes." Maintaining the balance is a "mutually acceptable criterion" which signifies that the United States must restrain itself.

In reply to a question about parity, another respondent said, with dramatic emphasis and pointing his finger at me pedantically, "Parity is a very important psychological concept." He said that the United States had enjoyed two hundred years of invulnerability and only recently lost its favored position. As a result of its history, the United States had an "inflated" self-confidence that led it to feel that it did not have to be constrained by the condition of mutual vulnerability. Only through maintaining parity can the Soviets hope to bring about a change in the American psyche. When the United States goes through the "psychological" process of accepting parity, only then will it also accept that we are "in the same boat." "Psychological equality" will then have the effect of "controlling against adventurism" on the part of the United States.

At least one respondent went a step further and argued that parity was a means of neutralizing efforts of American leaders to intimidate the Soviet Union by pretending to believe they can win a nuclear war.

He seemed to have a fairly good grasp of this kind of thinking in the West.

R: I would remind you of one concept which was published in the '70s or maybe even earlier. If I'm not mistaken the name is Schelling or something like that—the theory of conflict of this time. He says all the people are rational individuals. They wouldn't allow that—the people in general—that the war would happen. So if somebody in the international politics wishes to reach his own goals—egotistical goals—he should act irrationally.

I: So you're suggesting that in the United States there are people who have looked at a rational policy of appearing irrational and telling other countries—

R: I wouldn't say all the people, but among the people who are talking too much about the war, some of them, evidently, are of this type.

As I understood the argument he subsequently elaborated, he was saying that a condition of parity makes such irrational threats less credible and thereby weakens their effect.

Another recurrent perceptual rationale for parity stressed the importance of third parties. Several respondents claimed that the United States had built up its forces beyond the military requirements to impress allies and, more important, third world countries. Once again using greater-fool logic, they confirmed that third parties do misperceive the significance of the balance. As one respondent explained, "Other countries do look at numbers. This assumption is valid." The Soviet Union, they argued, was then forced to match the American buildup lest it appear to be "lagging behind."

In at least one case there seemed to be some confusion about whether or not the Soviet Union was following such a greater-fool strategy. First this respondent explained that parity is important because of its "political aspects." The side with superiority has "more respect" in the eyes of the rest of the world. In discussing this type of thinking further, however, he seemed to become uncomfortable and attributed it solely to Americans, calling it an "American belief." He discounted the idea that third parties are responsive to the balance, saying, "This is not true," and affirming that the Soviet Union does not "follow" this kind of thinking. Nevertheless, he shortly reasserted that the Soviet Union must "match" the United States because it is trying to impress third world countries and this time said, "Third parties have been impressed by numbers." Most likely, what he was trying to say is that the Soviet Union does not seek an advantage through addressing perceptions of third parties—just a neutralizing effect. Nevertheless he seemed unclear about whether third parties do, in fact, have such perceptions.

A few respondents began with a perceptual rationale for parity but gradually seemed to slide into taking on the belief in its military significance. One respondent first said that the concern for balance is "psychological." Unilateral reductions would be unacceptable for "political reasons" and it would "look like capitulation." But then, as he elaborated on this last point, his tone became more serious. Such capitulation would be like the response to Hitler that led to World War II. Then, growing emotional, he said, "Unilateral reductions would make us defenseless!" Therefore, he said, parity must be maintained.

There also seemed to be some confusion about whether SDI could upset the balance in a militarily significant way. One respondent initially said that the concern for the balance was "terrible nonsense" because of high levels of "overkill." He dismissed SDI as only relevant because of its "political connotations." But as he started talking about the offensive potential of SDI he seemed to become more worried and also brought in the idea that a combination of a "shield" and "offensive" could be problematic. When I tried to tie this to his original comment that all of this was only relevant in terms of political perceptions, he interrupted me, saying, "It's real!"

SEEKING ADVANTAGEOUS TERMINATION

In a few interviews respondents interpreted Soviet war-fighting plans and war-winning rhetoric in terms of a perceptual strategy. One respondent explained, "I would say that those statements were aimed more at Americans . . . so we give more a warning . . . like saying, 'You'd better not touch us because if you do, you'll live to regret it.' " Another respondent explained that military doctrine, such as war-winning objectives, is "not a real plan" but, rather, is "ingrained with political meaning." And yet another respondent explained that such military doctrine was something highly "politicized," designed to "take into account" the perceptions of "the other side." He saw such efforts as lying behind the military doctrine of the United States as well. He noted, though, that more recently, political considerations have led the Soviet Union to downplay references to "offensive" doctrine and the notion of "prevailing."

Public statements and published writings also hint that the Soviets may see a victory as a perceptual strategy designed to enhance the credibility of threats. Khrushchev made the statement: "I think that the people with the strongest nerves will be the winners. That is the most important consideration in the power struggle of our time. The people with weak nerves will go to the wall."[4] Bochkarev, a proponent of war-winning rhetoric, stressed that deterrence requires the perceived resolve to use nuclear weapons.[5] More recently, Georgi Arbatov regretfully embraced Western concepts that deterrence intrinsically requires both sides to appear somewhat irrational.

> . . . for the sake of maintaining your deterrent . . . you have to maintain your credibility, which in this case means showing and proving your readiness to stage a holocaust. . . . And this means not only threats, saber rattling and blackmail, but, from time to time, also practical actions designed to prove one's capacity for irresponsible action (like in a game of chicken), adventure, unpredictable behavior . . . the moral aspect aside. . . . We have here an example of that monstrously perverse logic imposed by the balance of terror.[6]

HARD-TARGET KILL CAPABILITY

The most frequently cited rationale for hard-target kill capability was that it would prevent the United States from thinking it can achieve escalation dominance by having advantages at specific levels on the ladder of escalation. The SS-20s are needed, it was said, to prevent the United States from thinking it can gain an advantage by making a counterforce attack using only its forward-based systems. Without the SS-20s American leaders might think they could extract Soviet concessions because the Soviet Union would have only the options to escalate to the strategic level or to submit. A few respondents also argued that high numbers of SS-18s and 19s are necessary to prevent the United States from thinking that it can make an all-out strike against Soviet ICBMs, thus forcing the Soviets to escalate to countervalue targets or capitulate. One respondent said, "Maybe it's our turn to be concerned about the window of vulnerability."

A dominant theme was that all of these efforts are part of a greater-fool strategy. American beliefs in the concept of escalation dominance were roundly dismissed as dangerous fatuity because escalation to an all-out war is all but certain. Georgi Arbatov worried that American missiles in Europe might "creat[e] an illusion that the United States can acquire the capability to wage a war against the USSR on a regional level, leaving safe U. S. territory."[7] Soviet efforts to fill in the rungs on the ladder of escalation were rationalized as necessary to prevent Americans from getting "crazy ideas."

A second perceptual rationale for hard-target kill capability was that it would enhance the American perception that a nuclear war would go all out. It was felt that a Soviet ability to "destroy all targets," especially military targets, would be particularly intimidating to Americans. When I raised the possibility that Americans might launch out from under a counterforce attack, most respondents assumed that the United States is on a general launch-on-warning policy, which only confirmed their point about the certainty of escalation.

There were several indications that this declaratory dedication to an all-out response was *primarily* a perceptual strategy. When one respondent asserted the certainty that a Soviet nuclear response invariably would be to "destroy all targets," I asked,

What if it was a limited nuclear attack?
R: Even then.
I: Would it be against cities too?
R: Everything.
I: Why?
R: Because we don't want the U.S. to think it could get away with it.

Another respondent was even more direct. With unusual objectivity he explained that both the Soviet Union and the United States are "playing the game of chicken. We are playing it militarily, while the U. S. is playing it politically." He elaborated, saying that "the U. S. presents the impression that the Soviet Union should retreat politically because [the U. S.] is prepared to fight a limited nuclear war. While from the military point of view the Soviet Union says if war starts it will be all out and therefore the U. S. should retreat militarily."*

These two perceptual rationales—filling in the ladder of escalation to prevent the United States from thinking it can gain escalation dominance and enhancing the United States's perception that a war will be all out—are different but in principle not entirely incompatible. However, in practice they do enter into conflict in a variety of ways.

For example, the way Soviets participate in the ladder-of-escalation framework ultimately weakens the perceived certainty that the Soviets will "destroy all targets" once the first nuclear weapons are used. There was a palpable interest in keeping a nuclear war limited. When asked what the Soviets would do if deterrence fails, respondents *predicted* that a war would go all out, but in at least half the cases they said the Soviet Union would first respond to American aggression in a limited way, with the "hope" that the exchange would stay limited.

Several respondents developed fairly elaborate concepts of escalation control within a "ladder" concept. One respondent used terms and phrases that could be drawn right out of American strategic literature. For example, he said, "Imbalances at any level have their effects at every level"; "imbalances at any level push escalation to the next level"; and "we never want to be frustrated at lower levels because this frees the hands of the U. S. to use force." When asked to describe the levels of escalation, he took out a pen and mapped out an eight-level ladder of escalation. He also pointed out that Brezhnev had spoken of "response in kind" and Andropov of "corresponding responses." He said that these concepts applied to war-fighting plans as well as to force posture. Another respondent said that "a counterforce exchange might be feasible" and that the Soviet Union sees three rungs on the ladder of escalation (one more than the two rungs traditionally recognized— that is, conventional and nuclear) rather than the twelve rungs he attributed the United States with seeing. Another individual said that having counterforce increases the probability of keeping a nuclear war under control.

Naturally these comments were quite surprising because they were so discrepant from the more traditional Soviet posture that rejects all

---

*This is reminiscent of Khrushchev's comment that "the people with the strongest nerves will be the winners." (Quoted in Mohammed Heikal, *Sphinx and Commissar: The Rise and Fall of Soviet Influence in the Arab World* [London: Collins and Sons, 1978], 97)

escalation-control thinking, and, indeed, in each case they reiterated, at some point, the familiar assertion that any war will probably go out of control. It is still unclear if these respondents were simply anomolies, if they were articulating thinking that is widespread but largely concealed from the West (which is doubtful), or if they signify an emerging trend. If an emerging trend, it is hard to say whether this is occurring by osmosis from Western thinking or whether the behavior of building weapons consistent with the ladder-of-escalation concept has in effect led the Soviets to take on corresponding belief systems even though the original intention was to accommodate American misconceptions. In any case, such trends seem contrary to the objective of convincing Americans that any use of nuclear weapons will be met with an unrestrained response.

Furthermore, if the wish to keep a nuclear war limited (should it occur) is becoming consolidated as a Soviet interest—and it is hard to believe it is not—then this interest does enter into conflict with the perceptual strategy of convincing Americans that the Soviets will necessarily escalate. To the extent that Americans are convinced the Soviets will escalate, the Americans will be given greater incentives to escalate first, thus undermining the possibility of limitation.

In summary, Soviet efforts to advantageously manipulate American perceptions by building hard-target-capable weapons runs into many of the same problems as American efforts, though there are some significant differences in emphasis.* Here again, by trying to do several things at once, their efforts tend to cancel them out.

Rationales Based on Psychological Needs

In some ways it seemed that the Soviets were not entirely comfortable with the rationalistic slant of my questions. They made efforts to give a logical basis to Soviet policies, but at times it seemed that they were trying to adapt their answers to a Westerner's orientation more than really explaining how they arrived at their own conclusions. When

---

*For example, Soviets put no emphasis on trying to enhance the credibility of their threats to use nuclear weapons per se. In fact, they tend to discount American concerns on this score as disingenuous.

they, instead, gave answers based on psychological needs, it seemed more natural to them, and they did so proportionally much more often than Americans.

An orientation to psychological needs was implicit in some of the arguments already discussed. Respondents often explained that Soviets were attached to maintaining the balance because they did not really feel confident in their nuclear military power in relation to the United States; they seemed to embrace this as a valid reason for a policy of maintaining the balance. Even when they were quite explicit about the fact that they saw this lack of confidence based on an illusion and expressed hope that this illusion would be overcome, still they saw Soviet policies to attend to domestic needs for self-confidence as appropriate.

Several respondents used the term *inferiority complex* to describe the Soviet psychology. This stemmed from the traumatic experience of being in a unilaterally vulnerable position, particularly in the 1950s. Several respondents became very emotional as they explained how frightful this period was, and seemed to be imploring me to be more understanding of Soviet policies that may have come out of an effort to "compensate." Speaking about the policy of seeking to win a nuclear war, one respondent said:

> Back in the '60s, when the United States did have the military superiority, I can understand the human emotional need to make that kind of statement. . . . [Now] we do have the power to strike back, and therefore there's no longer this emotional need to scream. That's how I see it psychologically.

The current policy of maintaining a balance was also seen as an effort to compensate for residual feelings of inferiority.

Closely related were rationales based on concerns for status and prestige. When I asked one respondent why parity is so important, he replied, "We don't want to be perceived as weak." I asked, "By whom?" He answered in very global terms: "By anyone, third world countries, Russians, Americans." Then, as if this made the point completely clear, "We're proud of being a superpower!" Similarly, when Arbatov was asked why the Soviet Union modernized its INF force with SS-20s, he first stressed that they did not grant any new military capability, saying, "The mission of these rockets hasn't changed." Then he asked rhetorically, "Well, what would the West think of the USSR if we replaced twenty-year-old missiles with something other than new and better missiles?"

The concern for status was not focused entirely on what other nations might think but also on how Soviet leaders might feel. A loss of status might weaken their resolve to maintain their position as a superpower. One respondent suggested that Soviet leaders might react to the nuclear balance as reflecting "political weight." An adverse development in the balance might lead Soviet leaders to be "coerced." He did not appear to be arguing that Soviet leaders would misperceive the military significance of the balance; rather, he seemed to believe that simply the emotional effects of a loss of status would have a major influence on Soviet leaders.

Some Soviets seemed to feel quite comfortable speaking about such status concerns. When one respondent spoke about the need to "save face" and expressed concerns about "what our friends will think," I asked him why that was important. He seemed to regard the question as odd and said, as if it were self-evident, "Every nation has an image it wants to maintain."

In other cases, Soviet efforts to gain status by building nuclear weapons were described with a mixed tone that conveyed some mockery of the attitude at the same time that it was embraced. For example, one respondent depicted Soviet desires for a large ICBM force, saying, with obvious exaggerated affect, "We must have the biggest and the best." Then, with a slightly more sympathetic tone, he made a cradling movement and said about the Soviet ICBM building program: "It was our beloved child. To have the best." And finally, with persisting embarrassment but apparent pride, "And we have it!"

Another psychological need cited in support of competitive policies was morale. A widespread argument was that the policy of pursuing victory in the event of a nuclear war was essential for military morale. As one respondent said sympathetically, "The military is bewildered by the concept that it is impossible to win." They are "concerned about the psychological impact on the troops." Therefore, the strong implication was, it is appropriate for the military to maintain concepts that reduce such bewilderment and "keep morale high." Another respondent said that war-winning objectives were necessary for military morale because "what would be the sense of weapons without people who think about how to use them?" The assumption, apparently, was that the military could think only in terms of traditional objectives or it would become apathetic.

A recurring theme was that the very identity of the army is built on an imperative logic of seeking victory. One respondent said, "Military people can't think in other terms. Otherwise they would be bad military people." He rejected the idea that the military might adapt to the new condition of mutual vulnerability, saying, "It is not their job to calculate costs and benefits." Another respondent explained, "The military has its own logic" and it is "only natural" that they will not easily "give up victory" as their goal. Perhaps the most apt explanation came from one respondent who shrugged and said, "The army is the army." All of them seemed to regard as foolish any idea of tampering with this situation.

Such thinking has also appeared in published literature. In a 1980 article Henry Trofimenko, after quoting Ogarkov on the goal of "defeating" the opponent, in a defensive tone insisted that such thinking is generic to the military: "The American military also prepares to fight efficiently. It is certainly not getting ready to capitulate and surrender to the enemy . . . the military in every country has one and the same mission . . . to ensure its country the favorable outcome of every battle and of the war."[8] This idea has been particularly promoted in Soviet military writings. Major General Bochkarev in 1968 rejected the notion that nuclear war cannot be won because accepting this idea would undermine the logic of the military. The implications, he writes, would be that "our military science should not even work out a strategy for the conduct of war since the latter has lost its meaning. . . . In this case the very call to raise the combat readiness of our armed forces and improve their capability to defeat any aggressor is senseless."[9] Others have labeled the belief "disorienting."[10] Rear Admiral Shelyag categorically asserted that the proper Marxist-Leninist view is not "one of futility and pessimism."[11] Colonel Rybkin warned that "class and defensive vigilance" would be weakened by such a belief.[12] A recurring theme, echoed by Grechko in 1975, was that the Soviet military, for purposes of morale, must not "lose . . . the belief in victory over the enemy."[13] In this context it becomes questionable whether these writers at all believe a nuclear war can be won, or if they are simply prescribing the belief.

More recently (in 1984), in an anonymous interview with the magazine *Détente,* a Soviet colonel tried to explain how such thinking is essential to the military despite the reality of mutual vulnerability.

> *Col. X:* All of us, more or less, know that nuclear war would be the end. All our theoreticians say that there is no way of preventing nuclear war from escalating to the global level, that you cannot win a nuclear war. That is our *general theoretical* position.
>
> But from a *professional military* point of view, such a position is impossible. Can a professional military man say that nuclear war is inconceivable? No, because some fool of an American President may really start a nuclear war. A professional military man must consider what to do in that event.
>
> *D: What difference does it make what you do in that event?*
>
> *Col. X:* Ah, *you* can say that. Mr. General cannot say that.
>
> *D: I am still confused.*
>
> *Col. X:* Consider the point of view of another professional, the doctor who knows that his patient is suffering from an incurable disease. He cannot for that reason abandon further efforts. . . . To make no plans for [a nuclear war] . . . would be openly to proclaim our helplessness. It would be *psychologically* wrong [emphases in original].[14]

Numerous Soviets—sometimes explicitly, sometimes implicitly—rationalized policies in terms of their value for assuaging fearful feelings in the public. As any foreigner who has been to the Soviet Union knows, Soviets have an intense need to tell the story of their suffering in World War II. In the interviews, when I pressed respondents to explain why they felt a need to maintain nuclear parity they would sometimes abruptly start talking about the trauma of World War II. It took me a while to understand that they were not simply changing the subject but were actually answering my question.

In some cases they would make the connection more explicit, explaining how they had not been prepared for Hitler and they want to make certain that they do not repeat the mistake. Some gave a very psychological analysis.

> I think you have to look at it from the viewpoint of, I'm not going to call it paranoia, but the viewpoint that this country—or this system—ever since its inception has been threatened. I mean, it has been attacked, and it has lived under the threat of attack for most of its sixty-seven years. It has had the very, very traumatic experience of being left alone, initially, to the mercy of Hitler. As you probably know, the Soviet Union, in the thirties, did everything they could to create an anti-Hitlerite coalition, asking for a kind of mutual treaty with France and England against Hitler. And nothing happened. And this is well documented. As a result it was forced into a pact with the Germans. I think that, psychologically (not only that, but that too), has had a great effect on the Soviet outlook. Plus, the immediate postwar situation, when the United States developed and used nuclear weapons, topped with the A-bomb, which immediately was seen by Truman as a sword to hold over the Soviets' heads. Again they found themselves threatened. And I think that this very, very powerful motivation—never again to be in a weaker position—has motivated the Soviets into this absolute desire for equality. That's the way I understand it. . . . [It's] historically based.
>
> I: More historically based than it is militarily based?
> R: Than it is militarily necessary.
> I: It's not important necessarily?
> R: I would agree with you, but you cannot dispel the human equation.

In general, though, there was an expressed optimism that the Soviets were gaining more confidence and would soon be less preoccupied with the balance. One respondent explained, "It is easier to arrive at a more sophisticated understanding when we are strong. . . . Now we're more secure."

This kind of thinking was also used in support of deploying hand-target kill-capable weapons. One respondent explained that without the ability to threaten hard targets, the Soviets did not really feel that the United States was vulnerable: "It was very hard to convince us about deterrence. We have always perceived ourselves as vulnerable" but the "U. S. was invulnerable." Only recently, with the development of counterforce weapons, did the Soviets finally become confident that the United States was really vulnerable. As a result, he said, "now we're happy."

Georgi Arbatov, in a published interview, also seemed to suggest that the purpose of Soviet hard-target-capable weapons was to allay Soviet anxieties rather than to fill a genuine military need.

> The MX missile and new warheads like the MK-12A . . . increase the worries of the other side, which, it can be assumed, will consider these programs threatening . . . and will therefore take appropriate measures in response . . . even if such anxieties are based on illusions."[15]

However, in general, respondents did not hold firmly to the position that developing hard-target-capable weapons or maintaining the balance was not necessary militarily. If a question pushed them to be too unambiguous, they shifted and began to give some credence to the official idea that the balance is, in fact, significant.

This kind of shifting has also been described as a form of *vranyo*, which, as Hingley explains, arises from a "two compartment mentality," allowing Soviets to shift between mindsets. He illustrates his point by describing a story by the Soviet author Alexander Yashin:

> members of a certain collective farm's Party organization are first found discussing the appalling condition of their fief: the widespread poverty, the shortage of livestock, the squalor, the mess, the meaninglessness of official catch-phrases. But then they suddenly pull themselves up, reverting with the ease born of long practice from real speech to the musical currency of official *vranyo*, and begin intoning those same meaningless catchwords which, in the previous phase, they themselves had been holding up to ridicule.[16]

A typical Western interpretation of this behavior is that Soviets feel coerced into mouthing the Party line even when they do not believe it. In the course of doing so, and as a means of further fulfilling what is demanded of them, they even try to convince themselves that they do believe it. While this interpretation may apply well to some cases, my experience in the interviews suggests that it misses what is most essential in this behavior. My impression was that the Soviets interviewed for this study did not feel coerced into supporting the Party line but genuinely supported it. They also recognized that the Party line was not entirely valid in an intellectual sense, but nevertheless felt that it was *emotionally* valid for the collective and therefore commanded their respect, even intellectually.

As a result, when they spoke to me, at times they seemed to be speaking with two voices, each with a different identification. The voice that expressed and defended the official conventionalized policies was derived from a group identification. The voice that discounted these arguments was derived from an individual identity—sometimes an individual who wanted to demonstrate his intellectual sophistication by making clear that he recognized the speciousness of the arguments. This does not mean, however, that respondents presented this individual self as their "real self." If I went too far in trying to consolidate my relationship with their "individual self" by asking them to amplify their critique, they would strengthen their "group self" voice and defend the policy. It seemed as if they wanted to remind me that they also "mean what they say" when they speak from their "group self."

This double-voice phenomenon had a slightly different texture from the way Americans shifted between positions. When Americans made inconsistent statements, they seemed more uncomfortable with them and tried harder either to suppress awareness of the inconsistencies or to resolve them in a higher-order framework. Even if unable to articulate such a framework, they seemed to feel a confidence that there must be one. Soviets, on the other hand, did not seem to expect that there would necessarily be a way to reconcile their positions intellectually. In a way, it seemed, the positions were reconciled for them simply by the fact that one arose from their individual perspective and one from collective psychological needs.

Among the Soviets interviewed it was very rare for them to explain policies (like some Americans did) in terms of philosophical concepts about the nature of being. Presumably this is partly because the underlying assumptions about the roots of international conflict have been carefully defined in Marxist-Leninist ideology. Most respondents were not willing to elaborate on these fundamental perspectives, and would brush off questions by saying that certainly I already knew the Marxist-Leninist view of such matters. Nevertheless there were several cases in which respondents implicitly communicated a richer sense of their view of the meaning of the Soviet-American conflict and the competitive policies that flow from it.

A particularly interesting example evolved out of a discussion of the reason for the Soviet Union's development of hard-target kill capability. This respondent's basic explanation was based on the perceptual rationale that the Soviet Union needs to fill in the rungs on the ladder of escalation lest the United States get the crazy idea that it can achieve escalation dominance. I pointed out a potentially problematic side effect, asking whether there was any concern that by doing so they might be "playing into the hands" of American hard-liners who insist that the Soviet Union, through developing its hard-target kill capability, is trying to open a window of vulnerability. He had clearly thought about this question because he then launched into a rapid-fire analysis of how every effort to enhance deterrence by trying to affect perceptions in some way "plays into the hands" of the other side. He went so fast that it was impossible to take notes, but he covered quite a few of the side-effect problems—for both the United States and the Soviet Union—that have been discussed in previous chapters. Finally he said, with some bewilderment, "So we're all playing into each other's hands all the time."

This was very interesting but I wondered whether he was being a bit facetious. To set a slightly more serious tone, I brought up an article he had written, in which he had argued that America's efforts to develop counterforce capabilities proved its intentions of trying to acquire a disarming first-strike capability. He recalled the point. I asked him if the Soviet Union had developed counterforce capabilities. He agreed that it had. I waited silently while he looked at me unperturbedly. Finally he said, "So, what, you hear a contradiction?" I answered, "Well, I suppose that it could be interpreted that way." Pausing a moment, with a look of annoyance for my obtuseness, he finally said, palms turned upward, "It's simple. We're white and you're black!"

Soon after he blew up in a fit of exasperation, saying that he had "had it up to here with Soviet-American relations" (drawing a line across his forehead) so much that he was "walking on the walls" (I think he meant "climbing the walls"). I tried to find out what this meant for him personally, but this question seemed odd to him. He realized that he could try to get out of the field of Soviet-American relations, but this seemed pointless—it would hardly solve anything. With a resigned shrug, he seemed resolved to continue to participate in the process of the Soviet-American conflict, which for him meant, among other things, writing articles that he knew were one-sided. There was a mixture of sadness and an almost cosmic humor that oscillated between bitterness and a genuine sense of playfulness. Clearly he felt that the Soviet-American competition was an inevitable manifestation of the peculiarities of human nature and that the only natural thing to do was to swim along with this tide, perhaps injecting some flair and intelligence along the way.

CHAPTER 13

Conclusion

THIS STUDY grew out of an attempt to understand how American and Soviet defense policymakers cope with the changes in international relations resulting from the emergence of nuclear weapons. Most centrally, it has been an effort to understand how defense policymakers come to terms with the condition of mutual vulnerability. It was observed that in both the United States and the USSR there are two streams in defense thinking, each with a distinctly different orientation to the problem of coping with nuclear reality.

One stream seeks to adapt to this new condition through fundamental changes in the role of military force in international relations. Ultimately it seeks to develop an international regime for resolving conflicts between nations that does not require the use of force.* Meanwhile it supports putting constraints on the military options available to states primarily through arms control and through a variety of confidence-building measures that marginally decrease the ability to take surprise actions.

The second stream downplays or even denies the fundamental significance of nuclear weapons. It supports a traditional perspective on the role of military force in international relations. It is suspicious of

---

*The concept of *international regimes* refers to a pattern of explicit and implicit norms, rules, and decision-making procedures that constrain the behavior of participating states and around which their expectations converge. The concept has been applied primarily to the realm of international political economy, though in recent years it has been increasingly applied to security issues and specifically to the realm of Soviet-American security relations. (See Joseph S. Nye, "Nuclear Learning and U.S.-Soviet Security Regimes," *International Organization* 41:3 [Summer 1987]: 371–402, and Alexander L. George, Philip J. Farley, and Alexander Dallin, *U.S.-Soviet Security Cooperation: Achievements, Failures, Lessons* [New York: Oxford University Press, 1988])

efforts to develop international regimes for regulating national behavior and most of all resists constraints on national autonomy.

These streams have distinctly different orientations to specific military policy questions. The adaptive stream tends to downplay the significance of relative levels of nuclear capabilities as long as one's own side has an adequate survivable retaliatory capability. In response to aggression, its goal would be limited to restoring the status quo ante with the minimum use of force, and it eschews any effort to seek advantages from a military conflict. It opposes the development of hard-target kill capability because it is destabilizing and provocative. The effort to defend populations with strategic defenses tends to be dismissed as simply unfeasible.

The traditional stream differs on each of these points. It supports a policy of maintaining a relatively exact balance of nuclear forces relative to the adversary. In the event of a superpower war, it supports the pursuit of an advantageous outcome. It favors the development of hard-target-capable weapons, and it sometimes regards the defense of populations with strategic defenses as a viable goal.

Because the policies supported by the traditional stream of thinking seemed inconsistent, in various ways, with nuclear reality, I undertook a study of the rationales given in their support. My assumption was that exploring these rationales might offer some insight into the difficulties involved in coping with nuclear reality.

As a totality the rationales given had a kind of leveled structure. Many respondents moved through these levels in a fairly sequential fashion during the interview. Other respondents moved back and forth between the levels in a more quixotic fashion. The most immediate level consisted of traditional military rationales that emphasized the pursuit of competitive advantages. These rationales could be characterized as "conventionalized" in that they largely ignored fundamental features of nuclear reality. However, when these features were pointed out, respondents rarely disagreed. Instead, they generally moved to another level, where these critical features were clearly recognized. This position, though, was not always stable. Some respondents shifted back and forth between recognizing nuclear reality and supporting inconsistent policies with little apparent awareness of the inconsistency.

When the inconsistency was indicated to respondents, they frequently moved to a third level, where they recognized the inconsistency but presented another type of rationale based on the strategic manipulation of perceptions. One of these perceptual rationales emphasized that there are key audiences who do not grasp nuclear reality and therefore it is necessary to maintain policies appropriate to a pre-nuclear context. Another argued that there may be strategic value in being perceived by an adversary as not fully grasping the significance of nuclear reality. Yet another stressed that pursuing traditional policies, even when they are generally recognized as invalid, is still important as a means of making certain symbolic gestures. The net effect of each of these rationales was to support policy behavior consistent with traditional, pre-nuclear orientation, even though the policymakers, much of the time, recognized that in fact such behavior was essentially inappropriate, given that fundamental changes have occurred.

Each of these perceptual rationales had some logical problems. These problems did not entirely undermine the basis of the rationale, but in each case it was not clear that the desired effects derived from the perceptual manipulations are any greater than the side effects resulting from the same effort. The net effect, then, may well be something close to a wash (that is, neither a net gain or a net loss) or possibly even a net loss. When I pointed out such problems in the interviews, a few respondents offered some very complex and sophisticated concepts suggesting how, with the proper political acumen, one could control such effects advantageously. However, even in these cases it was not clear that this perceptual strategy would necessarily produce a net gain.

One could end the analysis here and simply conclude that policymakers do not have a firm enough grasp on their arguments to recognize that they contradict themselves—that they are perhaps just "in over their heads." But I did not find this entirely satisfying. It seemed that policymakers were fully capable, intellectually, of grasping such problems. My conjecture was that there were deeper reasons for not seeing the problems more fully.

For this reason I was particularly interested in another level of rationales that went beyond such arguments. These emerged sometimes spontaneously and sometimes when respondents recognized the logical problems in the perceptual rationales. At this other level, rationales were based not on security interests but rather on the fulfillment of more psychologically oriented interests. Some of these centered around gratifying emotions—fulfilling the desire for status and prestige, sustaining national morale, and alleviating fear. Others emphasized that competitive policies were a means of blending with and fulfilling the inherently competitive nature of being.

A unique feature of such rationales is that they are not subject to the same kinds of cost/benefit analysis of other rationales. When one respondent recognized that a cost/benefit analysis, oriented to security concerns, did not really support the policy of maintaining a balance, he nonetheless asserted his preference for it, saying, "I just feel better that way."

This suggests that there may be an emotional resistance to recognizing nuclear reality inasmuch as it is perceived as interfering with the fulfillment of psychological needs. This can lead to a simple defensive response that resists recognizing the changes derived from nuclear weapons (conventionalization) or a more complex defensive response that justifies on political grounds behaving as if the nuclear revolution has not occurred. Some respondents seemed to be quite aware of the resistance to nuclear reality and could describe it. This emerged in a discussion of the window of vulnerability with a strategic analyst who had played a key role in its formulation. To my surprise, he rejected all the familiar military and perceptual arguments in support of the "window" idea. A bit perplexed, I said:

So it sounds like . . . when you talk about the window of vulnerability, you're not really saying that deterrence is threatened.

R: No. Let's put it this way, in more understandable terms. All roads in the strategic equation lead to MAD. All the other ones . . . are games, are window dressings, and they are window dressings for upmanship. . . . But when you take away all these layers of cloth, at the bottom of the thing, basically, is MAD, and no one likes it.

The Resistance to Nuclear Reality

A key question is, Why does "no one like" MAD? It may be useful to speculate about what the consequences might be if there were a fuller and unambiguous recognition of nuclear reality. This would mean first of all a greater awareness of the condition of mutual vulnerability. The fact that the survival of both superpowers rests in the other's hands would make the condition of interdependence more salient. The image of the nation as truly sovereign and autonomous would decline. The sense of the two nations inextricably bound together in a web of shared fate would grow. The image of mutual adversaries would be superseded by an image of profound interdependence, of each side simultaneously holding the other one at its mercy. Perhaps most centrally, competition would lose its pre-eminent position in superpower relations, and they would become at least as heavily conditioned by the felt need for such cooperation as would enhance mutual security.

This image is not without its attraction. Humans have an intrinsic urge for affiliation, to unite with ever-widening spheres of identity. However, those who think that this is a purely rosy image have a one-sided understanding of human motivation. In many ways this image is also highly repugnant. It suggests constraints on autonomous action, constant compromises, and a diffusion of the sense of identity into a morass of ambiguities. The paramount drama of human life, rather than being a clear-cut battle between good and evil moving toward an ultimate resolution, dissolves into a continuous and non-climactic negotiation in which the multiplicity of possible viewpoints becomes painfully apparent.

If the traditional image of the mythical battle is attractive enough or if the image of dissolving into a mire of complexities is repugnant enough, it may well impel individuals to resist recognizing the nuclear reality that may spawn such changes. Such feelings may even be so strong that they override concerns about security and survival. They may lead individuals to support policies consistent with pre-nuclear reality even if they semiconsciously or even consciously recognize that such policies marginally increase threats to security or obstruct possibilities for marginally improving security. On a day-to-day basis they may lead defense policymakers to suppress awareness of the fact that

Conclusion

nuclear reality undermines much of traditional military planning and to proceed as if nothing has changed.

In some interviews respondents were even candid enough to recognize some of these processes. One congressional defense analyst explained in a faintly sad voice why he avoided doing work on strategic issues. Referring to himself, he said:

> You're talking about a guy who, in fact, eschews [strategic analysis] . . . I think it's because I come from a military historical background, and, as an army colonel friend of mine once said, "Military men don't like nuclear weapons." I said, "Why?" He said, "Because they prevent us from getting on our horses and shroving our lances and charging the enemy."
>
> I: Do you feel some of that sentiment yourself?
> R: I think so.

Complaining again about analyses involving strategic weapons, he said, "I do not think there is much scope for the traditional . . . ways in which one studies things military."* He then described one possible solution to the problem as the effort to conventionalize strategic analysis but rejected it as nonsensical (though he also seemed to admire the effort). "One is sort of the assumption that nuclear weapons are like any other kind of weapons—they just have bigger bangs—which, it seems to me, is *valiantly* nonsensical [emphasis added]." Asked for rationales for various competitive defense policies, he did not defend the policies in military terms but described intrinsically motivated competitive feelings. "I am viscerally unwilling to give away an advantage over an adversary." Apparently uncomfortable with the boldness of his state-

---

*A similarly candid comment appeared in an article in the magazine *Proceedings* (April 1987, p. 39) titled "The *Nuclear* Maritime Strategy" by Captain Linton F. Brook (USN), who is presently director of defense programs on the staff of the National Security Council. Although the article is ostensibly about nuclear maritime strategy, the conclusion states in bold terms the suggestion that the subject be ignored:

The immense destructiveness of nuclear weapons and the ease of their delivery suggests such radical changes in the nature of war that it seems impossible to visualize their employment. The most *comfortable* way to deal with such weapons and their impact on naval strategy is to *ignore* them . . . a global war remaining at the conventional level [is] a contingency for which we have a well thought-out, coherent, well-understood strategy. . . . It seems a sterile exercise to discuss the strategic implications of nuclear war at sea. Should we not concentrate on continuing to improve the conventional Maritime Strategy? We should do exactly that [emphases added].

ments, he began to try to rationalize his competitive orientation in terms of security threats. "I do think that the Soviet Union poses the greatest threat to liberal democracy that the world has seen because they are more systematic, very rational, less spasmodic than something like Nazi Germany under Hitler." But then, catching himself in the middle of his next sentence, he paused for a moment and then said thoughtfully: "Maybe the threat isn't that great. Maybe that visceral feeling's so strong, maybe it overrides some of the more rational, analytical things you're talking about."

How Security Motives Are Overridden

The notion that there are motives that can override motives for security runs against a widely held model of human motivation. This model says that all biological life has an instinctive urge to survive, with all other motives being subordinate to it. Life forms that succeed in fulfilling this urge to survive thrive and reproduce. However, this model is actually a simplified way of describing a more complex process. Life forms do not have an innate survival instinct. Rather, they have certain genetically coded behavior patterns that are repeated. Life forms that have behavior patterns that, in a specific ecological context, result in survival and procreation are selected by evolution. This does not mean that the biological form is "trying" to survive. This is evidenced by the fact that when environmental conditions change, life forms will persevere in their established patterns even when it costs them their survival.

The conscious effort to survive is a uniquely human trait derived from the development of the brain's cortex. Human behavior is much less dominated by genetic coding and is therefore considerably more flexible than the behavior of other life forms. As a result, humans are remarkably adaptive and can adjust to changes in the environment. To adapt effectively, humans must exercise their cognitive understanding of the environment and direct their behavior accordingly.

Nevertheless survival-oriented cognitive processes are not the only factor influencing human behavior. There are other factors that have the capability to override the concern for individual survival or collec-

Conclusion

tive security. These include (1) competitive and fearful emotions, and (2) the urge to blend with and fulfill the essential nature of being.

COMPETITIVE AND FEARFUL EMOTIONS

At times emotions may serve survival interests. Competitive urges will often lead humans to take actions that give them a competitive edge in a struggle for limited resources. Fear may lead humans to avoid life-threatening situations. However, this does not mean that emotions are actually "trying" to enhance survival. Emotions will often prompt humans to persist in certain behaviors even when such behaviors threaten survival.

Competitive emotions will often lead individuals to engage in behavior that they know is life-threatening. In fact, competitive emotions at times are specifically drawn to life-threatening situations. In some cases individuals and groups that are more drawn to such competition may gain an edge over another individual or group less willing to take such risks. However, this does not mean that the advantage thereby gained is the goal of the survival-jeopardizing behavior. The willingness to take risks is not simply a form of bluffing. Humans will sometimes follow through on threats even when they know it will result in their death. Furthermore the culture that forms around such competitive posturing often puts much greater value on the intrinsic value of competitive behavior (pride, honor) than on the potential gains of posturing. Individuals who follow through on threats to the bloody end or who volunteer for suicidal missions are revered as exemplary.

Even the emotion of fear is not completely subordinate to survival-oriented cognitive processes. Fear seeks to reduce the *feeling* of insecurity. It does not necessarily seek to reduce real threats to security. Indeed, it may even lead one to take actions that increase threats. For example, a businessman whose company is in the midst of a crisis that threatens his livelihood may feel fearful and anxious and decide to take several drinks. This produces a lessening of the feeling that he is threatened, but it does not reduce the threat. In fact, it may even effectively increase it because the alcohol may weaken his ability to cope with the threat. While deciding to have the drinks, he may even be well aware that this weakening will occur. Nevertheless, he feels a strong emotional desire to drink.

Instances when emotions prompt behavior in stark contradiction with the promptings of reason are, however, fairly unusual. Such conflicts are unsettling. People may try to find a different way to satisfy their emotions that is consonant with their reality assessments, or they may simply try to inhibit the emotional urge. If both of these are ineffective, they may still try to reduce their experience of conflict by (1) *suppressing* or ignoring cognitions that suggest their emotionally gratifying behavior is not appropriate, or (2) developing complex *rationalizations* that explain how their emotionally gratifying behavior is objectively appropriate.

One of the reasons that suppressing or ignoring cognitions is so effective in releasing emotions is that emotions are only marginally responsive to cognitive considerations. Emotions respond primarily to conditioned associations. Cues and images that create associations to painful or traumatic experiences from the past will elicit aversive responses. Behaviors that were rewarding in the past will tend to be repeated. The associational logic of emotions is quite distinct from the more analytical logic of survival-oriented cognition.

As a result, emotions can be extraordinarily unresponsive to some of the most basic cognitions of present objective reality. For example, when watching a play or movie, people will often identify with the main character and will sit on the edge of their seats "hoping" that the story turns out well for that character. They will feel strong emotions toward the other characters depending on how they treat the main character. The objective fact that they are simply watching actors perform a predetermined story is temporarily suppressed. In rare cases, the feelings evoked by a performance are strong enough (and the reality cognition faint enough) to lead people to take action. Television actors often get letters addressed to the character they play, expressing strong feelings of approval or disapproval for their behavior within the television story. Soap opera stars are sometimes accosted in public and have even been physically assaulted in retribution for their on-screen behavior.

Not all defenses against reality are as primitive as suppression. When people *rationalize* the expression of their emotions, they may develop highly sophisticated and convoluted explanations for why certain behaviors are objectively appropriate. They may even convince themselves that their inclination to pursue a course of action has nothing to do with any of the intrinsic gratifications it offers, but is dictated entirely by external circumstances. It is only by noting a pervasive, though sometimes subtle, pattern of biases and contradictions in their arguments that an outside observer can deduce that rationalization may be occurring.

All of these patterns, arguably, were present in the rationales given for defense policies. When respondents used pre-nuclear, conventional principles to rationalize nuclear policies, they may well have been prompted by the conditioning effects of collective memories and images associated with past experiences.* They often made references to past traumatic experiences; for Soviets it was primarily the Nazi invasion, for Americans the failure of British Prime Minister Neville Chamberlain's appeasement policy or the bombing of Pearl Harbor. The policies proposed, such as maintaining an equal level of military power, would have been effective in these earlier experiences and therefore seem attractive now. Other policies, such as seeking military victory, striking at the enemy's military assets, or protecting populations, have also been positively conditioned by earlier experiences and therefore, by the logic of emotions, seem appropriate in the present.

The idea that such policies are derived from a unique emotional logic is further supported by the fact that virtually all respondents would at some points recognize that, given the military realities of the nuclear era, the policies they were proposing were questionable or even invalid. To elicit this second perspective, I simply had to direct their attention to key features of nuclear reality that they were ignoring or suppressing. From this perspective, they were more apt to approach defense problems in ways appropriate to the present reality. However, with time, they tended to gravitate back to the traditional pre-nuclear perspective and once again ignore critical features of nuclear reality. Doing so, presumably, reduced the unnerving feeling of vulnerability and gave rein to a competitive approach to defense policy.

When respondents used perceptual rationales for traditional defense policies, this may well have been a means of rationalizing their own desire to pursue such policies. Ostensibly, their argument was that

---

*Past experiences can have a conditioning effect in a society even when many individuals have not directly experienced the conditioning events. Highly emotional memories and images become part of the collective experience of a culture that individuals are assimilated into.

certain policies, though perhaps irrational in a military sense, were nonetheless dictated by "political realities." Although, when presenting such rationales, they were clearly cognizant of nuclear reality, the rationales justified behaving as if one were not aware of nuclear reality. This raises the possibility that such rationales may actually arise from a desire to liberate emotionally derived motives from the constraints imposed by security-motivated cognitions of nuclear reality.

This perspective is supported by two observations. One is that in the course of talking about how other key audiences do not grasp nuclear reality, respondents would unwittingly slip into taking on the perspective they were describing. Because they were clearly capable intellectually of grasping nuclear reality, their gravitation toward a conventional mindset suggests that there is something emotionally gratifying about it. Presumably this gratification arises from the fact that the conventional mindset suppresses the unnerving awareness of vulnerability and supports the fantasies associated with competitive policies. Second, the fact that even the most sophisticated respondents—the ones who consistently sustained a nuclear mindset and fashioned increasingly complex rationales—were not able to explain how perceptual manipulations produced a net gain in terms of security interests suggests that the motive for their rationales was perhaps not entirely based on security interests. All this is not to say that these respondents were consciously motivated by emotional interests. While this may have been so in some cases, I think that for the most part it is more accurate to say that security-oriented cognitive functions were being unconsciously subverted by emotion-oriented motives.

THE URGE TO FULFILL THE NATURE OF BEING

In chapter 10 we explored the argument that competitive policies should be pursued because competition is inherent in the nature of human beings, nation-states, and being itself. This argument goes beyond a simple desire to gratify emotions and apparently involves motives similar to those involved in religious activity. The central urge seems to be to blend with and fulfill the essential nature of being.

In the interviews, this urge could be differentiated from the concern for security. Although some respondents first rationalized competitive policies in terms of security, they would sometimes recognize that competitive policies were not necessarily the best way to pursue security. Some openly described a kind of tragic vision, saying that military competition was very dangerous in today's world but nonetheless still natural. Aligning oneself with the competitive nature of being by behaving competitively was not held out as necessarily the best means for preserving security. Rather, it appears that the desire to blend with the fundamental character of being may be more basic than the desire to preserve survival.

While such motives may sound somewhat idiosyncratic, they may actually be similar to some of the motives that prompted the first wars. A popular conception is that war has been a perennial feature of human behavior growing out of the pervasive competition for limited resources. However, a substantial body of evidence suggests that war is a relatively recent and advanced development in human evolution, appearing approximately 13,000 years ago, and having little or nothing to do with the competition for resources.[1] These early wars were ritual wars that involved an enactment of fundamental mythical and religious themes. The battles were (and in some primitive cultures continue to be) highly formalized competitions, similar to a sports match, and were often terminated as soon as one person was killed. The winning side did not usually acquire additional resources and would sometimes even send gifts to the losing side. Apparently such wars grew out of earlier rituals in which the origins of the universe were reenacted by portraying first the original chaos and then the reimposition of order. In ritual wars, the chaos was reenacted through a competitive battle, while the conclusion of the battle signified the reimposition of order. Presumably the rewards for the winner were found in the increased confidence that the ordering principles of their tribe were, in fact, the true reflection of the ordering principles of the universe.

It was only after the rise of agrarianism, some 6,000 to 7,000 years ago, that the element of conquest appeared and war as it is presently conceived began to take shape. However, even in these wars, it appears that these earlier ritual elements have played a major role. Lewis F. Richardson, in a study of the wars from the middle of the nineteenth to the middle of the twentieth centuries, found that the majority were not related to economic or security issues but rather to religion and national pride.[2] Wars have often been described as being the enactment of transcendental processes, for example, as described in the "Battle Hymn of the Republic."

Mine eyes have seen the glory of the coming of the Lord
He is trampling out the vintage where the grapes of wrath are stored
He has loosed the fateful lightning of his terrible swift sword
His truth is marching on.

There is no reference here to any material or security rewards that might flow from the war effort. In fact, the soldiers express not only their willingness but their intention to die in the service of this transcendental process.

In the beauties of the lilies Christ was born across the sea
With a glory in his bosom that transfigures you and me
As he died to make men holy *let us die* to make men free
While God is marching on. [Emphasis added.]

The gratifying sense of participating in a transcendental process also seems to carry over to the general population. In times of war, emotional contentment seems to improve, as is suggested, for example, by the fact that suicide rates plummet during wartime.[3] Also in times of war, even though a major part of a nation's productive capability is, in economic terms, being wasted, the economy sometimes improves. It was not until the United States entered World War II that it finally pulled out of the Depression.

The combination of the satisfying sense of meaning plus the positive domestic side effects creates a strong incentive for policymakers to try to sustain a tension with an outside adversary that is imbued with transcendental significance. It has been reported that John Foster Dulles's highly Manichaean approach—good versus evil—to the Soviets was influenced by Arnold Toynbee's suggestion that without an external challenge civilizations will decline.[4] President Reagan seemed to be following a similar line of thought in his now-famous "evil empire" speech. Denouncing the nuclear freeze, he said:

So in your discussion of the nuclear freeze proposals, I urge you to beware the temptation of pride—the temptation blithely to declare yourselves above it all and label both sides equally at fault . . . to simply call the arms race a giant misunderstanding and thereby remove yourself from the struggle between right and wrong, good and evil.[5]

Conclusion

Richard Nixon, in his book *The Real War*, also explicitly prescribes the belief that the United States is good and the Soviet Union is evil. He writes:

> It may seem melodramatic to treat the twin poles of human experience represented by the United States and the Soviet Union as the equivalent of Good and Evil, Light and Darkness, God and the Devil. . . .

But then, rather then asserting that these appraisals are, in fact, correct, he quotes a comment by Malcolm Muggeridge that such a belief sustains human order:

> As the British writer Malcolm Muggeridge has pointed out, "Good and evil . . . provide the theme of the drama of mortal existence. In this sense, they may be compared with the positive and negative points which generate an electric current; transpose the points and the current fails, the lights go out, darkness falls and all is confusion."[6]

Several interview respondents expressed similar ideas. Their concern seemed to be that the condition of mutual vulnerability was dampening the vitality of the collective will. A high-level State Department official expressing concerns about the untoward trends derived from the fear of nuclear war exclaimed emotionally, "We've got to believe we're right! We've got to be willing to sacrifice!"

The fact that these beliefs were prescribed by such individuals does not necessarily mean that they are simply being promoted for manipulative purposes. There are reasons to believe that some policymakers do see international relations as a context within which transcendental forces are played out. A study of John Foster Dulles reported that close associates of Dulles described him as seeing "the world as an arena in which the forces of good and evil were continuously at war."[7] In a recent study of U.S. congressmen, 35 percent agreed that "God has chosen America to be a light to the world" (a belief, incidentally, that was found to correlate strongly with support for high levels of defense spending).[8]

However, my impression is that many policymakers, while regarding the Manichaean description of the Soviet-American relationship as appropriate for the masses, see it as a crude approximation of a more neutral image based on the inevitability of conflict.

Very few of the interview respondents used overt Manichaean language. Much more common was an abstract and tragic vision of nature as inevitably spawning conflictual relations.* In its sparest form it was simply asserted that the nature of international relations is inherently competitive. This does not mean, though, that this vision is simply an intellectual concept. The role it plays in policymaking demonstrates that it is something akin to a religious belief. When respondents were asked why certain competitive policies were necessary, they answered that it is natural for nations to compete. The argument, being a tautology (the nation should compete because nations compete), was irreducible. These respondents did not say that competition is the best means for pursuing other interests, such as security. Some recognized that competitive policies actually jeopardize security. Competition was seen as an interest in itself and in a way even superordinate to security.

In some ways it may seem counter-intuitive to conclude that such ontological beliefs play such a significant role in the highly secular world of defense policymaking. Defense policymakers on the whole do not seem like such zealots that they would be willing to sacrifice the nation to fulfill such esoteric urges. However, the untold millions of individuals who willingly sacrificed their lives in religious wars over the centuries were probably not all religious zealots either. Ontological beliefs, to play a critical role in shaping behavior, do not even have to be fully conscious. As fundamental assumptions they form the bedrock of culture from which arise values and ultimately concepts of the national interest. The desire to behave in ways that are consonant with these deeply held structures is quite powerful and, as has been demonstrated again and again over the centuries, can be more fundamental than the desire to survive.

---

*While this neutral vision of conflict may be somewhat unusual in a Christian culture that emphasizes the conflict of good and evil, it does appear in other cultures. For example, in the ancient Hindu text, the *Bhagavad Gita*, the warrior Arjuna, in the midst of a war between two parts of his family, questions the seeming purposelessness of the war. The god Vishnu immediately appears to him and explains that the war is the wish of the gods, and that it is Arjuna's duty not to question such mysteries but to play his role in the divine order.

The Potential for Further Adaptation

If these psychological factors are so powerful that they can override security interests, does this mean that there is little hope for reducing the risk of a superpower war? Does this mean that progress in the security-oriented efforts to adapt to the condition of mutual vulnerability through greater Soviet-American cooperation and mutual restraint has reached a ceiling? My answer to these questions is "not necessarily." There are several reasons to believe that it is psychologically possible for Americans and Soviets to reduce further the probability of a war.

1. *Security motives are indeed powerful.* Even though security motives are not always the dominant motive in human behavior, they are nonetheless very powerful. The potential for a general nuclear war has bred a great deal of concern and has been the major force to generate and sustain the adaptive stream in American and Soviet defense thinking. This stream has gained increasing influence even though it runs against the grain of many of the psychological factors we have been exploring.

The concern for the potential consequences of a nuclear war has also led the superpowers to be considerably more restrained in their use of force than they might otherwise have been. There have been no direct military conflicts between Soviet and American forces throughout the nuclear era. Both sides have been careful to buffer the military competition by using proxy forces. While the risk of war is still significant, I tend to believe it is lower than it would be were it not for the fear of nuclear war. (All this is not meant to offer any moral redemption to nuclear weapons, but simply to underscore how powerful the security motive can be.)

2. *Collective defense mechanisms are difficult to sustain over time.* Abraham Lincoln said that "you can't fool all the people all the time," to which I would add, "even if they unconsciously want to be fooled." Although defense mechanisms may effectively serve to enable the individual to gratify emotions, there are other psychological forces that encourage individuals to seek out correct information about the envi-

ronment even if it is emotionally unsettling. This was demonstrated in the interview study by the fact that not a single respondent consistently presented a conventional mindset perspective; all would at some point recognize the key features of nuclear reality.

In the modern era, with high levels of information widely available, it becomes increasingly difficult to sustain collective self-deceptions for an extended period. Even when government leaders actively participate in promoting such deceptions, they are often short-lived. Witness the widespread incredulity when members of the Reagan administration suggested that the United States can survive or prevail in a nuclear war. The idea that someday it will be feasible to protect populations with strategic defense has fared a bit better with the general public, but among most defense specialists and even some high-level members of the Reagan administration such hopes are discounted as unrealistic. Reality exerts a persistent and implacable force on the human psyche.

3. *People are able to come to terms with the condition of vulnerability.* At the inter-individual level, people are completely vulnerable to one another and have somehow learned to accept this. When they drive down the street they are completely vulnerable to any one of the oncoming cars veering across the lane and killing them. And yet, they do not worry about it much. Usually it is adequate for people simply to realize that the drivers of the other cars probably do not intend to have a crash. They do not apply the maxim (applied by some defense analysts) that one should consider "capabilities, not intentions." If people constantly applied worst-case principles to their daily lives, they would soon become paralyzed.

However, when people are exposed to a new condition that puts them at risk in a new way, they find it unsettling. In the past, nations were not entirely invulnerable to each other, but they had a protective military shell around them that people could plausibly believe would at least retard advancing military forces. This shell has been shattered by the delivery capabilities of nuclear weapons. The uneasy feeling this new condition generates makes people susceptible to suggestions that they can "do something" to alleviate it, whether through building offensive or defensive weapons. They do not like hearing political leaders say (and therefore political leaders do not like to say) that "there is nothing we can do about it." However, as people come to accept this new condition, they may, in fact, learn to live with it and be less prone to pursue will-of-the-wisp schemes that generate the illusion of reducing vulnerability. They may become increasingly oriented to adapting effectively to this new condition.*

4. *People can come to terms with constraints on competitive behavior.* Of course, this is not an easy or cheerful process. Often it requires something akin to a period of mourning, something that both Americans and Soviets may be presently undergoing.

For Americans, accepting such constraints represents a substantial decline from the dominant position after World War II. Evidently, for a period of time, Americans experienced an inflated sense of their own power and potential. To accept the loss of such a feeling gracefully is not easy. These difficulties have been noted even by relatively hard-line policymakers. James Schlesinger wrote with a mixture of self-chiding and sadness, "Perhaps we are no longer of 'that strength that in the old days moved heaven and earth.' "[9] Jeane Kirkpatrick assailed her cohorts, saying, "Strange assumptions . . . are made concerning our power, our vulnerability and our resources. Often discussion sounds as though we were omnipotent, invulnerable . . . when we are, in fact, none of these. We are vulnerable, capable of being destroyed in minutes."[10]

It is, of course, tempting for American leaders to suggest to the American public that such acceptance is not necessary, that indeed American dominance can be regained. American leaders who have recognized this decline too baldly have suffered politically. The challenge for an American leader may be to find a way to help Americans come to terms with the reality of necessary constraints without evoking such a strong reaction that they become attracted instead to another leader's unrealistic, but more emotionally satisfying, vision of America's options.

For Soviets, the demand for constraints on competitive behavior disrupts a long-held image of their future. The fact that the capitalist

---

*This does not mean that one cannot hope that someday the nuclear sword of Damocles hanging over humanity will finally be removed. However, this sword can be removed only within the context of a cooperative effort built on the acceptance of the condition of vulnerability. Even if all nuclear weapons were dismantled, they could still be rebuilt in a matter of weeks. Therefore, though nuclear disarmament would, in effect, greatly lengthen the delivery time of nuclear weapons, it would not remove the essential condition of vulnerability.

West will apparently hold the Soviet Union at risk for the indefinite future dampens confidence in the Marxist-Leninist belief about the West's ultimate demise. Much of Soviet "new thinking" is an effort to come to terms with this new situation. But there is also an emotional component to this process of adaptation. One Soviet respondent told me that there have been discussions in the Young Communist League (Komsomol) about how a young socialist finds meaning in life now that it appears there will be no revolutionary breakthrough in the foreseeable future; instead, socialists must learn better how to co-exist with capitalism. (The idea of enjoying life more was eyed dubiously as a potential slide toward decadence.)

5. *Competition can be redirected away from the military arena.*
Because competitive feelings are not inherently oriented to objective security interests, they have the potential for being directed or redirected to different fields of activity. Redirection is particularly apt to occur when the potential for competition is obstructed by objective conditions. Such redirection rarely happens in a conscious way. Political leaders cannot directly say, "Let's forget about competing for African countries and instead invest more in our Olympic athletes." Rather, there tends to be a gradual decathexis, a lessening of emotional preoccupation, of one field of activity and simultaneously, though perhaps not consciously linked, a growing cathexis of another field of activity. The critical change that is needed in the process of adaptation to nuclear reality is a decathexis of the field of military competition. This may lead to a growing cathexis of other fields of competition.*

There are reasons to believe that the beginnings of such a redirection may be occurring. Several American respondents recognized, with some bewilderment, that there is a growing attitude in the American

---

*There is a popular idea that human competitiveness will inevitably express itself in lethal behavior because competitiveness is rooted in a killer instinct handed down in the course of evolution. Oddly, this idea is sometimes grossly misattributed to Konrad Lorenz. While Lorenz did suggest that aggressive behavior is instinctually derived, he also found that intraspecies lethal aggression is exceedingly rare. Complex inhibitory mechanisms prevent intraspecies aggression from becoming lethal. He speculated that the anomalous appearance of lethal aggression among humans is due to the fact that, with their rapid increase in aggressive capabilities, they have not had enough time to evolve corresponding inhibitory mechanisms. Lorenz did feel that human aggression could be effectively redirected away from lethal activity and advocated, among other things, competitive sports for this purpose. (Konrad Lorenz, *On Aggression*, trans. M. K. Wilson [New York: Harcourt, 1966])

public that competition in the military domain has reached a "dead end" because both sides are "overbuilt." These respondents were concerned that this loss of interest might lead to a weakening of support for defense spending. And, indeed, there is an increasing number of voices in the American business community arguing that defense spending should be diminished so as to compete more effectively in the economic realm. In a recent poll the American public agreed by a margin of more than three to one that "Economic power is more important than military power in determining a nation's influence."[11]

Equally interesting is the increasing Soviet interest in lowering defense spending. Soviet respondents said that this was so that they can redirect resources to building their economy. But why are the Soviets more interested in doing so now than they were in the past? No doubt there are many reasons for such a shift, but a comment by a Soviet respondent suggests that one reason may be because they see that the prestige of nations is being measured increasingly in terms of their economic capability and less in terms of military capability. Speaking about the significance that Soviet leaders attach to "face" and "prestige," he commented that currently Japan has the "best image" of all nations. This comment was surprising, because in the past the Soviets have had a derisive attitude toward Japan because of its weak military. If the attitude that Japan now has more prestige than the superpowers is, in fact, representative, it signifies a major change and may elucidate why the Soviets have recently begun to shift the focus of their attention to economic concerns even at the potential cost of military strength.

6. *People are capable of relinquishing images of the nature of being.* The desire to grasp the nature of being and to behave in a way that is in accord with it is not in itself maladaptive. Problems arise, though, when the image of the nature of being becomes crystallized. Such an image blocks out disconfirming evidence, exaggerates the significance of confirming evidence, and narrows the range of perceived options.

The process of relinquishing such images is often difficult and painful. It usually occurs only when external events consistently contradict deeply held assumptions or, more important, when the course of the action dictated by the image consistently frustrates particular motives (and even these conditions are often not sufficient). Relinquishing such images is often seen as entering into chaos, confusion, and disorientation. Religious and philosophical systems can play different roles in this process. They can bolster the image in a way that helps suppress disconfirming experiences. On the other hand, they can actually encourage individuals to relinquish their image, emphasizing that all images of the nature of being are necessarily limited and therefore one must repeatedly enter into the realm of not-knowing, of the void, of darkness, as the pathway to greater illumination. Despite the psychological rigors of the process, people at times do relinquish their images and allow them to change and to accommodate experience in a new way.

A critical step in the process of relinquishing images is simply the recognition of the image as such. In the United States the image of the battle of good versus evil being played out in the Soviet-American relationship is clearly recognized. Perhaps partly because of this recognition, the image seems to be having declining influence. Interview respondents generally made reference to it in a ridiculing fashion, clearly dissociating themselves from it. President Reagan's "evil empire" speech was widely considered a laughing matter. The few respondents who tried to sustain even a toned-down version of such a perspective obviously felt beleaguered. Among Soviets interviewed a recurring theme was the idea that the perceptions of both Soviets and Americans are distorted by the "enemy image." Many Soviet respondents were visibly embarrassed by the Manichaean character of some Soviet rhetoric, and took pains to convince me that there is a growing attitude that this kind of thinking is unsophisticated and passé. This does not mean these Soviet and American respondents do not view Soviet-American relations through a normative lens. But the idea that the relationship is an arena for a Manichaean clash between morally unalloyed and mythical forces was seen as simplistic and artificial.

However, even with some of these respondents a more subtle image persisted—that of nations as inevitably pursuing competition despite the security consequences. Perhaps this image continues to exert influence partly because it is not fully recognized. It was often muddled with the image of nations as fundamentally pursuing security, even though respondents, at some moments, would also say that nations pursue competitive policies even when they are not the best way to pursue security.

Nevertheless the image of international relations as necessarily and fundamentally competitive does not seem to be irrevocably fixed. A few American respondents described the Soviet-American relationship as being a "mix" of competition and cooperation. Soviet respondents (like current Soviet leaders) denounced the idea that the Soviet-American relationship is necessarily a zero-sum game. The image of the superpowers as being *interdependent* and therefore needing to show, and indeed showing, greater restraint is gaining currency in both countries.

This suggests that deeply held images can change. The desire for security or even the desire to see reality more clearly can prompt people to attend to features of the environment that disconfirm basic images. For some defense policymakers this may mean attending to indications that the condition of mutual vulnerability is beginning to prompt the superpowers to subordinate the competitive aspects of their relationship to a cooperative regime of mutual restraint. While movements in this direction may seem frail, and can be easily discounted by those who wish to, the perception of this trend may itself enhance the trend by gradually transforming images of how nations necessarily behave.

In closing I am suggesting that a greater adaptation to nuclear reality not only is possible but to some extent is already occurring. The fact that even the most traditionally minded defense policymakers would at some point recognize the profound significance of the nuclear revolution may mean that the psychological forces pressing for greater adaptation are inexorable. As we have seen, though, there are also deeply held resistances. Both Americans and Soviets are highly ambivalent about the prospect of mutual restraint, and thus their policies have a disjointed and at times even contradictory quality to them. However, nowhere did I find any individuals who consistently denied that the condition of mutual vulnerability ultimately points to the need for fundamental changes in the way nations use military force.

This does not mean, of course, that the possibility of a nuclear war between the superpowers has been eliminated. The regime of mutual restraint is not yet robust enough to preclude the possibility that some combination of unfortunate and improbable events could lead to a confrontation. As such a regime grows, such probabilities decline, but presently the probabilities are not insignificant. For this reason continued efforts to facilitate the emergence of such a regime may well be critical. Of course, not all the problems such efforts encounter arise from psychological resistances. Indeed there are many and complex objective difficulties that demand substantial attention. We can, however, hope that as the underlying ambivalence that hinders such adaptive efforts is recognized and gradually resolved, they can increasingly move forward with a steadiness and earnestness appropriate to the magnitude of their significance.

NOTES

Chapter 1

1. For an interesting first-person account of this period, see David Lillienthal, *Change, Hope and the Bomb* (Princeton, N.J.: Princeton University Press, 1963).

2. *Pravda*, February 24, 1981; quoted in David Holloway, *The Soviet Union and the Arms Race* (New Haven, Conn.: Yale University Press, 1983), 48.

3. Richard M. Nixon, "The Pillars of Peace: Soviet-American Relations," speech delivered before the Los Angeles World Affairs Council, March 6, 1986, cited in *Vital Speeches of the Day*, 52: 19 (July 15, 1986), 587.

4. Quoted in Strobe Talbott, *The Russians and Reagan* (New York: Vintage Books, 1984), 133.

5. Quoted in Lawrence Freedman, *The Evolution of Nuclear Strategy* (New York: St. Martin's Press, 1983), 44.

6. Quoted in John Lewis Gaddis, *Strategies of Containment* (Oxford: Oxford University Press, 1982), 80.

7. Ibid., 174.

8. Ibid., 192.

9. Ibid., 187.

10. Ibid., 188.

11. Ibid., 187.

12. Ibid., 283.

13. Dean Acheson, *Present at the Creation: My Years in the State Department* (New York: Norton, 1969), 374.

14. U. S. National Security Council, "NSC-68: A Report to the National Security Council, April 14, 1950," *Naval War College Review*, May/June, 1975, 68.

15. Ibid., 99.

16. Ibid., 68.

17. Ibid., 91.

18. Ibid.

19. Ibid., 98–99.

20. Quoted in Jerry Sanders, *Peddlers of Crisis: The Committee on the Present Danger* (Boston: South End Press, 1983), 202.

21. Ibid., 149.

22. Hedrick Smith, "Taking the Churchill View of Defense," *New York Times Magazine*, November 1, 1981, 79.

23. *Foreign Relations of the United States, 1952–1954*, vol. 2, "Statement of Policy by the National Security Council, June 10, 1953," 379, 381.

24. Quoted in Gaddis, *Strategies of Containment*, 149.

25. Senate Hearings, Committee on Foreign Relations, *Analysis of Effects of Limited Nuclear Warfare* (Washington, D.C.: GPO, 1975), 105.

26. Charles Mohr, "Carter Orders Steps to Increase Ability to Meet War Threats," *New York Times*, August 26, 1977, A8.

27. U. S. Department of Defense, Caspar Weinberger, *Annual Report to Congress FY 1984* (Washington, D.C.: GPO, 1983), 3.

28. Richard Halloran, "Pentagon Draws Up First Strategy for Fighting a Long Nuclear War," *New York Times*, May 30, 1982, A1.

29. Quoted in Richard Halloran, "Weinberger Angered by Reports on War Strategy," *New York Times*, August 24, 1982, B8.

30. Robert W. Tucker, "The Nuclear Debate," *Foreign Affairs* (Fall 1984): 9.

31. U. S. Army Headquarters, FM-100-30 (TEST), *Tactical Nuclear Operations* 12: 4 (August 1971), 83.

32. U. S. Army Headquarters, FM-3-87, *Nuclear, Biological, and Chemical (NBC) Reconnaissance Decontamination Operations* 22 (February 1980), 1–2. U. S. GPO, 1980.

33. General John D. Ryan, "A Rationale for Adequate U. S. Aerospace Forces," *Air Force* (May 1972): 51.

34. General Donn A. Starry, "Extending the Battlefield," *Military Review* (March 1981): 32, 34.

35. Henry A. Kissinger, *Nuclear Weapons and Foreign Policy*, excerpted in Robert J. Art and Kenneth N. Waltz, eds. *The Use of Force: International Politics and Foreign Policy* (Boston: Little, Brown, 1971), 107–9, 111, 113, 115.

36. Quoted in The Arms Control Association, *Star Wars Quotes* (Washington, D.C.: Arms Control Association, 1986), 54.

37. Freedman, *The Evolution of Nuclear Strategy*, 182.

38. Michael D. Kuhlman and Alfred F. J. Marshello, "Individual Differences in Game Motivation as Moderators of Preprogrammed Strategy Effects in Prisoner's Dilemma," *Journal of Personality and Social Psychology* 32 (1975): 922–31.

39. Robyn M. Dawes, Jeanne Mctavish, and Harriet Shaklee, "Behavior, Communication, and Assumptions About Other People's Behavior in a Commons Dilemma Situation," *Journal of Personality and Social Psychology* 35 (1977): 1–11.

40. See Lee Kennett and James LaVerve Anderson, *The Gun in America* (Westport, Conn.: Greenwood Press, 1975), 120.

41. Hans Morgenthau, "The Fallacy of Thinking Conventionally About Nuclear Weapons," in David Carlton and Carlo Schaerf, eds., *Arms Control and Technological Innovation* (New York: Wiley, 1976), 256–57, 260.

42. Robert Jervis, *The Illogic of American Nuclear Strategy* (Ithaca, N. Y.: Cornell University Press, 1984), 22, 36, 47.

43. Ibid., 56–57.

44. Lee Ross and Craig A. Anderson, "Shortcomings in the Attribution Process: On the Origins and Maintenance of Erroneous Social Assessments," cited in Daniel Kahneman, Paul Slovic, and Amos Tversky, *Judgment Under Uncertainty: Heuristics and Biases* (Cambridge: Cambridge University Press, 1982), 149.

45. Thomas Kuhn, *The Structure of Scientific Revolutions* (Chicago: University of Chicago Press, 1970).

46. Private communication.

47. Gaddis, *Strategies of Containment*, 149.

48. Public Agenda Foundation, *Voter Options on Nuclear Arms Policy: A Briefing Book for the 1984 Elections* (New York: Public Agenda Foundation, 1984), 24.

49. George Gallup, Jr., "American and Soviet Views on Nuclear War," *San Francisco Chronicle*, April 9, 1987, 18.

50. Public Agenda Foundation, *Voter Options*, 34.

51. U.S. Bureau of the Census, *Statistical Abstracts of the United States, 1987*, 107th ed. (Washington, D.C.: GPO, 1986), 75, 76.

52. Public Agenda Foundation, *Voter Options*, 31, 34.

Chapter 3

1. "Prepared Text of Reagan's Speech on Central America," *New York Times*, May 10, 1984, A6.

2. U. S. Department of Defense, Caspar Weinberger, *Annual Report to Congress FY 1984* (Washington, D.C.: GPO, 1983), 19.

3. Quoted in Strobe Talbott, *Deadly Gambits* (New York: Alfred A. Knopf, 1984), 172–73.

4. Quoted in John Lewis Gaddis, *Strategies of Containment* (Oxford: Oxford University Press, 1982), 321.

5. Quoted in Robert Scheer, *With Enough Shovels: Reagan, Bush, and Nuclear War* (New York: Random House, 1982), 89.

6. The Heritage Foundation, "The Nuclear Freeze: Myths and Realities," *The Backgrounder* 251 (March 3, 1983), 7.

7. Quoted in Mark Green and Gail MacColl, *There He Goes Again: Ronald Reagan's Reign of Error* (New York: Pantheon Books, 1983), 39.

8. Quoted in Scheer, *With Enough Shovels*, 245.

9. Brad Knickerbocker, "Weinberger on A-Weapons," *Christian Science Monitor*, October 10, 1984, 40.

10. Scheer, *With Enough Shovels*, 262.

11. Ibid., 234.

12. Bernard Weintraub, "Reagan Denies Cut Will Hurt Military," *New York Times*, December 19, 1985, B22.

13. Helmut Schmidt, "The 1977 Alastair Buchan Memorial Lecture," *Survival* 20: 1 (January/February 1978): 3.

14. Quoted in Robert Jervis, *The Illogic of American Nuclear Strategy* (Ithaca, N.Y.: Cornell University Press, 1984), 88.

15. The Heritage Foundation, "The Hard Facts the Nuclear Freeze Ignores," *The Backgrounder*, no. 225 (November 3, 1982): 11.

Chapter 4

1. Robert Scheer, *With Enough Shovels: Reagan, Bush, and Nuclear War* (New York: Random House, 1982), 18.

2. Paul Nitze, "Atoms, Strategy and Policy," *Foreign Affairs* (January 1956): 189–91.

3. Fred Kaplan, *The Wizards of Armageddon* (New York: Simon & Schuster, 1983), 246.

4. Nitze, "Atoms, Strategy and Policy," 190–91.

5. Leon Sloss and Marc Dean Millott, "U. S. Nuclear Strategy in Evolution," *Strategic Review* (Winter 1984): 23.

6. U. S. Department of Defense, Donald Rumsfeld, *Annual Report to Congress FY 1978* (Washington, D.C.: GPO, 1977), 68.

7. Senate Committee on Armed Services, *Hearings on FY 1978: Military Procurement, Research and Development, and Personnel Strengths*, pt. 2, 95th Cong., 1st sess. (Washington, D.C.: GPO, 1977), 829.

8. Quoted in Jerry W. Sanders, *Peddlers of Crisis* (Boston: South End Press, 1983), 291.

Chapter 5

1. Senate Committee on Foreign Relations, *Nuclear War Strategy*, Hearings on Presidential Directive 59, September 16, 1980 (Washington, D.C.: GPO, 1980), 18.

2. Daniel Ford, "The Button," *The New Yorker* (April 8, 1985), 53.

3. Ibid.

4. Herman Kahn, *On Escalation: Metaphors and Scenarios* (New York: Praeger, 1965).

5. Ibid.; see also Paul Nitze, "Assuring Strategic Stability in an Era of Detente," *Foreign Affairs* 54:2 (January 1976): 207–32.

6. U. S. Department of Defense, James Schlesinger, *Annual Report to Congress FY 1975 Defense Budget and FY 1975–1979 Defense Program* (Washington, D.C.: GPO, 1974), 5.

7. U. S. Department of Defense, Harold Brown, *Annual Report to Congress FY 1981* (Washington, D.C.: GPO, 1980), 67, 94.

Chapter 6

1. "Partial Transcript of Interview with President" (interviewers: William H. Lawrence, George Herman, Sander Vanocur), *Washington Post*, December 18, 1962, A13.

2. Senate Committee on Foreign Relations, Sparkman, *Hearings on Agreement on Limitation of Strategic Offensive Weapons* Calendar 929, Report 92–279, July 21, 1972, 8.

3. See *Congressional Record*, December 4, 1975, S. 21757 ff; also Donald Westervelt, "The Essence of Armed Futility," *Orbis* 18, (Fall 1974), 233 (reprinted in *Congressional Record*, December 4, 1975) for a further discussion of this point.

4. Edward N. Luttwak, *The Strategic Balance: The Washington Papers No. 3* (New York: Library Press for the Center for Strategic and International Studies, 1972), 69, 74–75.

5. U. S. Department of Defense, James Schlesinger, *Annual Report to Congress FY 1975* (Washington, D.C.: GPO, 1974), 6.

6. Ibid., 27.

7. U.S. Department of Defense, James Schlesinger, *Annual Report to Congress FY 1976* (Washington, D.C.: GPO, 1975), II:7.

8. Schlesinger, *FY 1975*, 5.

9. Senate Committee on Foreign Relations, *Analyses of Effects of Limited Nuclear Warfare*, September 1975 (Washington, D.C.: GPO, 1975), 31.

Notes

10. Admiral Thomas Moorer, *United States Military Posture Statement FY 1975* (Washington, D.C.: GPO, 1974), 2, 6, 41.

11. General George S. Brown, *United States Military Posture Statement FY 1978* (Washington, D.C.: GPO, 1977), 6.

12. Quoted in John Lewis Gaddis, *Strategies of Containment* (Oxford: Oxford University Press, 1982), 288.

13. Ray Cline, *World Power Assessment* (Washington, D.C.: Center for Strategic and International Studies, 1975), 8.

14. Edward Luttwak, "Perceptions of Military Force and U. S. Policy," in *Strategy and Politics: Collected Essays* (New Brunswick, N.J.: Transaction Books, 1980), 57–58.

15. Ibid., 60, 59, 54.

16. U. S. Department of Defense, Donald Rumsfeld, *Annual Report to Congress FY 1978* (Washington, D.C.: GPO, 1977), 74.

17. U. S. Department of Defense, Harold Brown, *Annual Report to Congress FY 1979* (Washington, D.C.: GPO, 1978), 64, 45.

18. U. S. Department of State, Alexander Haig, "Peace and Deterrence," *Current Policy* 383 (April 6, 1982): 3, quoted in Robert Jervis, *The Illogic of American Nuclear Strategy* (Ithaca, N.Y.: Cornell University Press, 1984), 68.

19. U. S. Department of Defense, Caspar Weinberger, *Annual Report to Congress FY 1988* (Washington, D.C.: GPO, 1987) 16, 14, 16, 44.

20. Quoted in Strobe Talbott, *Deadly Gambits* (New York: Alfred A. Knopf, 1984), 187.

21. Excerpts from "Report of the Commission on Strategic Forces," *New York Times*, April 12, 1983, A12–13.

22. Brown, *FY 1979*, 56.

23. Joyce E. Larson and William C. Bodie, "The Intelligent Layperson's Guide to the Nuclear Freeze and Peace Debate" (New York: National Strategy Information Center, 1983), 39.

24. Brown, *FY 1979*, 103.

25. Strobe Talbott, "The Vulnerability Factor," *Time*, August 31, 1981, 14.

26. Brown, *FY 1979*, 56.

27. Donald C. Daniel, ed., *International Perceptions of the Superpower Military Balance* (New York: Praeger, 1978), 190.

28. Ibid., 188, 185, 77.

29. Robert Jervis, "The Symbolic Nature of Nuclear Politics," The Edmund Jones James Lecture, November 7, 1985 (Department of Political Science, University of Illinois at Urbana-Champaign, 1987), 14, 15.

30. Steven Kull, "The Game of Perceptions in Arms Racing," *The Center* (September/October 1987): 54.

31. Paul Nitze, "Assuring Strategic Stability in an Era of Détente," *Foreign Affairs* 54:2 (January 1976): 207–32.

32. Quoted in Strobe Talbot, "The Vulnerability Factor," *Time* (August 31, 1981): 16.

33. Daniel, *International Perceptions of the Superpower Military Balance*, 187.

Chapter 7

1. Senate Committee on Foreign Relations, *Nuclear War Strategy*, Hearings on Presidential Directive 59, September 16, 1980 (Washington, D.C.: GPO), 12–14.

2. Daniel Ellsberg, "The Political Uses of Madness" (unpublished paper), 1959, 11.

3. Herman Kahn, *Thinking About the Unthinkable* (New York: Horizon Press, 1962), 45.

4. H. R. Haldeman, *The Ends of Power* (New York: Warner Books, 1980), 253, 255.

5. Richard Nixon, *RN: The Memoirs of Richard Nixon* (New York: Putman, 1978), 864; quoted in John Lewis Gaddis, *Strategies of Containment* (Oxford: Oxford University Press, 1982), 300.

6. Richard Nixon, *The Real War* (New York: Warner Books, 1980), 253, 255.

7. Kahn, *Thinking About the Unthinkable*, 49. The quote from Ambassador Smith was taken from *Time*, June 13, 1949.

8. Robert Scheer, *With Enough Shovels: Reagan, Bush and Nuclear War* (New York: Random House, 1982), 261–62.

9. Theodore Draper, "On Nuclear War: An Exchange with the Secretary of Defense," *The New York Review of Books*, August 18, 1983, 27.

Chapter 8

1. U. S. Department of Defense, Harold Brown, *Annual Report to Congress FY 1981* (Washington, D.C.: GPO, 1980), 7.

2. Paul Nitze, "Assuring Strategic Stability in an Era of Détente," *Foreign Affairs* 54: 2 (January 1976), 223; see also 226.

3. U.S. Department of Defense, Harold Brown, *Annual Report to Congress FY 1982* (Washington, D.C.: GPO, 1981), 41.

Chapter 9

1. The Arms Control Association, *Star Wars Quotes* (Washington, D.C.: The Arms Control Association, 1986), 1, 2, 3.

2. Ibid., 3, 24, 4, 5.

3. William Broad, "Space Weapon Idea Now Being Weighed Was Assailed in '82," *New York Times*, May 4, 1987, A18.

4. Arms Control Association, *Star Wars Quotes*, 8.

5. Ibid., 27.

6. Quoted in "You Can Quote Me on That," *Arms Control Today*, December 1986, 22.

7. Colin Campbell, "At Columbia, 3 Days of Arms Talks," *New York Times*, February 11, 1985, A3.

8. Arms Control Association, *Star Wars Quotes*, 5, 7, 27.

9. Ibid., 17.

10. Ibid., 51, 50.

11. Ibid., 54, 55.

12. Ibid., 30.

13. Ibid., 31.

14. Ibid., 32.

15. Ibid., 32, 33.

16. "Star Wars Stumbles on Itself," *New York Times*, March 10, 1987, A26.

17. "Teller Says 'Star Wars' Space Shield Need Not Actually Work," *The Institute* 11: 1 (January 1987): 1.

Notes

Chapter 10

1. Colin Gray, "The Urge to Compete: Rationales for Arms Racing," *World Politics* 26: 2 (January 1974): 215, 224–27.
2. U. S. Department of Defense, James Schlesinger, *Annual Report to Congress FY 1976* (Washington, D.C.: GPO, 1975), II: 7.
3. "U.S. Continues Political Discussion with Moscow," *New York Times*, September 16, 1986.
4. Elliot Negin, "Taking Credit," *Nuclear Times* (July/August 1987): 9.
5. From March 3, 1983, speech, quoted in Mark Green and Gail MacColl, *There He Goes Again: Ronald Reagan's Reign of Error* (New York: Pantheon Books, 1983), 43.
6. Seymour Hersch, *The Price of Power: Kissinger in the Nixon White House* (New York: Summit Books, 1983), 155.
7. Gray, "The Urge to Compete," 232–33.

Chapter 11

1. Quoted in David Holloway, *The Soviet Union and the Arms Race* (New Haven, Conn.: Yale University Press, 1983), 31.
2. Quoted in Harriet F. Scott and William F. Scott, *The Soviet Art of War: Doctrine, Strategy, and Tactics* (Boulder, Colo.: Westview, 1982), 124.
3. *Pravda*, January 15, 1960; quoted in Holloway, *The Soviet Union and the Arms Race*, 38.
4. Quoted in Bernard Brodie, *War and Politics* (New York: Macmillan, 1973), 375.
5. Quoted in Raymond L. Garthoff, "Mutual Deterrence and Strategic Arms Limitation in Soviet Policy," *International Security* (Summer 1978): 115.
6. General Lieutenant P. A. Zhilin, "Military Aspects of a Relaxation of Tensions," *International Life (Mezhdunarodnaya Zhizn')*, October 23, 1973, 19; cited in Joint Publications Research Service 60729 *Translations on USSR Political and Sociological Affairs* 469 (December 10, 1973), 19.
7. Lieutenant General P. A. Zhilin, "The Truth of History Is Irrefutable," *Red Star (Krasnaya Zvezda)*, September 1, 1976, 2–3; cited in Foreign Broadcast Information Service *Daily Report: Soviet Union* 3:182 (September 17, 1976), A4.
8. Marshal Nikolai V. Ogarkov, *History Teaches Vigilance* (Moscow: Voenizdat, 1985), 51.
9. Marshal N. V. Ogarkov, "A Reliable Defense for Peace," *Red Star (Krasnaya Zvezda)*, September 23, 1983, no. 219.
10. Quoted in Alexander Bovin, "Let's Speak Frankly" (Moscow: Novosti Press, 1985), 9.
11. *Red Star (Krasnaya Zvezda)*, September 23, 1983, 2; quoted in Holloway, *The Soviet Union and the Arms Race*, 166.
12. *Red Star (Krasnaya Zvezda)*, February 7, 1974; quoted in Holloway, *The Soviet Union and the Arms Race*, 166–67.
13. D. A. Volkogonov, ed., *Marxist-Leninist Doctrine on War and Army* (Moscow: Voenizdat, 1984), 28.
14. Col. I. Sidelnikov, "Peaceful Coexistence and the Security of the Peoples," *Red Star (Krasnaya Zvezda)*, August 14, 1973, 2–3, trans. *Current Digest of the Soviet Press* 25:34, 6–7, September 19, 1973.

15. *Military Thought (Voenn Mysl)* 10 (October 1968); quoted in Dan L. Strode and Rebecca V. Strode, "Diplomacy and Defense in Soviet National Security Policy," *International Security* 8:2 (Fall 1983): 114.

16. Quoted in Scott and Scott, *The Soviet Art of War,* 275.

17. Quoted in ibid., 277.

18. Ibid., 163, 213, 254.

19. "Secure Shield," *New Times (Novoye Vremya)* 51 (December 26, 1986), 14.

20. Ibid., 12.

21. "Marshal of the Soviet Union D. F. Ustinov, USSR Minister of Defense, Answers Questions from a Pravda Correspondent," *Pravda,* December 7, 1982, 4, trans. *Current Digest of the Soviet Press* 34:49, 8, January 5, 1983.

22. "Yu. V. Andropov Answers Questions from a Pravda Correspondent," *Pravda,* March 27, 1983, 1, trans. *Current Digest of the Soviet Press* 35:13, 4, April 27, 1983.

23. Quoted in Daniel Frei, *Perceived Images: U.S. and Soviet Assumptions and Perceptions in Disarmament* (Totowa, N.J.: Rowman and Allanheld, 1986), 47.

24. Quoted in Holloway, *The Soviet Union and the Arms Race,* 45.

25. M. Gladkov and B. Ivanov, "The Economy and Military Technological Policy," *Communist of the Armed Forces,* May 1972; quoted in Albert Weeks and William Bodie, "War and Peace: Soviet Russia Speaks" (New York: National Strategy Information Center, 1983), 35.

26. Quoted in Holloway, *The Soviet Union and the Arms Race,* 1135.

27. V. Kuznetsov, "According to the Laws of Détente," *New Times (Novoye Vremya)* 5 (January 28, 1977), 4–5; cited in Foreign Broadcast Information Service *Daily Report: Soviet Union* 3:21 (February 1, 1977), A4.

28. Major General Rair Georgiyevich Simonyan, "International Situation—Questions and Answers," Foreign Broadcast Information Service *Daily Report: Soviet Union* 3:119 (June 21, 1977), A8.

29. Nikolai Ogarkov, "Defense of Socialism: Historical Experience and the Present Day," *Red Star (Krasnaya Zvezda),* May 9, 1984, 3.

30. Tass-attributed report, Rebuttal to Carter's Annapolis Speech, June 16, 1978, B2; cited in Foreign Broadcast Information Service *Daily Report: Soviet Union* 3:118.

31. Quoted in Edward L. Warner III, *The Military in Contemporary Soviet Politics: An Institutional Analaysis* (New York: Praeger, 1977), 129.

32. Henry Trofimenko, "Changing Attitudes Toward Deterrence," ACIS Working Paper No. 25 (U.C.L.A.: Center for International and Strategic Affairs, July 1980), 15, 16, 18–19, 20, 31, 33, 34.

33. Quoted in Scott and Scott, *The Soviet Art of War,* 175.

34. Quoted in Thomas W. Wolfe, *Soviet Strategy at the Crossroads* (Cambridge, Mass.: Harvard University Press, 1964), 228.

35. Quoted in Scott and Scott, *The Soviet Art of War,* 236.

36. Lieutenant General V. Reznichenko, "Characteristic Features and Methods of Conducting an Offensive," *Military Thought (Voyenna Mysl)* 1 (January 1972); excerpted in Leon Goure and Michael J. Deane, "The Soviet Strategic View," *Strategic Review* 9:1 (Winter 1981): 74.

37. Scott and Scott, *The Soviet Art of War,* 168.

38. Ibid., 204.

39. Ibid., 223–25.

40. Ibid., 238.

41. Ibid., 175, 247.

42. Marshal Andrey Grechko, *The Armed Forces of the Soviet State* (Moscow, 1975), trans. and pub. U.S. Air Force Series *Soviet Military Thought* No. 12 (Washington, D.C.: GPO, 1975), 168.

Notes

43. Marshal Vasily Sokolovsky, *Soviet Military Strategy,* 3rd ed., trans. Harriet Fast Scott (New York: Crane, Russak, 1975), 208.

44. Colonel B. Byely et al., *Marxism-Leninism on War and Army* (Moscow: Progress Publishers, 1972); trans. and pub. U.S. Air Force Series *Soviet Military Thought* No. 2 (Washington, D.C.: GPO, 1974), 304.

45. Scott and Scott, *The Soviet Art of War,* 223–25.

46. Colonel General N. A. Lomov, ed., *Scientific Technical Progress and the Revolution in Military Affairs* (Moscow, 1973), trans. and pub. U.S. Air Force Series *Soviet Military Thought* No. 3 (Washington, D.C.: GPO, 1974), 144, 147.

47. Quoted in Stephen W. Van Evera, "Causes of War" (Ph.D. diss., University of California, Berkeley, 1984), 603.

48. Grechko, *Armed Forces of the Soviet State,* 91.

49. Ibid., 164, 167.

50. Quoted in James M. McConnell, "Shifts in Soviet Views on the Proper Focus of Military Development," *World Politics* 37:3 (Spring 1985): 325.

51. Quoted in ibid., 322, 324n.

52. Zhilin, "Military Aspects of a Relaxation of Tensions," 19.

53. Quoted in McConnell, "Shifts in Soviet Views," 322.

54. Ibid., 338–39.

55. Scott and Scott, *The Soviet Art of War,* 246–49, 248, 254.

56. Nikolai Ogarkov, "Always in Readiness to Defend the Homeland," chap. 2, trans. in *Soviet Press Selected Translations* (November/December 1982): 323.

57. Quoted in Strode and Strode, "Diplomacy and Defense in Soviet National Security Policy," 113n.

58. Quoted in McConnell, "Shifts in Soviet Views," 321, 322.

59. Lomov, *Scientific Technical Progress,* 188, 269.

60. Colonel Y. Rybkin, "The Leninist Conception of Contemporary War," *Communist of the Armed Forces* 20 (October 1973): 21–28; quoted in Robert L. Arnett, "Soviet Attitudes Toward Nuclear War: Do They Really Think They Can Win?" *Journal of Strategic Studies* 2: 2 (September 1979): 175.

61. Trofimenko, "Changing Attitudes Toward Deterrence," 31.

62. Scott and Scott, *The Soviet Art of War,* 222, 228.

63. M. Shirokov, "Military Geography of the Present Stage," *Military Thought (Voenna Mysl),* November 1966; excerpted in Systems Planning Corporation, *Selected Readings from Soviet Military Thought 1959–1973* SPC Report S84 (Arlington, Va.: Systems Planning Corporation, 1980), 202.

64. Quoted in Garthoff, "Mutual Deterrence," 129.

65. Trofimenko, "Changing Attitudes Toward Deterrence," 26.

66. Quoted in A. Gorokhov, "Within the Strategic Command Centers," *Pravda,* May 29, 1985, 6.

67. *Soviet Military Encyclopedia,* vol. 24 (1980), 98; quoted in Frei, *Perceived Images,* 57.

68. "Secure Shield," 13.

69. Quoted in Georgi Arbatov and Willem Oltmans, *The Soviet Viewpoint* (New York: Dodd, Mead, 1983), 97.

70. *Pravda,* November 3, 1981, trans. in *Soviet Press Selected Translations* (September/October 1982): 281.

71. Ogarkov, "Defense of Socialism," 3.

72. Arbatov and Oltmans, *The Soviet Viewpoint,* 124.

73. *Soviet Military Encyclopedia,* vol. 7 (1980), 32; quoted in Frei, *Perceived Images,* 56.

74. Trofimenko, "Changing Attitudes Toward Deterrence," 25.

75. Arbatov and Oltmans, *The Soviet Viewpoint,* 123, 101.

76. In William R. Kintner and Harriet Fast Scott, trans. and eds., *The Nuclear Revolution in Soviet Military Affairs* (Norman: University of Oklahoma Press, 1968), 166.

77. V. D. Sokolovsky and M. I. Cherednichenko, "Military Strategy and Its Problems," *Military Thought (Voenna Mysl)*, October 1968; excerpted in Systems Planning Corporation, *Selected Readings*, 383.

78. Col. A. A. Shirman, "Social Activity of the Masses and the Defense of Socialism," in A. S. Milovidov and V. G. Kozlov, eds., *The Philosophical Heritage of V. I. Lenin and Problems of Contemporary War* (Moscow: Voenizdat, 1972), trans. and pub. U.S. Air Force Series *Soviet Military Thought* 5 (Washington, D.C.: GPO, 1972), 127.

79. M. M. Kir'yan, ed., *Military-Technical Progress and the Armed Forces of the USSR* (Moscow: Voenizdat, 1982), 313, 326.

80. Colonel General N. A. Merimskiy, *Tactical Preparation of Motorized-Rifle and Tank Subunits* (Moscow: Voenizdat, 1984), 8.

81. D. T. Yazov, "The Military Doctrine of the Warsaw Pact Is the Doctrine of the Defense of Peace and Socialism," *Pravda*, July 27, 1987, 5; cited in Foreign Broadcast Information Service *Daily Report: Soviet Union*, July 27, 1987, BB 2.

82. Mikhail Gorbachev, *Political Report of the CPSU Central Committee to the Congress of the Communist Party of the Soviet Union* (Moscow: Novosti Press, 1986), 80–83.

83. Yazov, "The Military Doctrine of the Warsaw Pact," BB 1, BB 2, BB 3.

84. Ibid., BB 4.

85. "Secure Shield," 12.

86. Yazov, "The Military Doctrine of the Warsaw Pact," BB 4.

87. Ibid., BB 1, BB 7.

Chapter 12

1. David Shipler, *Russia: Broken Idols, Solemn Dreams* (New York: Times Books, 1983), 21.

2. Ronald Hingley, *The Russian Mind* (New York: Scribner's, 1977).

3. Marshall Nikolai Ogarkov, "Always in Readiness to Defend the Homeland," chap. 1, trans. in *Soviet Press Selected Translations* 82: 9–10 (September/October 1982), 282.

4. Quoted in Mohammed Heikal, *Sphinx and Commissar: The Rise and Fall of Soviet Influence in the Arab World* (London: Collins and Sons, 1978), 97–98.

5. Cited in James M. McConnell, "Shifts in Soviet Views on the Proper Focus of Military Development," *World Politics* 37:3 (Spring 1985): 327. McConnell interprets Bochkarev's comment as being derived from an effort to resolve the paradox of deterrence.

6. Georgi Arbatov and Willem Oltmans, *The Soviet Viewpoint* (New York: Dodd, Mead, 1983), 96.

7. Ibid., 124.

8. Henry Trofimenko, "Changing Attitudes Toward Deterrence," ACIS Working Paper No. 25 (UCLA Center for International and Strategic Affairs, July 1980), 23.

9. Quoted in Raymond Garthoff, "Mutual Deterrence and Strategic Arms Limitations in Soviet Policy," *International Security* (Summer 1978), 120.

10. General-Major A. S. Milovidov and Colonel V. G. Kozlov, eds., *The Philosophical Heritage of V. I. Lenin and Problems of Contemporary War* (Moscow: Voenizdat,

Notes

1972), trans. and pub. U.S. Air Force Series *Soviet Military Thought* 5 (Washington, D.C.: GPO, 1972), 17.

11. Rear Admiral V. V. Shelyag, "Two World Outlooks—Two Views on War," *Red Star (Krasnaya Zvezda)*, February 7, 1974, 2–3; cited in Foreign Broadcast Information Service *Daily Report: Soviet Union* 3:30 (February 12, 1974), A4.

12. Quoted in Edward L. Warner III, *The Military in Contemporary Soviet Politics: An Institutional Analysis* (New York: Praeger, 1977), 252.

13. Marshal A. A. Grechko, *The Armed Forces of the Soviet State*, trans. in *Soviet Military Thought* 12 (Washington, D.C.: GPO, 1975), 164.

14. "Colonel X's Warning: Our Mistakes Plus Your Hysteria," *Détente* (October 1984), 2–3.

15. Arbatov and Oltmans, *The Soviet Viewpoint*, 101.

16. Hingley, *The Russian Mind*, 107.

Chapter 13

1. Susan Mansfield, *The Gestalts of War* (New York: Dial Press, 1982).

2. Lewis F. Richardson, "Statistics of Deadly Quarrels," in T. H. Pear, ed., *Psychological Factors of Peace and War* (New York: Philosophical Library, 1950).

3. Jean Baechler, *Suicides* (New York: Basic Books, 1979), 319–20.

4. John Lewis Gaddis, *Strategies of Containment* (Oxford: Oxford University Press, 1982), 136.

5. From March 3, 1983, speech, quoted in Mark Green and Gail MacColl, *There He Goes Again: Ronald Reagan's Reign of Error* (New York: Pantheon Books, 1983), 43.

6. Richard Nixon, *The Real War* (New York: Warner Books, 1984), 314.

7. David Finlay, Ole R. Holsti, and Richard Fagen, *Enemies in Politics* (Chicago: Rand McNally, 1967), 37.

8. Peter L. Benson and Dorothy Williams, *Religion on Capitol Hill: Myths and Realities* (San Francisco: Harper & Row, 1982).

9. U. S. Department of Defense, James Schlesinger, *Annual Report to Congress FY 1976* (Washington D.C.: GPO, 1975), I-3.

10. Quoted in James Reston, "What's the National Interest?" *New York Times*, March 16, 1986, A25.

11. Hobart Rowen, "The Democrats Are Muffing It," *Washington Post* (nat'l. ed.), November 30, 1987, 5.

INDEX

ABM, *see* Antiballistic missile
Abrahamson, General James, 209, 212–13
Absolute Weapon, The (Brodie), 5
Accommodation: mutual, 8; perception of balance and, 130; of Soviet delusions and idiosyncrasies, 181–91
Acheson, Dean, 9–10
Achille Lauro, 54
Action policies, 156–57, 174
Adaptation: to nuclear reality, 3–29; potential for further, 311–14, 317
Adaptive stream, 5, 5n, 6–9, 27, 298; in Soviet military thinking, 248–68
Adelman, Kenneth, 210, 230
Advanced Strategic Missile Systems program, 213
Advantage: mutual, 8; punitive, 81; unilateral, 7–8
Advantageous termination of war: 12–13, 30, 39–41, 72–93; appearing to seek, 156–76; domestic morale and, 232–33; Soviet concept of, 254–61, 275–83
Adventurism, 51–53
Afghanistan, 52–53, 232
Aggression: 18–19; Soviet, 19, 86, 101, 104, 174n, 204
Air-breathing systems, 210–11
Air Force, U.S., 13, 85, 98
Allies: escalation control and, 205–6; European, 145, 166, 193
Alternative target coverage, 274
America, *see* United States
American Security Council, 34
Anderson, Craig, 24
Andropov, Yuri, 252, 285
Angola, 232
Annihilation, nuclear, 12, 191
Anti-ballistic missile (ABM), 67; treaty, 9, 60, 242
Approximate equality, 254
Arbatov, Georgi, 265–66, 283–84, 292
Armed Forces of the Soviet State (Grechko), 257
Arms control: competition and, 243–46; concept of, counter to human nature, 243–44; negotiations, 4, 11, 67, 111, 154–55; violations, Soviet, 70; *see also specific treaties*
Arms Control and Disarmament Agency (ACDA), 63, 109, 117, 137, 210, 216, 234
Arms race, 123–24, 144, 240–41, 245–47; offensive, 219; prestige and, 225–26
Arms reduction, 212
Army, U.S.: FM 100-30, 13; FM 100-5, 13; FM 3-87, 13
Arsenal(s): American, 6–8, 11, 15, 22, 27, 30–31, 41, 52, 57n, 64, 122, 126, 157, 273; categories, 11; design, 9, 39; French, 51; Soviet, 6–7, 11, 22, 39, 53, 124, 185, 237, 264, 273; weapons categories, 155
Assured destruction capability: 110; American, 47, 57, 57n, 60–61, 66; questioning, 57–71; Soviet, 10, 14, 53, 57, 59
Asymmetries, 280; marginal, 150–51, 253
Atomic bomb, 291; detonation of first, 5

B-1 bomber, 146
B-52D bomber, 128
Backfire bomber, 146
Balance of forces, 10–11, 30; maintaining, 38–39, 47–71, 114–55; misperception of, 138; as signaling device, 141–47; Soviet concept of, 252–54; Soviet interviewees on, 271–74
Balance of power, 30
Ban, MIRV (Multiple Independent Reentry Vehicle), 242
Basic Principles of Relations, 7–8
Behavior, *see* Competition
Being, nature of: competition and, 238–47; relinquishing images of, 315–17; urge to fulfill, 306–10
Beliefs, tendency to assume, 149–51
Benefit, mutual, 8
Bhagavad Gita, 310n
Blackjack bomber, 146
Bluff: American, 175; war-winning policies as, 175

Index

Holocaust, nuclear, 119
House Armed Services Committee, 34, 209
House of Commons, 49
Hudson Institute, 120
Hydrogen weapons, 3
Hyper-rationalism, 19

ICBM, *see* Intercontinental ballistic missiles
Ideology, differences in, 8
Idiosyncrasies, of defense policymakers, 18; Soviet, 177, 181–91
Illogic of American Nuclear Strategy, The (Jervis), 23–24, 186n
Illusion, playing along with, 137–41
Imbalance: favorable, 122; nuclear, 119
Imperative logic, traditional, 77–81
India, 118
Industry: American defense, 34; vulnerability of, 107
INF, *see* Intermediate Nuclear Force
Inferiority, strategic, 123–24; American, 5–8, 120, 237; Soviet, 52, 287–88
Inner conflict model, 27–29
Intercontinental ballistic missiles (ICBMs), 42, 54, 57n, 62–63, 65, 124, 149; American, 62, 65, 111, 120, 131, 146, 183, 242; land-based, 63, 65, 111; Soviet, 65, 70–71, 96, 118, 120, 123–24, 128, 134, 145–46, 185, 187, 200–201, 242, 264–65, 274, 284, 289; vulnerability of, 60, 65; *see also* Minuteman
Interdependence, condition of, 31, 300–301
Intermediate Nuclear Forces (INF), 49, 55n, 277; debates, 263; missiles, 186; treaty, 85n, 269; weapons, 146, 192–94, 198
Intermediate-range nuclear ballistic missiles, *see* Intermediate Nuclear Forces, Pershing II missile, SS-20 missile
International Institute of Strategic Studies, 70n
International morality, 243
International Perceptions of the Superpower Military Balance (Daniel), 141, 154
Interviewees: academics, 33, 240; ACDA officials, 63–64, 109, 117–19, 137–38, 216, 234; arms control negotiators, 188, 196–97, 228; CIA employee, 133; Committee on the Present Danger officials, 132–33; Congressional defense analysts, 214, 243, 301–2; congressmen, 33, 49, 56–60, 88, 133–34; CSIS analysts, 165, 231; defense analysts, 240–41; Geneva negotiators, 219; Joint Chiefs of Staff officials, 81–83, 92–93, 96, 98, 115–16, 130, 138, 152, 220, 229; military officers, 79, 234–35; NATO headquarters warplanners, 197–202; NSC officials, 80–81, 88–89, 143, 173, 179, 183, 185, 221;

Pentagon officials, 51–54, 69, 71, 73–75, 84, 99, 104, 108, 109, 111–12, 132–33, 135–36, 152–53, 157, 162–67, 171–72, 178, 182–83, 185–86, 188, 190, 194, 196, 203–6, 214, 216, 227, 230, 234–36, 238–39, 241–42, 244, 246–47; political analysts, 142–43, 245; presidential advisors, 144, 171, 243–45; Rand analysts, 55, 77–78, 89–92, 101, 104, 129–30, 138–39, 157, 162, 173–74, 186–87, 214–15, 219–20, 223–24, 229, 231, 233; Reagan administration officials, 60–62, 116–17, 159; Reagan advisors, 236–37; Scowcroft Commission members, 138, 215–16; SDIO officials, 217–18; Senate Armed Services Committee officials, 158, 179, 186, 216–17; Senate Foreign Relations Committee officials, 116, 143; senators, 33, 56, 64–66, 104, 189; senators' aides, 173, 180–81; START negotiators, 111, 169–70; State Department officials, 50–51, 151, 156–58, 219, 231–35, 239–41, 245, 309; strategic analysts, 60–61, 66–69, 80, 84, 86–88, 99–101, 105–7, 116, 178, 218–19, 227–28, 299; think-tank analysts, 33; women, 34
Intimidation: of Soviet Union, 159–66, 175–76; of United States, 165
Iran, 52, 232; *see also* Middle East
Italy, 129, 245

Jackson, Henry, 120–21, 226
Jackson Amendment, *see* SALT I
Japan, 136, 141, 236, 245, 315
Javits, Jacob, 158–59
Jefferson, Thomas, 244
Jervis, Robert, 23–24, 144
Joint Chiefs of Staff, 11, 32, 34, 75, 81, 92, 96, 98, 115, 123, 130, 138, 151, 220, 229
Jones, David, 85
Jones, T. K., 76, 76n

Kahn, Herman, 87, 102, 161, 165, 166n
Kalb, Marvin, 210–11
Kaplan, Fred, 84
Kennan, George, 5
Kennedy, Edward, 212
Kennedy, John, 120, 143
Keyworth, George, 209, 211
Khrushchev, Nikita, 52, 135, 143, 166, 248–49, 251, 259, 283, 285
Kirkpatrick, Jeane, 12, 313
Kiryan, General M. M., 267
Kissinger, Henry, 7, 14–15, 123, 130, 242
Komsomol, 314
Kremlin, *see* Soviet Union
Krylov, N. I., 263

Index